RESEARCH PROJECT MANAGEMENT AND LEADERSHIP

A Handbook for Everyone

The project management approaches, which are used by millions of people internationally, are often too detailed or constraining to be applied to research. In this handbook, project management expert P. Alison Paprica presents guidance specifically developed to help with the planning, management, and leadership of research.

Research Project Management and Leadership provides simplified versions of globally utilized project management tools, such as the work breakdown structure to visualize scope, and offers guidance on processes, including a five-step process to identify and respond to risks. The complementary leadership guidance in the handbook is presented in the form of interview write-ups with 19 Canadian and international research leaders, each of whom describes a situation where leadership skills were important, how they responded, and what they learned. The accessible language and practical guidance in the handbook make it a valuable resource for everyone from principal investigators leading multimillion-dollar projects to graduate students planning their thesis research. The book aims to help readers understand which management and leadership tools, processes, and practices are helpful in different circumstances, and how to implement them in research settings.

P. ALISON PAPRICA is an adjunct professor and senior fellow at the Institute for Health Policy, Management, and Evaluation at the University of Toronto.

Research Project Management and Leadership

A Handbook for Everyone

P. ALISON PAPRICA

UNIVERSITY OF TORONTO PRESS
Toronto Buffalo London

© University of Toronto Press 2024
Toronto Buffalo London
utorontopress.com
Printed and bound by CPI Group (UK) Ltd, Croydon, CR0 4YY

ISBN 978-1-4875-4451-5 (cloth) ISBN 978-1-4875-4433-1 (EPUB)
ISBN 978-1-4875-4446-1 (paper) ISBN 978-1-4875-4432-4 (PDF)

Library and Archives Canada Cataloguing in Publication

Title: Research project management and leadership : a handbook for everyone /
   P. Alison Paprica.
Names: Paprica, P. Alison, author.
Description: Includes bibliographical references and index.
Identifiers: Canadiana (print) 20230530796 | Canadiana (ebook) 20230530826 |
   ISBN 9781487544515 (cloth) | ISBN 9781487544461 (paper) |
   ISBN 9781487544324 (PDF) | ISBN 9781487544331 (EPUB)
Subjects: LCSH: Project management – Handbooks, manuals, etc. |
   LCSH: Leadership – Handbooks, manuals, etc. | LCGFT: Handbooks and manuals.
Classification: LCC HD69.P75 P37 2024 | DDC 658.4/04 – dc23

Cover design: Mary Beth MacLean
Cover image: istock.com/kid-a

We welcome comments and suggestions regarding any aspect of our publications –
please feel free to contact us at news@utorontopress.com or visit us at utorontopress.com.

Every effort has been made to contact copyright holders; in the event of an error or
omission, please notify the publisher.

We wish to acknowledge the land on which the University of Toronto Press
operates. This land is the traditional territory of the Wendat, the Anishnaabeg, the
Haudenosaunee, the Métis, and the Mississaugas of the Credit First Nation.

University of Toronto Press acknowledges the financial support of the Government of
Canada and the Ontario Arts Council, an agency of the Government of Ontario, for its
publishing activities.

ONTARIO ARTS COUNCIL
CONSEIL DES ARTS DE L'ONTARIO
an Ontario government agency
un organisme du gouvernement de l'Ontario

Funded by the   Financé par le
Government   gouvernement   Canadä
of Canada   du Canada

This handbook is dedicated to research leaders everywhere. I have been inspired by the ways in which they have stepped up, supported others, taken chances, led with compassion, stuck their necks out, and gone the extra mile. I admire them and thank them for their contributions to research.

Contents

Illustrations

Tables

Boxes

Leadership Advice Crosswalks

Overview of Research Project Management and Leadership

1.1 RESEARCH REQUIRES BOTH VISION AND PLANNING

Research, by its nature, tends to focus on the vision. It is about the potential to generate knowledge or improved products, processes, and services. For hundreds of years, however, people have realized that a vision alone is not enough; planning is also required (see Box 1.1). That is why this handbook presents a combination of advice from 19 research leaders and light-touch versions of globally accepted project management tools and processes to support research team members in planning and implementing projects to achieve their vision.

"Research" is a broad term that can include everything from the generation of new theories at universities to experimental development performed by businesses to refine or improve commercial products (Box 1.2). This handbook focuses on guidance for academic research – sometimes referred to as *higher education research and*

BOX 1.1. A VISION AND A TASK PROVERB

A vision without a task is but a dream. A task without a vision is drudgery. A vision and a task are the hope of the world. – Anonymous (often attributed to an unknown church in Sussex, England, c. 1730)

BOX 1.2. TYPES OF RESEARCH AND DEVELOPMENT

Basic research is experimental or theoretical work undertaken primarily to acquire new knowledge of the underlying foundation of phenomena and observable facts, without any particular application or use in view.

Applied research is original investigation undertaken in order to acquire new knowledge. It is, however, directed primarily toward a specific, practical aim or objective.

Experimental development is systematic work, drawing on knowledge gained from research and practical experience and producing additional knowledge, which is directed to producing new products or processes or to improving existing products or processes.

Source: Organisation for Economic Co-operation and Development (2015).

---

development (HERD) – which includes research performed at universities, colleges, research hospitals, and research institutes and centers that are under the control of tertiary education institutions (Organisation for Economic Co-operation and Development [OECD], n.d.-b). Academic research is primarily funded by governments and plays an important role in innovation systems by ensuring the provision of new knowledge from basic and applied research that businesses are unlikely to conduct because of the non-appropriable, public good, intangible character of knowledge and the risky nature of research (OECD, 2012).

There is a massive international investment in academic research each year. The OECD (n.d.-a) reports that more than US$300 billion of research is performed annually by the higher education sector, most of which is invested in eight countries that each have more than US$10 billion of annual HERD investment (see Table 1.1).

The specific objectives of the funders of academic research vary, but they generally include the generation of new foundational knowledge and research findings that will directly or indirectly address societal, economic, and security challenges (OECD, 2016). Of course, there are exceptions, but, overall, research has higher

Table 1.1. Countries with More Than US$10 Billion Annual Higher Education R&D

Country	Annual R&D Performed by the Higher Education Sector (US$, billions)	Latest Year for Which Data Are Available
United States	84.0 (D, P)	2021
China (People's Republic of)	34.5	2018
Germany	28.0 (P)	2021
Japan	21.0	2021
United Kingdom	20.2	2020
France	15.6	2021
Canada	13.0 (E, P)	2022
Korea	10.9	2021

D = difference in methodology; E = estimated value; P = provisional value; R&D = research and development.
Source: Organisation for Economic Co-operation and Development (n.d.-a).

uncertainty than other kinds of work. For example, at the beginning of a research project there may not be certainty about what the research questions will be, what methodology will be used, or whether the project will yield any conclusive results. This uncertainty is unavoidable and associated with the open and inquisitive nature of research. The uncertainty is highest for investigator-driven basic research, which is conducted to generate knowledge without any particular application in mind (Figure 1.1).

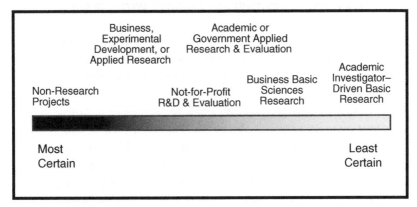

Figure 1.1. Continuum of Certainty for Research Projects (with Exceptions, of Course)

1.2 SUMMARY OF THE LITERATURE

Volumes have been written about project management and leadership. Among the thousands of project management books and textbooks that exist, two stand out because they guide the practice of millions of practitioners: the *Standard for Project Management and a Guide to the Project Management Body of Knowledge (PMBOK® Guide)* (Project Management Institute, 2021) and *Managing Successful Projects with PRINCE2®* (Axelos, 2017; see Box 1.3). These resources are complemented by many academic publications, including broad-scope journals (e.g., *International Journal of Project Management, Project Management Journal, International Journal of Project Organization and Management, Project Leadership and Society*) and journals focused on specific sectors (e.g., *International Journal of Managing Projects in Business, International Journal of Information Technology Project Management*). Within this large project management and leadership literature, only a small number of publications focus specifically on academic research; however, there is complementary literature focused on research and development (R&D), including academic journals such as *R&D Management* and *Higher Education Research and Development*, and thousands of books written about various aspects of R&D.

BOX 1.3. TWO DEFINITIVE RESOURCES: THE *PMBOK® GUIDE* AND *MANAGING SUCCESSFUL PROJECTS WITH PRINCE2®*

Two books are recognized as definitive resources for the practice of project management: *The Standard for Project Management and a Guide to the Project Management Body of Knowledge (PMBOK® Guide)*, published by the US-based Project Management Institute (PMI; 2021) and *Managing Successful Projects with PRINCE2®* (Axelos, 2017), published by the Stationary Office and supported by Axelos as joint venture with the UK government. PMI has more than one million certified project management professionals (PMPs), Axelos has more than one million PRINCE2® certified project managers, and both PMI and Axelos offer multiple different project management–related certification programs. The *PMBOK® Guide* and *Managing*

Successful Projects with PRINCE2® each provide hundreds of pages of guidance and are continuously reviewed and updated by thousands of contributing project managers.

The main difference between the two resources is that the *PMBOK® Guide* presents a framework of standards along with many options for tools and processes that can be applied to plan and manage projects, whereas *Managing Successful Projects with PRINCE2®* presents a specific but flexible method for planning and managing projects. The two resources use slightly different terminology, but both draw on and bring together project management tools and processes that predate the publication of the *PMBOK® Guide* and PRINCE2® resources, such as the work breakdown structure, Gantt charts, and responsibility assignment matrices. By their nature, the *PMBOK® Guide* and *Managing Successful Projects with PRINCE2®* are general resources that do not provide detailed guidance on, or examples of, the application of project management in research or other sectors. They both encourage the tailoring of project management to meet the needs of individual projects and different contexts.

Despite the large volume of written material, it is extremely challenging to identify publications focused specifically on academic research project management and leadership because most of the project management and leadership literature focuses on non-academic projects. On top of that, there are no standardized search terms that distinguish between publications focused on the leadership and management of academic research and publications that present academic research on project management in other sectors.

As part of the preparation of this handbook, a literature review was performed to identify scholarly publications focused on the leadership and management of academic research. The first step involved searching Scopus and Google Scholar using combinations of the terms "management," "project management," "leadership," and "academic research" to find articles that might be relevant, followed by a review of abstracts and full text to identify the subset of articles that focused on the leadership and management of academic research. From there, the snowball search method was used to identify additional relevant publications that cited, or were cited by, publications that had been confirmed to be relevant. This approach identified two literature reviews focused on academic research project management (Philbin, 2017; vom Brocke & Lippe, 2015), one literature review focused on academic research leadership (Anthony & Antony, 2017), and a small number of additional articles that warranted inclusion either because they were not included in previously published literature reviews or because relevant details in them were less emphasized in the published literature reviews.

To complement the peer-reviewed and indexed literature, a general internet search for resources related to academic research project management and leadership was performed, including a search of guidance provided by research funders. This identified one workshop report (Lemieux-Charles, 2005); one working group report (Canadian Health Services and Policy Research Alliance [CHSPRA], 2015); and several websites with program guides, guidance, reports, and case studies (Advance HE, n.d.; Canada Foundation for Innovation, n.d.; Canadian Institutes of Health Research [CIHR], 2016, 2017; European Commission, 2002; Memorial University of Newfoundland, 2018; Miller, 2019; OECD, n.d.-b). Note that internet search results change as new materials are posted, and research funders may have program guides and other relevant materials that are accessible only to researchers who register with them. Therefore, although the institutional and research funder internet resources cited here may have some helpful information for readers, they are included primarily to illustrate the existence of relevant online materials and to prompt readers to seek guidance from their own institutions and funders.

Taking all of the published material focused on the management and leadership of academic research together, two things can be said:

1 Not much has been published on the topic relative to the large investments made in academic research.
2 The degree of consistency of findings and recommendations is high, including consensus that project management and leadership are different for academic research than they are for other sectors (see Box 1.4).

BOX 1.4. FINDINGS FROM A LITERATURE REVIEW FOCUSED ON ACADEMIC RESEARCH PROJECT MANAGEMENT AND LEADERSHIP

* Many articles focused on the management or leadership of academic research cite or paraphrase Ernø-Kjølhede's (1999) statement from more than 20 years ago: "The management of a research project is full of uncertainty and complexity. Research has substantial elements of creativity and innovation and predicting the outcome of research in full is therefore very difficult."
* Additional major differences between general project management and research project management include the following: research project goals may be abstract and subject to change; research project team members have competing and possibly conflicting obligations, such as teaching and other projects; the purpose of a research project is to generate knowledge and the best achievable result (which may be different than the planned result); too much planning and control may be counterproductive for research projects; and the leadership and integration of research is more important than the rigid management of research project tasks (Huljenic et al., 2005; Riol & Thiullier, 2015).
* Authors have also noted that leadership of academic research differs from traditional leadership because of unique factors associated with the university context, the fact that leadership may be distributed across team members who come from different disciplines and sectors, and the graduate student–supervisor relationship (Anthony & Antony, 2017).
* Much of the work of academic research projects is performed by graduate students who need to be supported and provided with opportunities to learn (Lemieux-Charles, 2005; Riol & Thiullier, 2015).
* In addition to serving as the research lead and supervisor, the principal investigator of an academic research project may take on project management responsibilities (e.g., managing contracts, cost, time, scope, communications, and stakeholders), often without training (Cassanelli et al., 2017; Lemieux-Charles, 2005).
* Where there are dedicated research project managers (or equivalents, i.e., people with other titles who perform project management functions), they may be faced with resistance to basic project management processes and lack the ability to affect the behavior of

other research team members, in part because of challenges with project management techniques that are not suited to academic settings (Moore & Shangraw, 2011; Powers & Kerr, 2009).

* In describing how research project management and leadership operate now, the literature notes that project management tools and processes can be applied (Mustaro & Rossi, 2013) but that university culture can be "anti-management" (Moore & Shangraw, 2011).
* Academic research topics requiring more attention include time management, human resources management, risk management, partners, scope, and the project vision (Kuchta et al., 2017; Lemieux-Charles, 2005; vom Brocke & Lippe, 2015).
* Researchers have identified the need to pay more attention to the people side of research leadership to make science more productive, rigorous, and happy (Norris et al., 2018).
* In addition to developing their research and analytical skills, trainees need support in developing professional skills, including leadership and project management (CHSPRA, 2015; CIHR, 2017).
* Regarding future research and practice changes, the literature notes that improving research project management and leadership will require a mix of people-focused soft skills and technical skills and processes (Philbin, 2017; Riol & Thiullier, 2015).
* On the soft skills side, cooperation and compatibility among research project team members to make shared contributions to the research vision are critical, as are interpersonal and mentoring skills (Lippe & vom Brocke, 2016; Riol & Thiullier, 2015; vom Brocke & Lippe, 2015).
* In addition to soft skills, research projects also require flexible planning and monitoring, a clear understanding of responsibilities among team members, governance structures suited to academic environments, skilled project managers, and techniques tailored to academic settings (Cassanelli et al., 2017; Lemieux-Charles, 2005; Moore & Shangraw, 2011; Philbin, 2017; Powers & Kerr, 2009; Riol & Thiullier, 2015; vom Brocke & Lippe, 2015).
* On the basis of all of these findings, project management and leadership training and capacity building must be tailored to support skills development in academic settings (Lemieux-Charles, 2005; Philbin, 2017).
* The need for management and leadership capacities in the research sector is expected to grow as the size and complexity of research projects increase (Lemieux-Charles, 2005).

1.3 ORIGIN AND CONTENT OF THIS HANDBOOK

As the director responsible for up to $60 million in annual research funding from the Ontario Ministry of Health from 2010 to 2013, I saw how the lack of project management and leadership capacity threatened research performed at universities, research hospitals, and research institutes. I worked with many academic researchers who had excellent research and scientific skills but struggled to realize their visions or complete their projects on time. On reflection, this was not surprising, given that graduate school focuses almost exclusively on teaching trainees research methods for the sciences, arts, and humanities, leaving those who pursue careers in research to figure out research management and leadership on their own. But the status quo struck me as an inappropriate sink-or-swim approach when there is a clear need to build project management and leadership capacity in the research sector.

I decided to leverage my decades of experience as a certified project management professional, and what I had learned about leadership as a research funder, to develop training for research teams. My approach was informed by the report from a 2005 National Workshop on Research Leadership and Management planned by a team led by Professor Louise Lemieux-Charles (Lemieux-Charles, 2005). The workshop summary report made the point that everyone involved in academic research, from graduate students to senior researchers, has a role to play in research management and leadership (see Figure 1.2). I was also influenced by my participation in multiple non-academic career options panels that I had been part of and, later, by the work of the Canadian Health Services and Policy Research Alliance (CHSPRA, 2015; CIHR, 2017) on training modernization in health services and policy research.

On the basis of personal experience and the limited literature on the topic of academic research project management (see Box 1.4), it was clear to me that globally accepted project management and leadership practices would need to be tailored and adapted to work in academic research settings. As a certified project manager who began my career by working in international pharmaceutical R&D before moving to academic research roles, I realized that there was a significant disconnect between the project management guidance that works well for other sectors and what is needed for academic research projects. I also

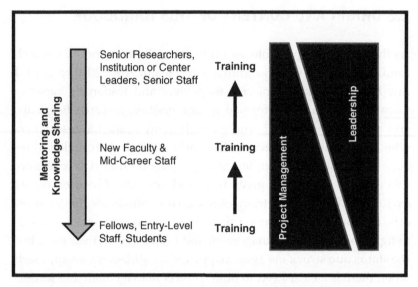

Figure 1.2. Everyone Has a Role to Play in Research Leadership and Management
Source: Adapted with permission from Lemieux-Charles (2005).

knew, firsthand, that leadership looks different in academic environments than it does in the innovative but highly regulated pharmaceutical sector where I had worked for 7 years. Paraphrasing the iconic baseball coach Tommy Lasorda, I believe that the effective leadership and management of academic research is like holding a dove – you need to hold it tightly enough that it does not fly away, but not so tightly that you crush it. Research projects need space to evolve and move in new directions, which means that the guidance that has been developed for other sectors needs to be tailored to be helpful and enabling, not constraining and burdensome. Therefore, the guidance and capacity building that I developed took the form of simplified and high-level versions of globally accepted project management tools and processes combined with complementary, less-structured advice from research leaders.

To start, I developed a graduate student course offered through the University of Toronto's Institute of Health Policy, Management and Evaluation. Participants included full-time graduate students and people pursuing graduate degrees on a part-time basis as they worked in public- and not-for-profit-sector organizations focused on health. The course material consisted primarily of well-known and globally accepted project management tools and processes that I had personally modified for my own use, complemented by guest lectures and informal question-and-answer sessions with research leaders from my network. Over time, I worked with a program advisory committee organized by the University of Toronto's School of Continuing Studies to develop a continuing education course that anyone (not just graduate students) could take, and I later developed shorter workshop and webinar versions of the training.

In total, more than 1,000 people have participated in the courses, workshops, and webinars on research project management and leadership that I have delivered since 2013. Most of the participants have been research staff, graduate students, and postdoctoral fellows working at universities, research hospitals, or research institutes, but approximately 10 percent have been principal investigators and early career researchers. In addition to providing training and services to more than 40 different university departments and not-for-profit organizations, I have occasionally provided customized training for not-for-profit organizations that specialize in developing or evaluating programs, and I have had people who work in the private sector attend my workshops.

At the end of each workshop or course, I use facilitated group discussions and polling combined with anonymous evaluation forms to learn what participants value the most and areas for improvement. Over the years, I have refined and modified the training content in response to the following things that I have learned from participants:

- A range of people in the academic sector, including graduate students, postdoctoral fellows, research staff, early career researchers, and experienced principal investigators, appreciate and make use of research project management and leadership guidance.
- Participants were the most interested in simplified versions of project management tools (e.g., the work breakdown structure [WBS]) and processes (e.g., risk management) that they could immediately begin using in planning and managing their own research.
- Participants appreciated seeing multiple (sometimes similar) examples of project management tools and processes being applied

to fictional or generic projects because those examples highlight the generalizability of the tools and increase the likelihood that one or more of the examples will be similar to what is required by their own projects.

- People inherently understood that tools and processes alone are not enough for personal or project success, and they valued the advice and stories of research leaders.
- Trainees, staff, and faculty who work on research projects benefit from guidance on topics that might seem obvious or unnecessary to people working in corporate roles or other sectors (e.g., how to plan and chair a meeting, the importance of project closure activities).

As I provided training and capacity-building sessions to hundreds of people, I also learned that there was no existing project management resource that was suitable for the research team members who attended my courses, workshops, and webinars. Of course, many comprehensive project management resources are available (see, e.g., Box 1.3), but in practice I found that those resources had a lot of detail that the research team members with whom I worked did not want or need, at least not to start with. I also realized that the lack of guidance fit for the purpose would pose an even bigger problem for people who did not want to attend a course or workshop and were seeking a stand-alone resource for research project management and leadership.

These observations led me to conceive of, and write, this handbook, beginning in 2021. In keeping with the feedback from course and workshop participants, the handbook is a practical resource that is light on concepts and theories and focuses instead on examples of research project management and leadership in practice.

1.4 SUMMARY OF PROJECT MANAGEMENT TOOLS AND PROCESSES FOR RESEARCH

1.4.1 Distinguishing Projects from Operations

It makes sense to start the discussion of academic research management and leadership with project management, because most research team members start building their management and leadership skills at the project level. Projects are temporary endeavors undertaken to create a unique product, service, or result. This means that every project has a beginning and an end and produces something that is, in some way, different from the outputs of other projects.

Consider a research project team studying the heat tolerance of crops. The lab may have specialized equipment and standard ways of performing studies, but if a heat wave hits, the research project team's project and project management will probably change in some ways. For example, some stakeholders may become more available and interested in being involved in the research, and others may be less available because they are actively involved in responding to the crisis. The research project team may also need to change its approach to sharing preliminary findings. Of course, no team ever wants to release preliminary research results that end up being disproven, but during a heat wave the stakes for the crop heat tolerance research team would be higher. If a team must retract or change preliminary findings, that can have very negative consequences for stakeholders who acted on preliminary findings or lead to loss of stakeholder trust in the research team.

In contrast with temporary, unique, and time-limited projects, operations are ongoing and may be repetitive. Making solar panels at a factory is one example of operations, and Table 1.2 presents others.

Because operations are about doing the same thing over and over again, approaches such as Lean Six Sigma (American Society for Quality, n.d.-b) may be used to perfect processes and minimize inefficiencies in how operations are conducted. However, because every project is unique in some way, project management cannot be about perfecting a single way of doing things. Instead, project management is about knowing how to adapt and apply project management tools and processes for the benefit of unique and individual projects. This handbook focuses mostly on project management for research, with some brief coverage of management related to research operations, research programs, and research portfolios in Section 5.2, "Applying Project Management Tools and Processes to Research Programs, Operations, and Portfolios."

Table 1.2. Contrasting Projects and Operations

Project	Operations
Applied research project to increase the efficiency of solar panels	Manufacturing solar panels at a factory
Running a clinical trial of a new drug product	Monitoring an approved drug for adverse drug effects
Buying and installing a new electron microscope	Supporting a community of scientists in using the electron microscope
Developing a policy for urban parks	Confirming that new proposed plans for urban parks comply with the policy
Developing a new method to improve detection of toxins in beach water	Monthly testing of toxins in beach water
Creating a new historically based opera	Operating a university theater
Launching a web portal with evidence-based resources for families of children with learning disabilities	Populating a web portal with new content every 2 weeks
Consulting with clinicians to develop a new guideline	Supporting the use of a guideline in practice

1.4.2 Project Management Tools and Processes

A stock chart (see Figure 1.3) is a good way to understand how project management tools and processes provide two major benefits. First, the stock chart tool is much better for presenting information than a narrative description would be. You could write pages and pages about how a stock price changes over time, but why would you? The visual presentation in the stock chart is much easier to make sense of and the chart helps people quickly understand whether the general trend for the stock price is positive or negative and how volatile the price is.

The second benefit of the stock chart tool may be less obvious – it serves as a prompt for people to capture standardized information about the stock price at regular intervals. In this way, the stock chart promotes a more thorough process for capturing and analyzing stock price data than would be possible with irregular and ad hoc written descriptions of the changes in stock price.

In the absence of project management guidance that is suitable for research, I have seen many research teams do the equivalent of writing pages and pages of text (or emails) to manage and lead their projects. Despite the time and effort required to do all of this writing, these bits

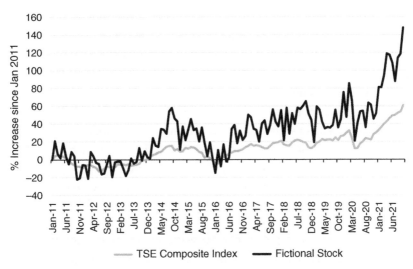

Figure 1.3. Fictional Stock Chart as an Example of a Tool Used in the Financial Services Sector
Source: Author.

and pieces of disconnected project information captured with ad hoc methods rarely cover basic project information needs, such as what the project will produce, who is responsible for what work, and how the project is progressing.

It does not have to be this way. Just like the financial services community has developed tools such as the stock chart, the project management community has developed tools for collecting and organizing information about projects. Once adapted to work for research projects, project management tools can help with sense-making, and the processes used to apply the tools ensure a comprehensive and consistent approach to managing research.

1.4.3 Overview of the Research Project Management Tools Presented in This Handbook

Because of their uncertainty, many academic research projects do not have the amount of detail that would be required to apply project management tools and processes in traditional ways. Instead, I recommend, and personally use, modified versions of project management tools and processes that are higher level than would be used for projects with more known details. I call this approach "light-touch" project management (see Box 1.5).

Even when using light-touch tools and processes, research teams should begin with the minimum amount of project management documentation that is needed and only add more when there is benefit in doing so. Figure 1.4 presents, at a high level, the light-touch tools that are most likely to add value to academic research projects, based on my own experience and feedback from people who have participated

BOX 1.5. WHAT IS LIGHT-TOUCH PROJECT MANAGEMENT?

"Light touch" means that I have taken project management tools and practices that could lead to the generation of tens to hundreds of pages of documentation and modified them to be as high-level and non-constraining as they can be while still providing value in the context of research.

Because of the variation in the certainty of research projects (see Figure 1.1), there will be variation in the length and detail of project documentation for research projects. In the pharmaceutical sector, I personally developed multipage project Gantt charts that had 400 or more tasks. In contrast, of the many high-level adapted Gantt charts that I have prepared for academic research projects, none have exceeded two pages in length.

As a rule of thumb, the greater the inherent uncertainty of a research project, the fewer the number of pages of planning and management documents. For example, an investigator-driven academic research project with high uncertainty might have a high-level plan with as few as three pages of planning and management documentation.

Of course, some research projects require pages of details that are captured in other mandatory documents such as regulatory submissions, permit applications, research protocols, research ethics board or internal review board submissions, and reports to funders and governments. Still, the overarching project management plan – the one that all team members and stakeholders need to understand and buy into – can be very short because it focuses on the high-level information that all the research team members and stakeholders need to know and agree on in order to work together effectively.

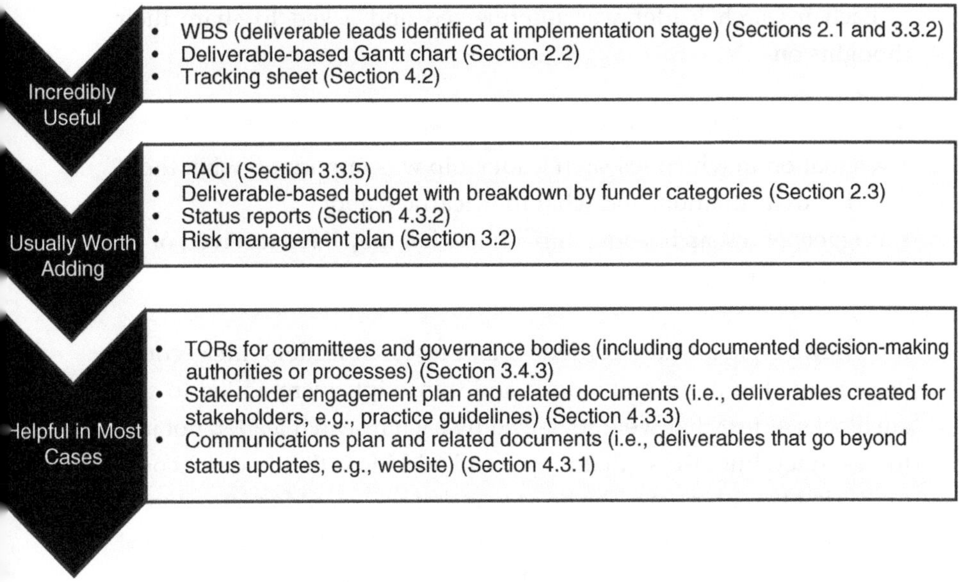

Incredibly Useful	• WBS (deliverable leads identified at implementation stage) (Sections 2.1 and 3.3.2) • Deliverable-based Gantt chart (Section 2.2) • Tracking sheet (Section 4.2)
Usually Worth Adding	• RACI (Section 3.3.5) • Deliverable-based budget with breakdown by funder categories (Section 2.3) • Status reports (Section 4.3.2) • Risk management plan (Section 3.2)
Helpful in Most Cases	• TORs for committees and governance bodies (including documented decision-making authorities or processes) (Section 3.4.3) • Stakeholder engagement plan and related documents (i.e., deliverables created for stakeholders, e.g., practice guidelines) (Section 4.3.3) • Communications plan and related documents (i.e., deliverables that go beyond status updates, e.g., website) (Section 4.3.1)

Figure 1.4. 20,000-Foot View of High-Impact Light-Touch Project Management Tools
RACI = Resource–Approver–Consulted–Informed; TORs = terms of reference; WBS = work breakdown structure.

in my courses and workshops. As noted in Figure 1.4, three tools – the work breakdown structure (WBS), deliverable-based Gantt chart, and tracking sheet – are incredibly useful. Even so, that does not mean that those three tools will be the most valuable and helpful for every reader's situation. Section 1.6, "How to Use This Handbook," provides guidance on how readers in various roles may want to start using this handbook.

1.5 MAIN THEMES FROM RESEARCH LEADER INTERVIEWS

Notwithstanding that project management tools and processes can be very helpful, success and impact in research requires much more than using templates and following processes. For that reason, in addition to presenting adapted project management tools and processes, this handbook includes advice from 19 research leaders.

Each research leader was interviewed and asked to share their thoughts on

- what research leadership means to them;
- a situation in which research leadership was important, what they did in that situation, and what they learned; and
- nuggets of research leadership advice that they have received or given over the years.

Interviews were audio recorded so that research leaders' ideas could be presented in their own words, and transcripts were edited to create blocks of text that were reviewed by each research leader, not just for accuracy, but also so that they could add ideas that had not come up during the interview. The hope was that this would create content that was similar to the unstructured and off-the-cuff advice that guest lecturer research leaders provided during my courses.

Interestingly, although there were differences in how the interviewees defined research leadership, almost every person interviewed spoke about the role of the research leader in mobilizing and supporting people with complementary skills in working together toward a common goal. The full write-ups of each research leader's interview are presented in Section 6, "Interviews with Research Leaders." In Box 1.6, I highlight that, taking the 19 interviews together, 10 themes emerged.

BOX 1.6. MAIN THEMES FROM RESEARCH LEADER INTERVIEWS

1 *It's the team that matters.* Research leadership is mostly about bringing together other people and providing them with the resources and support that they need to make their best contributions. It is less about what the research leader knows or does themselves. No research leader, no matter how smart they are, can accomplish on their own what a team of people with complementary skills can do together.

2 *Leadership is about passion, empathy, and inspiring others.* Being a research leader is much more than task delegation and project

management. Research leaders who relate to and inspire others on a personal level are the ones who have the biggest impact, in terms of both their research productivity and their effect on the people they help mentor and develop.

3 *Nothing happens without funding*. Even research leaders who have tenured academic positions must obtain their own (non-institutional) funding to pay for students, research staff, supplies, and other direct costs of research. Research leaders need to understand their role in securing funding and have an entrepreneurial spirit.

4 *Research leaders build and sustain communities.* Research advances through communities that are fueled by voluntary contributions of time and expertise from research. The more diverse research communities have better research outputs. When it comes to research leadership, you get what you give.

5 *Invest in long-term relationships with collaborators and stakeholders*. Relationships with collaborating researchers and partners in the public sector, not-for-profit, and business sectors are key to research leaders' successes. These relationships are one of the main sources of ideas and innovation and a big part of how research leaders have an impact. Research leaders should invest time in building and maintaining relationships with people with whom they click because relationships are most fruitful when people get along well together.

6 *Develop and support the next generation of researchers*. Research leaders have a responsibility to mentor and develop the researchers of tomorrow. Part of that is knowing when to step back and make room for new leaders to take over. One of the most gratifying and rewarding things about being a research leader is seeing research programs be strengthened and taken in new directions by the people one has mentored.

7 *Watch out for human resources and interpersonal issues*. No details are provided in the interview write-ups to protect confidentiality, but several research leaders spoke about how damaging it can be to have someone on the research project team who is not a good fit because of that person's poor interpersonal skills or insufficient technical or research skills. When this happens, the issue can spread and affect many relationships within the team and with external collaborators and stakeholders. It is important to move quickly to address interpersonal and performance issues

when they arise and to take whatever time is needed when filling roles on research teams.

8 ***Do not say yes to every potential partnership or project.*** If you come to be known as one of the leaders in your field, you will probably find that the opportunities to collaborate and partner outweigh the time you have for those activities. Research leaders are naturally inquisitive people with many interests. If they do not know how to say no nicely, they will not have time for the things that matter the most to them. This does not mean having a closed door when it comes to new opportunities, but it does mean being thoughtful and intentional so that you only say yes to the right things.

9 ***Stay true to your vision.*** A research leader's vision is one of the most important things they can contribute to their teams, to the communities that they build and support, and to society. But that does not mean that everyone will agree with the leader's vision or on how to achieve it. No matter what direction a research leader takes, there will always be some people who see things differently. Research leaders need to be mindful of not being pulled in directions that do not align with their vision or with the essence of what they are trying to accomplish. They may also need to develop a thick skin to stay true to their vision in the face of criticism.

10 ***Research leaders need to be flexible, adaptive, and constantly learning.*** Staying true to your vision as a research leader does not mean resisting change or others' advice. Research leaders know that they do not have all the answers, and they often spend more time listening than talking. If you are being innovative as a research leader, and if you are working with bright and inquisitive people at various stages of their careers, you should be adapting and changing how you approach your research and research leadership over time.

Each of these 10 themes was present in multiple interviews, although sometimes expressed in different ways. To direct readers to points of connection and complementarity between the research leaders' interview write-ups in Section 6 and the project management content of the handbook, "Leadership Advice Crosswalks" have been added throughout Sections 2 to 5.

1.6 HOW TO USE THIS HANDBOOK

As the handbook's title implies, it is intended to be a practical resource for anyone who wants to build their project management and leadership skills related to research. There is no right or wrong way to use the handbook, but it may help for people to think of it as a practical resource that they can use in the same way as they would consult a user's manual for a new piece of equipment.

Like the beginning of a user's manual, Section 1 of this handbook helps readers orient themselves to the content, and the Table of Contents includes descriptive headings for sections, subsections, research leader interviews, figures, tables, and text boxes that are designed to help readers find the guidance that will benefit them the most. For example, if you are involved in a project that is repeatedly being surprised by new negative risks, Section 3.2, "Processes to Identify and Manage Risks," would be a good place to start; if you are beginning to prepare a grant application, Section 3.5, "Using Project Management to Strengthen Grant Applications," can help; and if ineffective meetings are a source of frustration, you may want to begin with Section 5.1, "Running Effective Meetings." The nature of project management is that tools build upon each other, but, overall, the handbook is written in such a way that you can implement whatever subset of tools and processes adds value in your environment in the short term without having to read about multiple other tools and processes beforehand.

From the courses, workshops, and team coaching sessions that I have provided, I have learned that, depending on their role, people are interested in different content. Box 1.7 provides some suggestions about what handbook content might be particularly relevant to students, research staff, early career researchers, and seasoned principal investigators. These suggestions are not meant to be constraining. For example, nothing prevents students from focusing on the research leader interviews or experienced researchers from focusing on the project management content. Readers should feel free to use the handbook in whatever ways make sense for them.

None of the project management tools and processes described in this handbook require specialized software. Commercially available specialized project management software options do exist, including Microsoft Project (https://www.microsoft.com/en-ca/microsoft-365/project/project-management-software), Monday.com

BOX 1.7. SUGGESTIONS FOR DIFFERENT RESEARCH PROJECT TEAM MEMBERS' USE OF THIS HANDBOOK

- **Students** may want to begin by looking at the deliverables outlined in Appendix A, Figure A.1, "Work Breakdown Structure for a Fictional Graduate Student Thesis Project," and then, consistent with the guidance in Figure 1.4, follow Sections 2.1, 2.2, and 4.2 to use Figure A.1 as the foundation for their own WBS, deliverable-based Gantt chart, and deliverable-based tracking sheet.
- **Early career researchers** might similarly use and adapt Figure 5.3, "Work Breakdown Structure for a Fictional New Investigator's Research Portfolio," following the guidance in Sections 2.1, 2.2, and 4.2. They are also likely to find the 19 research leader interviews in Section 6 informative and (hopefully) inspiring.
- **Research staff** (e.g., research associates, project managers, co-ordinators, program administrators, research assistants) are often the ones who take on project management responsibilities and may be positioned to put a lot of the handbook's guidance into practice immediately. Instead of trying to implement everything at once, they should scan the Table of Contents, List of Illustrations, and List of Tables and identify one or two topics that relate to immediate risks or opportunities in their environments, try implementing guidance for those topics, and then consider adding more tools and processes.
- **Principal investigators and other senior researchers** are often interested in advice that helps them formalize and improve governance (see Section 3.4, "Decision Making, Governance, and Oversight"), communications (see Section 4.3, "Communications and Stakeholder Involvement during Implementation"), and negative risk management (see Section 3.2, "Processes to Identify and Manage Risks") for the large initiatives they lead. They may also appreciate advice on developing their teams (see Section 3.3.6, "Building Capacity across the Research Project Team") and find it helpful to see examples of how multiple projects can be organized into programs or portfolios of research (see Section 5.2, "Applying Project Management Tools and Processes to Research Programs, Operations, and Portfolios").

(https://monday.com/), Asana (https://asana.com/), Confluence (https://www.atlassian.com/software/confluence), Team Gantt (https://www.teamgantt.com/), and others. Depending on the project manager's and team's needs, the built-in functions of these applications may be useful in some cases. However, the examples presented in this handbook have intentionally been created with Microsoft Office applications (see Box 1.8, "Examples of Microsoft Office Suite Features that Can Be Used to Create and Populate Project Management Tools"), which offer several advantages, including the following:

- It is usually the case that everyone on the research project team has Microsoft Office applications (or equivalents such as Google Slides and Google Sheets), which means that everyone on the team can view and edit documents created with those applications; this makes it easier for the team to collaborate when creating and using project management tools.
- Unlike Microsoft Office applications, some purpose-built project management applications rely on a significant amount of detail that does not exist for many academic research projects. For example, in my experience, the natural unit of planning academic research projects is the half-month (e.g., a team might commit to having a deliverable completed in the first or second half of April as opposed to the 10th week of a project), but most project management applications require users to plan in terms of hours, days, or weeks.
- Research project team members often bring specialized skills and the capacity to lead deliverables over weeks and months and may not respond well to the daily or weekly assigned tasks generated by some specialized project management software.
- It can take many hours to learn how to use project management software, such as Microsoft Project, correctly, and it is probably more beneficial for team members to put those hours toward project work than toward learning project management software.

I also encourage readers to reach out to me if they think of modifications or additional content that would be helpful. In the same way that the courses, workshops, and webinars I deliver have been strengthened by feedback from participants, this handbook will become better and more useful as it evolves and expands alongside the needs of research team members.

BOX 1.8. MICROSOFT OFFICE SOFTWARE FEATURES THAT CAN BE USED TO CREATE AND POPULATE PROJECT MANAGEMENT TOOLS

- The SmartArt Hierarchy option that is designed to create organizational structures in Microsoft PowerPoint can also be used to create work breakdown structures (WBSs; see Section 2.1).
  - ° The Microsoft PowerPoint SmartArt Text Pane makes it easy to add or modify workstreams and deliverables to a WBS (e.g., using the promote/demote and move up/move down features).
  - ° The SmartArt Design menu includes layout options (e.g., right-hanging, both) that help maximize the font size on a one-page WBS.
  - ° Finishing touches can be put on the WBS by using the SmartArt Design "Convert to Shapes" function, which offers more flexibility in terms of font size and deliverable placement.
- Once the workstreams and deliverables of the WBS have been established in Microsoft PowerPoint SmartArt, the commands "Copy" and "Paste Special – [Unformatted] Text" can be used to transfer deliverables into other software, so text never needs to be rekeyed.
- The standard features of Microsoft Excel make it easy to create a deliverable-based Gantt chart (see Section 2.2):
  - ° The workstreams and deliverables can be "pasted" from the WBS into the first column(s) of a Microsoft Excel tab to create the vertical axis of the Gantt chart.
  - ° Cell shading and drawings of lines can be added in Microsoft Excel to show the start and end date of each workstream, deliverable, and subdeliverable.
  - ° The diamond symbol for milestones can be added using the "Draw" function of Microsoft Excel.
  - ° Text can be added, in deliverable bars or in footnotes, to provide additional details about the schedule.
- The standard features of Microsoft Excel also make it easy to create a deliverable-based tracking sheet (see Section 4.2) beginning by "pasting" the deliverables from the WBS into the first column(s).
- Modifiable templates for project management tools created using the Microsoft Office Suite are available for download from the Research Project Management (RPM) website (https://www.researchpm.com/tools-resources/).

Scoping and Planning Research Projects

2.1 SCOPE AND THE WORK BREAKDOWN STRUCTURE

2.1.1 Project Management Mindset of "Define, Then Deliver"

The project management mindset of "define, then deliver" (Box 2.1) is at the heart of the tailored project management guidance presented in this handbook. That mindset prompts research teams to think and plan in terms of the concrete things – also known as the deliverables – that their projects will produce. "Define, then deliver" means that even when a research team believes that they know what their near-term activities are, they take the time to define the project deliverables before they move on to project implementation and delivery.

BOX 2.1. PROJECT MANAGEMENT MINDSET: "DEFINE, THEN DELIVER"

- **Define:** Before you begin the work of your project, work with the research team and stakeholders to establish a common understanding of the deliverables that the project will produce.
- **Then deliver:** Assign qualified leads to all deliverables and support them in working together, using their judgment and expertise, to produce the deliverables.

For the "define" step, it may help research teams to think about all the documents and images of things that are not documents that they might want to have in a special folder at the end of their project. Most research team members have an intuitive understanding of the deliverables that will be the final products of a research project, such as peer-reviewed publications, reports, conference presentations, books, websites, and other knowledge dissemination products. However, the team should also be prompted to define interim or temporary deliverables, such as the documents that will be required for external approvals, terms of reference for committees, data collection instruments, inclusion and exclusion criteria, and so forth.

To identify all the deliverables of a research project, it may also help the team to think of the "nouns" that the project will produce, as opposed to the activities, or verbs, that will be undertaken. For example, instead of stating that a project will "perform public engagement" (an activity including the verb "perform"), the team might articulate specific deliverables (nouns), such as two town halls and 20 one-on-one interviews. By articulating these specific public engagement deliverables, the team is likely to uncover any variation in team members' understanding of what constitutes complete public engagement and also to be positioned to identify a lead for public engagement who is qualified to do the work to complete the deliverables.

Interim deliverables help in that they serve as stakes in the ground that help the team know how they are progressing toward completing the agreed-on project scope (see Figure 2.1). Outside of the research sector, people sometimes use the metaphors of a blueprint or a road map to describe the output of project planning. For many research projects, however, the team may not want a plan that is too detailed or fixed. The metaphor of deliverables as stakes in the ground works better for research because the stakes orient the research team toward a common goal without implying that the final destination, or the route to get there, is rigid or set in stone.

2.1.2 The Work Breakdown Structure as a Tool to Articulate Project Scope

"Project scope" is the work required to complete a project. Many research project team members intuitively understand that they need

Figure 2.1. Deliverables as Stakes in the Ground for Research Project Planning and Implementation
Source: Illustration by Juliet Di Carlo.

to be able to describe the research project's scope in concrete terms if they want to lead and inspire others and secure research funding to achieve their vision. However, because many research project managers are self-taught, they often do not benefit from tools and processes that assist them in defining scope in a way that is 100 percent complete.

The work breakdown structure (WBS) is a project management tool that helps the research project team and project stakeholders visualize scope in terms of deliverables. The WBS was hands down identified as the single most helpful personal takeaway by hundreds of participants in research project management courses and workshops that I delivered from 2013 to 2022.

In terms of appearance, the WBS resembles a hierarchical organizational structure diagram. However, instead of having the chief executive office or president at the top with a column for each of the vice presidents and departments beneath them, a research project WBS

LEADERSHIP ADVICE CROSSWALK

2.1. RELATIONSHIP BETWEEN SCOPE AND VISION

Research leaders Beth Coleman, Michael Schull, and David Wolfe spoke about the importance of translating their vision into manageable chunks of scope that help focus effort and provide clarity about what people are working to achieve together. That is not to say that the documents that define deliverables constitute the complete vision, just that they help to promote a common understanding of some concrete deliverables that contribute to the vision. A research leader's vision is broader and greater than the scope and deliverables of any one project. The vision often involves pushing boundaries, asking new questions, and bringing research skills to bear on societal problems (see, e.g., interviews with Sharon Straus, Jutta Treviranus, and Stefaan Verhulst).

has the project name at the top and columns with work-streams[1] (identified in Figure 2.2 with the letters A, B, C, etc.) and deliverables beneath the workstreams (identified in Figure 2.2 with letter–number combinations, e.g., A1, C2).[2]

Just like a corporate organizational structure, the WBS is much easier to test for completeness than a list of items because of its visual format. Imagine you are presented with a numbered list of 200 names and asked whether it accurately presents a company's entire staff. Apart from being able to assess whether the total count of names on the list is the same as the total count of people on the company's payroll, it would be very hard to know much about the completeness of the list. Alternatively, if an organizational structure is created that has the count or names of employees assigned to each department, it is more likely that you would be able to identify whether all staff in every department have been included, and it enables a simple process to test for completeness – you can ask the lead for each department to confirm the accuracy and completeness of their portion of the organizational structure to make sure that no staff person has been missed.

---

1   The *Horizon Europe Programme Guide* (European Commission, 2022) uses the term "work packages" in place of "workstreams." In this handbook, I use "workstream" instead of "work package" because the *PMBOK® Guide* (Project Management Institute, 2021) and *Managing Successful Projects with PRINCE 2®* (Axelos, 2017) use the term "work package" in ways that differ from the *Horizon Europe Programme Guide* and from each other.

2   The use of this, or any other, hierarchical numbering scheme is optional, but it can create a helpful shorthand for referring to specific research project deliverables.

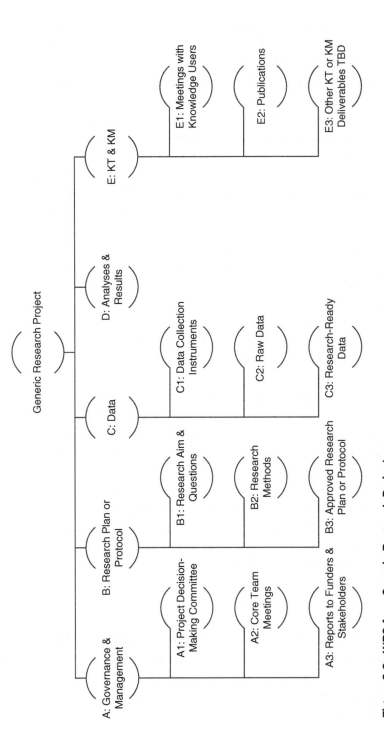

Figure 2.2. WBS for a Generic Research Project

Notes: KM = knowledge mobilization; KT = knowledge translation; TBD = to be determined; WBS = work breakdown structure.

The same is true when it comes to assessing the completeness of research project deliverables. If something is necessary for your project scope and your project planning has inadvertently missed it, people are more likely to notice its absence on a WBS than they would in a list of deliverables, milestones, or project activities.

As illustrated in Figure 2.2, the WBSs for research projects will often present workstreams and deliverables at a very high level. This is because the WBS helps the research project team establish a common understanding of what deliverables a research project will produce without getting into the details of how those deliverables will be produced. For research projects that are very innovative, the research project team may not know exactly how the deliverables will be produced at the start of the project, and that is okay. Deliverable leads are chosen on the basis of their knowledge and capacity to figure out how to produce deliverables (see Section 3.3, "Roles and Responsibilities"). Even if the future is uncertain, the deliverable-based WBS helps the whole research project team get on the same page in terms of what the interim and final products of a research project are likely to be, and it provides a simple visual way to communicate any changes in scope that arise during project implementation.

The key to high-level deliverable-based scoping is to create a WBS that covers the entire project with the level of detail that everyone needs to know and agree on. Many research projects will have additional documents that are more detailed than the WBS and used by a subset of the research project team members (e.g., detailed study protocols required by regulators, ethics submissions, permit applications). However, you do not want those detailed planning documents to be your only articulation of scope because (a) you do not want to burden the entire research project team with updates as those detailed documents are developed and refined and (b) there are usually research team members and stakeholders who do not want, or need to understand, all the details in those documents.

2.1.3 Deliverable-Based Scoping Drives Activities to the Point at Which They Produce Something Tangible

Before discussing the five workstreams presented in Figure 2.2, it is worth noting how the process of using a WBS to define scope ensures that activities are taken to the point at which they have produced something tangible. I use the deliverable "B1: Research Aim and Questions" to illustrate this benefit of WBSs. Regardless of whether there is a WBS or not, most, if not all, research project teams will work together to agree on their aims and research questions some time near the start of a research project. However, when project management is informal and ad hoc, the aim and research questions are not always expressed in a tangible and distinct way. For example, they may be communicated in meeting minutes, via emails, or orally during a meeting of the research project team. Having a WBS with a deliverable named "B1: Research Aim and Questions" prompts the research project team to produce a stand-alone document containing the research aim and questions, and that tangible document produces other benefits. For example, the "B1: Research Aim and Questions" document can be shared across the team, including when students and new members join, to make sure that everybody understands what the research aim and questions are. The document can also be shared with stakeholders, funders, and potential partners to confirm alignment or explore collaboration in ways that would not be possible with meeting minutes or a forwarded email. In these ways, the small amount of extra work it takes to convert information that exists about the research aim and questions into a distinct and tangible deliverable produces the large benefit of making it easier to communicate project scope and decreasing the likelihood of misunderstandings about deliverables among research team members, stakeholders, and partners.

2.1.4 Common Workstreams and Deliverables for Research Projects

Of course, every research project is different, but there are some workstreams and deliverables that many academic research projects have in common. Also, because the WBS presents stakes in the ground for the tangible deliverables that the project will produce, as opposed to the detailed content of the deliverables, the WBSs for two very different projects can be quite similar. I use a generic research project to do a high-level walk-through of the five workstreams presented in the WBS that are common across many academic research projects (see Figure 2.2).

The first workstream, A: Governance and Management, might be the one that is least familiar to many readers because research project teams often cover it informally. The governance and management workstream does not usually represent a lot of additional work for the research project team beyond what would happen in the absence of a WBS, but articulating specific governance and management deliverables helps to ensure a thorough and complete project plan and a well-governed and well-managed project during the implementation phase. Section 3.3, "Roles and Responsibilities," and Section 3.4, "Decision Making, Governance, and Oversight," provide more guidance about the governance and management workstream, so for now I just note three governance and management deliverables that it helps to include in the scope of most research projects:

- *A1: Project Decision-Making Committee:* the group of people who are identified, up front, as being responsible for making major decisions about the project (e.g., a steering committee or research executive committee)
- *A2: Core Team Meetings:* regular meetings of the group of people who work on the project on a regular basis (i.e., the people who do some work on the project in most weeks)
- *A3: Reports to Funders and Stakeholders:* distinct project outputs that provide information to people outside of the research project team about project progress, risks, opportunities, issues, and accomplishments.

The deliverables for Workstream B: Research Plan or Protocol, illustrate, at a high level, how the research plan or protocol will be developed. Often this will start with articulation of B1: Research Aim and Questions, followed by B2: Research Methods, that is, a document that presents the methodology or methodologies that will be used for the research. For highly uncertain research projects, the methods document created at the start of the project may be very high level – for example, it may simply state whether the research will use quantitative, qualitative, or mixed methods or whether it will be descriptive or experimental in nature. When the project moves into the implementation phase, the details of the methodology will become more defined for the people who are directly involved in performing the work, but the high-level deliverables in the WBS may not change unless the high-level choices about the methods change. The final deliverable under Workstream B: Approved Research Plan or Protocol is the protocol or plan document itself. Depending on the nature and circumstances of the project, there may be subdeliverables

> **LEADERSHIP ADVICE CROSSWALK**
>
> **2.2. THE VALUE OF REGULARLY SCHEDULED MEETINGS**
> Colleen Flood spoke about the value of having scheduled dates and times for the team to connect every 1 to 2 weeks, even if there is no formal agenda for those meetings. Including meetings in the project schedule creates time and space for team members to come together and exchange ideas.

as the plan or protocol is finalized. For example, for research with human subjects, the WBS might include B3a: Draft Research Ethics Board Application, 3b: Final Research Ethics Board Application, and B3c: Approved Research Ethics Board Application.

The third workstream, C: Data, maps out the stakes in the ground for research projects that involve quantitative or qualitative data. The "instruments" in C1: Data Collection Instruments could refer to standardized tools for collecting or organizing qualitative research data (e.g., focus group interview guides) or physical instruments (e.g., thermometers, balances, spectrometers, and other laboratory equipment). Regardless of the nature of the research data, Figure 2.2 distinguishes between C2: Raw Data and C3: Research-Ready Data to ensure that team members and stakeholders understand the distinction between, and work associated with, raw data at the point of collection and data that are ready for research and analysis.

It is important to note that the number of deliverables on the WBS is not necessarily an indication of the amount of work associated with a workstream. To emphasize this point, Figure 2.2 does not include any specific deliverables for Workstream D: Analyses and Results. Even if most of the project work will fall under this workstream, if the lead for that workstream, the research project team, and the project stakeholders all have a common understanding of what needs to be done in terms of analyses and results, the WBS may not need to include any breakdown. In other cases, it may be necessary to break D: Analyses and

Results down into deliverables, particularly if the project includes more than one kind of analysis, for example, qualitative coding and statistical analyses of data. Section 2.1.5, "Using the Work Breakdown Structure to Establish a Shared Understanding of the Research Project's Scope," and the Appendices provide some examples of deliverables that research project WBSs might identify under D: Analyses and Results.

The final workstream in Figure 2.2 is E: Knowledge Translation (KT) and Knowledge Mobilization (KM). Depending on the research discipline, other labels and abbreviations can be applied to this workstream, such as knowledge translation and exchange (KTE). Regardless of the label applied to it, this workstream is the place to include deliverables that help the knowledge and outputs generated by the research project turn into action and impact.

In courses and workshops with academic research team members, peer-reviewed publications are almost always identified as a key deliverable under the KT and KM workstream, but E1: Meetings with Knowledge Users is also included in Figure 2.2 to reflect the growing recognition that it is important to have deep involvement of the groups and individuals who are positioned to act on research findings and outputs, that is, the knowledge users and people who would be affected by the project (CIHR, n.d., 2016). The final deliverable of Figure 2.2, E3: Other KT and KM Deliverables TBD, has been included for two reasons. First, it reflects the fact that research projects that have publications and meetings as their only KT or KM outputs are becoming increasingly rare. Second, it highlights that it is acceptable, and logical, to include a placeholder if you know that additional deliverables will be produced, but you do not yet know what those deliverables are.

2.1.5 Using the Work Breakdown Structure to Establish a Common Understanding of a Research Project's Scope

The extraordinary benefit of the WBS is that it, in a single page, helps the research project team and project stakeholders establish a common understanding of the deliverables that constitute the complete project scope. The WBS also helps to provide clarification about deliverables that might reasonably be considered within or outside of the project's scope. I use the non-research example of bathroom renovation to illustrate this point.

The WBS for a new bathroom would almost certainly include deliverables labeled "toilet," "sink," and "mirror." You would not need to include "door" as a deliverable on the WBS because every bathroom has one of those, but you might want to have a deliverable named "locking doorknob" if you want to make sure everyone understands that the door must have a lock. Most important, you would want your WBS to be clear about whether the bathroom includes a bathtub, a shower, or both because there is a lot of variation in terms of whether individual bathrooms have those items.

Because the WBS presents scope in visual terms, it is easier for people to process than lists or blocks of text, especially if it is kept to a single page. Figure 2.3 shows how the WBS for the research project in Figure 2.2 would change if a Workstream F: Training and Capacity Building is added. Consider how apparent the additional training and capacity-building workstream in Figure 2.3 is, and how much harder it would be for people to process the additional deliverables if they were presented as one or two new sentences in a written project description.

To develop your WBS, it is often easiest to begin with an existing WBS that bears some resemblance to your project. This could be a WBS from one of the Appendices to this handbook, a downloadable WBS template (https://researchpm.com/tools-resources/), or, even better, a WBS that your research project team has used for a previous project. The next step is to modify or add deliverables so that the WBS reflects the unique scope of your project as you understand it. There is no single correct way to create a WBS, and nobody is bound to use the five or six workstreams presented in Figures 2.2 and 2.3. What is important is that you present workstreams and deliverables that the team will have the skills and knowledge to produce.

At the planning or grant application stage of a research project, you do not need to have all the workstream and deliverable leads identified, but you should present the scope in such a way that leads could be identified at some point (see Section 3.3.2, "Work Breakdown Structure with the Leads' Initials as a Tool for Identifying Workstream and Deliverable Leads"). In other words, you would not want to create a deliverable or workstream that you cannot imagine any single individual having the skill to lead.

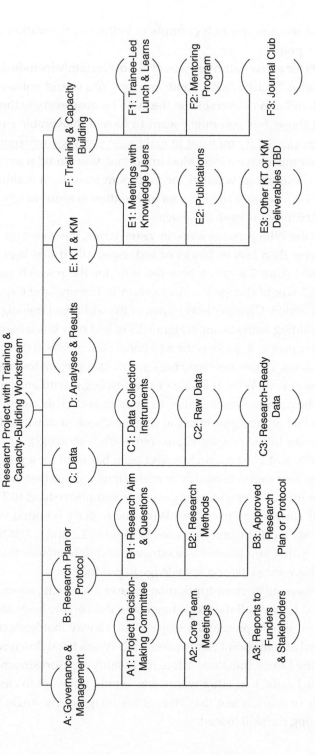

Figure 2.3. WBS for a Generic Research Project with a Training and Capacity-Building Workstream

Note: KM = knowledge mobilization; KT = knowledge translation; TBD = to be determined; WBS = work breakdown structure.

To support capacity building, deliverables on the WBS can be broken down into narrow-scope subdeliverables that less-experienced team members can lead. This can help early-career team members build their curriculum vitae or résumé and leading a subdeliverable can be a step on their personal paths to leading research projects, research programs, and even research institutions.

Once you have created a preliminary draft WBS, the next step is to begin circulating it for comment, beginning with one or two people who will provide honest and constructive feedback. Ask all the reviewers two questions – "Do you know what these labels mean?" and "If we produce this, and only this, will the project be complete?" – and expect that their responses will change your WBS, potentially in major ways. It is not uncommon for reviewer feedback to lead to different labels for deliverables, the breakdown of deliverables into subdeliverables to clarify scope, or both. If your reviewers feel that anything major is missing, or mislabeled, the odds are good that your WBS will be unclear or open to different interpretations by other people, too.

To illustrate how a WBS will reflect the unique deliverables of a research project, two fictional examples are provided in Boxes 2.2 and 2.3 and in Figures 2.4 and 2.5, respectively, with additional examples in the Appendices. The inclusion of B4: Permits in the WBS for a pollution monitoring project (see Box 2.2 and Figure 2.4) is an example of a deliverable that other research projects might not need but that would be essential to include in the scope for a drone-based pollution monitoring study. The second example WBS is for the evaluation of a seniors' health clinics project (see Box 2.3 and Figure 2.5), and it includes details aligned with government funder needs, that is, a steering committee and six specific subdeliverables for the evaluation plan.

One thing to be aware of is that some reviewers on the team may suggest extensive details for the deliverables and workstreams that they know the best. This is a natural phenomenon, particularly if these reviewers are also the leads for workstreams and deliverables. Generally, the best approach in this case is to distinguish between the details that the subset of research project team members working on a deliverable would need to know and the information that the whole research project team and stakeholders would need to know.

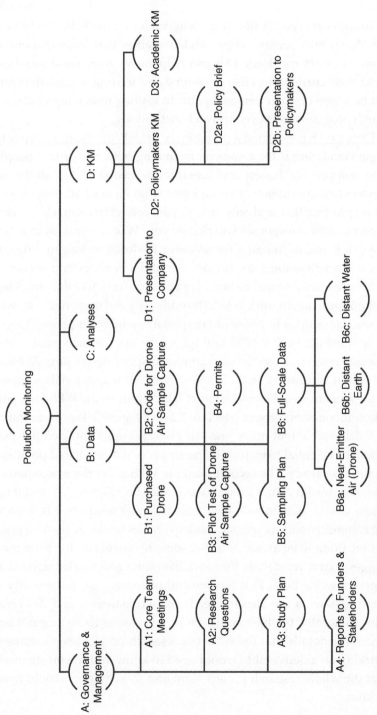

Figure 2.4. WBS for a Fictional Pollution Research Project

Notes: KM = knowledge mobilization; WBS = work breakdown structure.

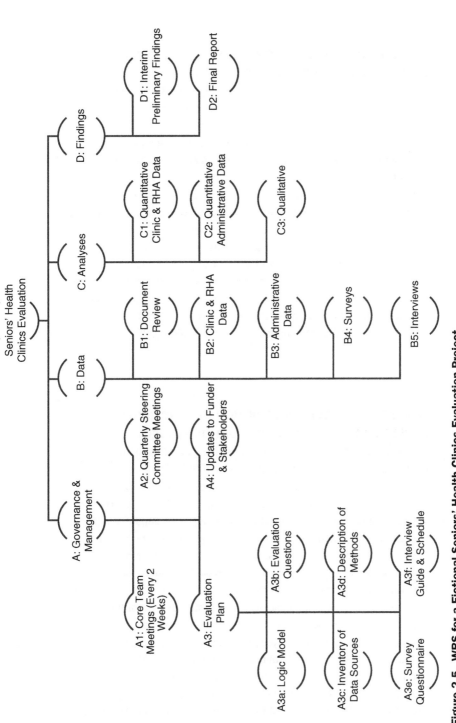

Figure 2.5. WBS for a Fictional Seniors' Health Clinics Evaluation Project

Notes: RHA = regional health authority; WBS = work breakdown structure.

BOX 2.2. HIGH-LEVEL DESCRIPTION OF A FICTIONAL POLLUTION RESEARCH PROJECT

Pollution monitoring of major emitters, such as electrical power generation plants or smelters, is important to assess the environmental impact of their operations. A three-dimensional profile of the spread of pollution from such sites during various weather conditions is needed to enable the development of mitigation and remediation strategies. A research team plans to measure pollutants in the air within 2 kilometers of an emission site using a drone and to compare and correlate the air pollution results with pollution measured in water and soil at sites distant from the emitter. Completion of the project will require the purchase and programming of the drone and air sampling equipment, drone-based air sampling, physical collection of water and soil samples, analyses of all samples, and comparison and correlation of near-emitter drone-based measurements with distant air and water pollution results. This project is funded by the federal government at $150,000 annually for 2 years ($300,000 total).

BOX 2.3. HIGH-LEVEL DESCRIPTION OF A FICTIONAL SENIORS' HEALTH CLINICS EVALUATION PROJECT

A regional health authority (RHA) has established 15 seniors' health clinics for individuals aged older than 65 years to receive comprehensive assessments, immunizations, preventive care, and other health care services. One year after the funding started, anecdotal information suggests that there has been variation in the success of the program's implementation. Some sites are reporting large numbers of older adults served; other sites have established only a fraction of their programming and have few clients. Both the RHA and the Ministry of Health are interested in a formative evaluation study to address questions, including the status of each of the clinics, the extent to which they are following the planned model of service delivery, the activities and outputs of each clinic, and the impact of these services on other health system metrics. In addition to quantitative analyses, the evaluation should use qualitative methods to shed light on how and why different sites are experiencing and implementing the program in different ways. The budget is $90,000, and the RHA has requested the results in 9 months.

As a rule of thumb, a WBS for a research project will usually fit on a single page with 10-point type or larger. This is in stark contrast to the 8/80 rule of thumb for (non-research) WBSs (see, e.g., Donato, 2022) which recommends that project work should be broken down into individual work packages that are between 8 and 80 hours of work each. One full-time person will work approximately 1,700 to 2,000 hours per year, assuming 15 vacation days and a work week that is between 35 and 40 hours long. On the basis of those estimates, the WBS for a 2-year, 5,000-hour research project with two graduate students, one part-time postdoctoral fellow, and some research faculty time would include between 60 and 600 deliverables! Clearly, many research projects, and most of those in academic settings, never put that level of detail into writing. A research project plan with that many pages of deliverables would be mostly fiction and not helpful for implementation.

However, occasionally, you may need to create one or more separate pages for some workstreams or deliverables in the same way that company organizational structures may have separate pages that break down departments. Additionally, or alternatively, your research project team and stakeholders may benefit from a WBS dictionary that provides a few lines of detail about each of the workstreams and deliverables in the WBS (see Appendix F, "Example Full Project Plan for a Fictional Natural Sciences Research Project That Is Part of a Multidisciplinary Program" for an example).

As with all project management, you should be guided by what makes sense for your project and research project team and be mindful of the fact that if your WBS becomes long and detailed, people may not engage with it. One of the benefits of a single-page WBS is that people are more likely to read and process it than they would a multipage document. Nothing prevents you from adding details about scope beyond the WBS if needed or requested, but starting with the minimum documentation that adds value and increasing the level of detail when needed is generally better than starting with a long and detailed document, particularly if the details are likely to change during the implementation phase of the project.

As your WBS is improved by feedback, widen the circle of people who receive copies to include key external stakeholders (see Section 2.4, "Involving Stakeholders in Project Planning") and make sure to provide anyone that you consult with a copy of the WBS once it has been finalized.

If you find that the WBS is very intuitive, you are not alone. For many, the WBS is a powerful communication tool that conveys, in a single page, the complete essence of a project even in the absence of any narrative description of it (see the Appendices for additional examples). For others, the WBS may be more like the plumbing or wiring of a building – something that indirectly helps them achieve their objectives, but not something that they give a lot of thought to. Regardless of whether it is in the foreground or the background, the WBS provides many benefits.

For example, the WBS is an excellent tool to get people on the same page regarding what the project will produce. If there are any differences of opinion about project deliverables, it is much better to have them surface and be resolved while working with a one-page WBS than later in the project when you have invested resources. Most important, the WBS serves as a complete foundation for other project planning and implementation tools, such as the schedule, budget, and risk management plan.

Box 2.4 summarizes the things you want to do, and avoid doing, when you are creating and using a WBS in research project planning.

BOX 2.4. WORK BREAKDOWN STRUCTURE DOS AND DON'TS

- **Do** use previously completed work breakdown structures (WBSs) for related projects as a starting point for new WBSs.
- **Do** feel free to have "Other – to be determined" as a deliverable on your WBS if you know that additional deliverables will be produced but are not sure what they will be.
- **Do** use the WBS to establish a common understanding of the project's scope and to provide clarification about deliverables that might reasonably be considered within or outside of its scope.
- **Do** use the WBS to check for completeness.
  - Circulate the WBS to a few team members, then the whole team, and then stakeholders, and ask the question "If we

produce this – and only this – will the project be complete?" Adjust the WBS on the basis of the feedback you receive.

○ Also ask people whether the elements of the WBS are clear and have intuitive labels, and make changes or add footnotes until you have text that is understood by the entire research project team and project stakeholders.

• **Do** identify leads for workstreams and deliverables, or at least define workstreams and deliverables in such a way that a qualified lead can be identified in the future.

• **Don't** go into a level of detail that is needed by only a subset of the people leading or working on a deliverable.

• **Do** use the WBS as the foundation for all other research project planning and implementation activities.

2.2 DELIVERABLE-BASED SCHEDULE

2.2.1 Using Work Breakdown Structure Deliverables to Create a Schedule That Covers the Project's Entire Scope

The project schedule, often presented in a Gantt chart format, is a visual sequenced presentation of the work required to complete a project. A deliverable-based Gantt chart is, as its name implies, a schedule that visually presents the time required for the deliverables of a project to be completed. Using the deliverables of the WBS as the vertical axis for a Gantt chart ensures that the schedule will cover 100 percent of your project scope (see Figure 2.6). In contrast, if you use a list of activities or milestones as the vertical axis of a Gantt chart, the schedule may inadvertently leave out important project work.

Figure 2.6 presents the deliverable-based Gantt chart for the fictional pollution research project identified in Box 2.2 and Figure 2.4. The hierarchical structure of the WBS is preserved in the chart using color, shading, and variation in the thickness of the bars. There is no set format for a Gantt chart but, as is the case for Figure 2.6, most Gantt charts have darker or thicker bars and lines for the workstreams and highest-level deliverables. For example, in Figure 2.6, the workstreams are presented as black bars, the first-level deliverables as gray bars, and the second-level deliverables (also known as subdeliverables) as black lines.

2.2.2 Benefits of a Schedule

Given the uncertain nature of research, it is understandable that some research project teams might resist or resent the project schedule, potentially perceiving it as an administrative burden intended to hold the team accountable for things that are beyond their control. For that reason, I begin the discussion of the schedule with some reasons why a research project team might want to establish a schedule, even if their funder or host institution does not require one.

First and foremost, research project teams need a schedule so that they do not run out of time to complete their project. Much of the quality of the final products of a research project is directly related to how much time is available to review and improve the project outputs in the final stage. Without a schedule, research project teams are more likely to be rushed near the end of the project, which increases the risk of mistakes.

Second, all project schedules include dependencies – in other words, they have deliverables that cannot start until other deliverables have been completed (or at least nearly completed). Just like the WBS helps the team get on the same page with respect to scope, the schedule helps the team have a common understanding of dependencies. This is important because deliverable leads need to be able to distinguish between situations in which they can take extra weeks or months to complete their work and situations in which any delay will have a negative effect on other deliverables and workstreams. In this way, the schedule is the project management tool that facilitates collaboration and coordination between research project team members.

The schedule also helps research project team members understand which deliverables are constrained (e.g., if a report to a funder is due by a specific date) and which deliverables are not constrained. Examples of non-time-constrained deliverables include preparatory work for knowledge translation products or events and advance work (e.g., on the background sections of publications and reports to funders).

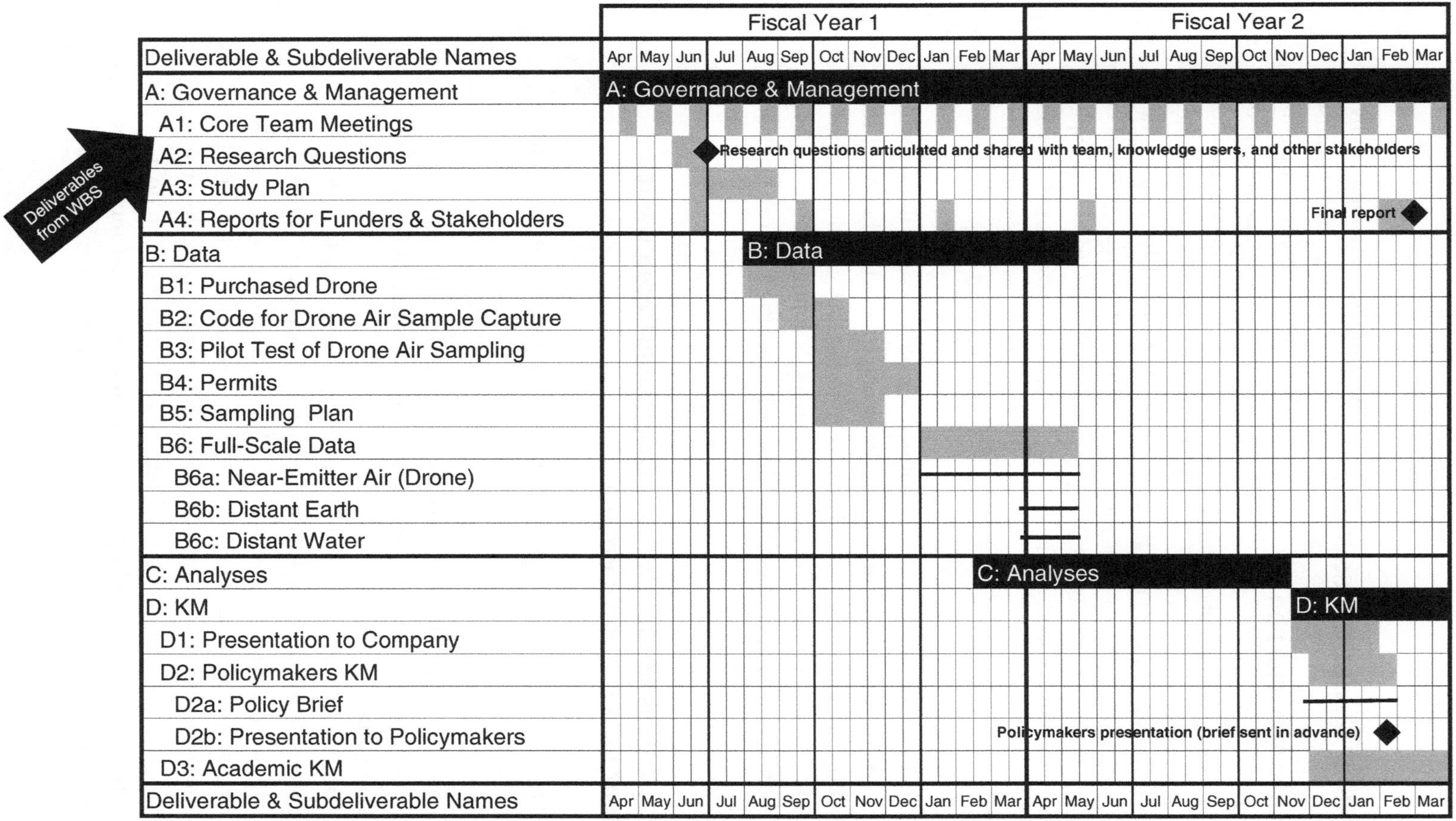

Figure 2.6. Deliverable-Based Gantt Chart for a Fictional Pollution Research Project
Note: KM = knowledge mobilization.

Non-time-constrained deliverables are important because they are a major source of flexibility. For research projects, it is not uncommon for time-constrained deliverables to be delayed for reasons beyond the team's control. For example, the team may experience delays related to participant recruitment, research ethics board approval, permits and regulatory approvals, delivery of materials, or equipment breakdowns. In those cases, you do not want team members to be sitting idle while they wait for work on a time-constrained deliverable to restart, because that is equivalent to building a future deficit of resources. It is much better to have identified non-time-constrained deliverables that the team can work on when time-constrained deliverables become delayed.

2.2.3 Steps for Developing a Deliverable-Based Gantt Chart for a Research Project

There are five general steps in establishing a research project deliverable-based Gantt chart:

1 Enter or "paste" the names of the deliverables from the WBS in the first column (the vertical axis) of the deliverable-based Gantt chart.
2 Estimate the total amount of time required to complete each deliverable identified in the WBS (i.e., the time between the start date and finish date of the deliverable). The duration is not necessarily a reflection of the work effort required to complete a deliverable. For example, if a statistician external to the team estimates that they will need to perform 36 hours of work and they can do it between March 1 and March 15, the duration is 1 half-month, not 36 hours. You can estimate the deliverable duration on the basis

of historical experience, expert judgment (i.e., the advice of some-one who would be in a position to know on the basis of their past experience), or a simple parametric estimate calculation that takes several possible durations into account and weights the most common one more heavily (see Figure 2.7).

3   Even though it may feel counterintuitive, establish the schedule working backward, beginning with the last deliverable and the project end date and plotting the durations for each deliverable, honoring dependencies and hard constraints.

- Whenever possible, start by building in buffer at the end of the project because this can make a big difference in the quality of final project deliverables.

4   Check the unadjusted start date, and if it falls before the actual start date of your project funding, compress the schedule until you have a planned schedule that completes the deliverables in the allowed time with no major resource bottlenecks (see Section 2.2.4, "Schedule Compression").

5   Add key milestones – tasks of zero duration that show an important achievement at a specific point in time – that you want to draw attention to. For example, the deliverable-based Gantt chart for the pollution research project in Figure 2.6 includes three milestones expressed as black diamonds. Some common milestones for research projects are the establishment of a funding agreement or memorandum of understanding, the articulation of research questions, the start or finish of data collection, and the delivery of interim and final reports.

2.2.4 Schedule Compression

In Figure 2.6, work on several of the deliverables is set to start before their predecessor deliverables have been completed. This is called fast-tracking, and it is common in all project scheduling, not just research project scheduling. It is also one of the reasons you want to establish your schedule by working backward from the end date. If you begin with the tasks and deliverables that you know best – that is, the ones your team is planning to do in the upcoming weeks and months – the natural tendency is to have a relaxed schedule for the

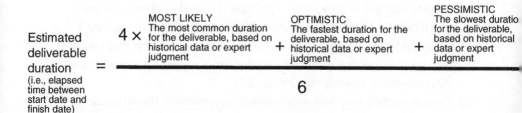

Figure 2.7. Parametric Estimates of Deliverable Duration

first months or year of your project, that is, one in which no deliverables start before their predecessors end. However, that can directly lead to a highly compressed and overly optimistic schedule at the end of the project.

In Figures 2.8 and 2.9, two deliverable-based Gantt charts for the fictional pollution research project illustrate the downside of relaxed scheduling at the start of the project. In Figure 2.8, the recommended schedule includes two examples of fast-tracking identified with arrow symbols: (a) work is initiated to purchase a drone for air sample collection in early August before the study plan is finalized in late August and (b) the analyses of samples start in mid-February before sample collection ends in mid-April. Because of this fast-tracking, Figure 2.8 includes 8 months for sample analyses out of a 24-month project.

In contrast, Figure 2.9 presents a deliverable-based Gantt chart that starts at a relaxed pace without any fast-tracking. Notably, in Figure 2.9 only 7 months are allowed for analyses (vs. 8 months when fast-tracking is applied) and, even more significant, much less time is included for knowledge mobilization – 2.5 months compared with 4.5 months. Also, the schedule without fast-tracking in Figure 2.9 has no buffer at the end of the schedule, with the final report being produced in the last 2 weeks of the project. This is extremely risky. If analyses are delayed or people are unable to complete analyses during the holiday period, the schedule in Figure 2.9 risks a situation in which analyses are still being conducted even as presentations to external stakeholders are being made. If a research project team makes its results public, even in small circles, and they end up being wrong, the consequences can be very serious in terms of knowledge user trust and researchers' reputation. Nothing in research project management is entirely risk free, but it is better to take on known risks early in the project (when possible), because if fast-tracking does not work as planned, the team will have more time and options to bring the project back on track.

Fast-tracking is just one option for schedule compression (see Box 2.5). Others include "crashing" the schedule by adding resources to complete deliverables in less time or drawing on the skill of other groups and organizations so that you buy or partner on deliverables instead of having your team "make" them all. However, as noted in Box 2.5, crashing is not always an option for research project teams consisting of highly skilled individuals, and your team will always give something up if they switch from producing a deliverable themselves to buying it or partnering with others to produce it.

When compressing a schedule, you may have to resist the urge to compress the schedule only enough to complete the last deliverable just under the wire. Academic research projects are often highly uncertain with unpredictable timing. A schedule with zero buffer includes the risky assumption that everything will go exactly as planned, and that is rare for innovative research projects. Including buffer in your schedule is analogous to including a contingency fund for a home renovation. You include it because you expect to use it. It gives you some flexibility and makes it less likely that you will have to make decisions that threaten the viability of your project if things do not go exactly as planned.

Figure 2.10 presents the schedule for the fictional seniors' health clinics evaluation described in Box 2.3 and Figure 2.5. As with the pollution research deliverable-based Gantt chart (Figure 2.6), the schedule in Figure 2.10 is built up from the deliverables in the WBS and includes fast-tracking. Specifically, (a) data collection starts before the evaluation plan is finalized, (b) analyses start while data collection is still in progress, and (c) there is a plan to share preliminary findings before analyses have been completed.

Even though the fictional seniors' health clinics evaluation project is only 9 months long, the schedule follows the accepted best practice of including buffer at the end (although only 2 weeks of buffer are available, given the short duration of the entire project). To illustrate the fact that there may be variation in the level of detail

Deliverable & Subdeliverable Names	Year 1												Year 2											
	Apr	May	Jun	Jul	Aug	Sep	Oct	Nov	Dec	Jan	Feb	Mar	Apr	May	Jun	Jul	Aug	Sep	Oct	Nov	Dec	Jan	Feb	Mar
A: Governance & Management																								
A1: Core Team Meetings																								
A2: Research Questions																								
A3: Study Plan																								
A4: Reports for Funders & Stakeholders																								
B: Data																								
B1: Purchased Drone																								
B2: Code for Drone Air Sample Capture																								
B3: Pilot Test of Drone Air Sampling																								
B4: Permits																								
B5: Sampling Plan																								
B6: Full-Scale Data																								
B6a: Near-Emitter Air (Drone)																								
B6b: Distant Earth																								
B6c: Distant Water																								
C: Analyses																								
D: KMb																								
D1: Presentation to Company																								
D2: Policymakers KMb																								
D2a: Policy Brief																								
D2b: Presentation to Policymakers																								
D3: Academic KMb																								
Deliverable & Subdeliverable Names	Apr	May	Jun	Jul	Aug	Sep	Oct	Nov	Dec	Jan	Feb	Mar	Apr	May	Jun	Jul	Aug	Sep	Oct	Nov	Dec	Jan	Feb	Mar

Annotations within chart:
- A: Research questions articulated and shared with team, knowledge users, and other stakeholders
- Final report
- B: Data — Compression
- C: Analyses (8 months) — Compression
- D: KMb
- Policymakers presentation (brief sent in advance)

Figure 2.8. Fast-Tracked Deliverable-Based Gantt Chart for a Fictional Pollution Research Project with Fast-Tracking in Year 1 to Ensure Time for Quality Final Deliverables at the End of the Project

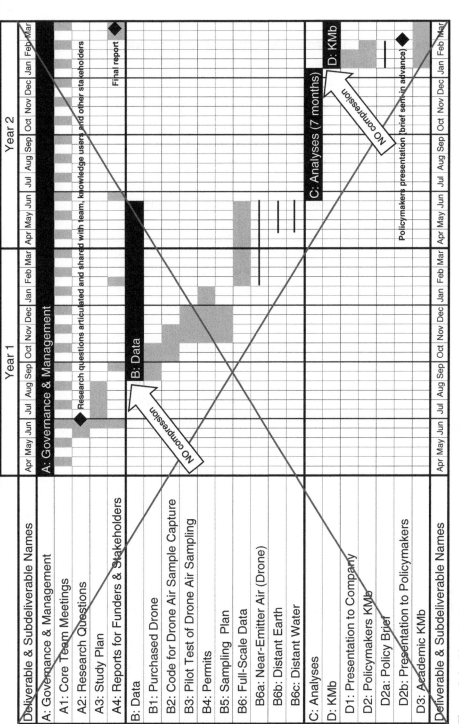

Figure 2.9. Risky Deliverable-Based Gantt Chart for a Fictional Pollution Research Project with Relaxed Schedule in Year 1

BOX 2.5. OPTIONS FOR COMPRESSING THE RESEARCH PROJECT SCHEDULE

* Fast-tracking
    ° Start some deliverables before the preceding deliverables end.
    ° Sacrifice preferred logic in that you perform some work in parallel that would ideally be performed in sequence.
    ° Include fast-tracking in almost all projects.

* Crashing
    ° Decrease the duration of time required to complete a deliverable by adding more resources (people) to it.
    ° In practice, the research project team may not include multiple people with the skills required to contribute to a deliverable, so you must be mindful of the risk of adding people to a deliverable and slowing progress because the people who do know how to do the work are shifted from doing work to training others.

* Revisit and reconsider make, buy, or partner decisions for deliverables.
    ° Instead of having students and staff make or create a deliverable (e.g., an app, website, or data capture instrument or code built from scratch), it may be possible to condense your schedule in major ways by using commercial products or partnering with a more experienced group or organization to do the work.
    ° This will always cost something (money, standard vs. desired features, less control), but it may be worth it or necessary to complete the project in the time available.

---

expressed for deliverables in different project management tools, Figure 2.10 also includes some changes relative to the WBS. The WBS for the health clinics evaluation project identifies six subdeliverables for the evaluation plan, but the schedule does not include a separate row for each of them. Instead, Figure 2.10 has a footnote referencing the six subdeliverables. This is okay. Even without the footnote, the schedule in Figure 2.10 covers 100 percent of the scope at the high level. Project management practitioners should feel free to provide different levels of detail for workstreams and deliverables in different project management tools and during different phases of the project.

A final noteworthy feature of the deliverable-based Gantt chart in Figure 2.10 is the scheduling in the month of December. Given the holidays in that month in Europe and North America, it is not usually realistic for people working on those continents to plan for important meetings or extensive progress on deliverables in late December. Therefore, instead of following the recurring schedule, which would result in a steering committee meeting and update for funders and stakeholders at the end of December, those two deliverables are moved to the first half of January.

2.2.5 Avoiding Unnecessary Multitasking

One of the benefits of deliverable-based project planning is that work can be delegated and distributed across multiple qualified people in parallel to reduce bottlenecks and decrease the time required to complete the project. In contrast, multitasking – having one individual work on multiple deliverables (or projects) at the same time – can have a negative impact on project progress.

Consider three fictional deliverables, each of which requires approximately 1.5 months to complete. Figure 2.11a is a representation of how long it would take to complete the three deliverables if the same person is the lead for all of them and that person multitasks by alternating which deliverable they are working on each half-month. Figure 2.11b shows how the work would be completed without multitasking when Deliverable 1 is assigned priority status, and the lead works on it exclusively without interruption, then on Deliverable 2, and then on Deliverable 3. The key takeaway from Figure 2.11 is that eliminating multitasking means that Deliverable 1 can be completed 2.5 months earlier without negatively affecting the amount of time required to complete Deliverable 3. Moreover, in reality, Deliverable 3 would probably be completed later when there is multitasking because it is rare for people to switch gears with 100 percent efficiency.

When I first learned about this way of thinking about multitasking in Goldratt's (1997) novel *The Critical Chain*, it was new to me. Before

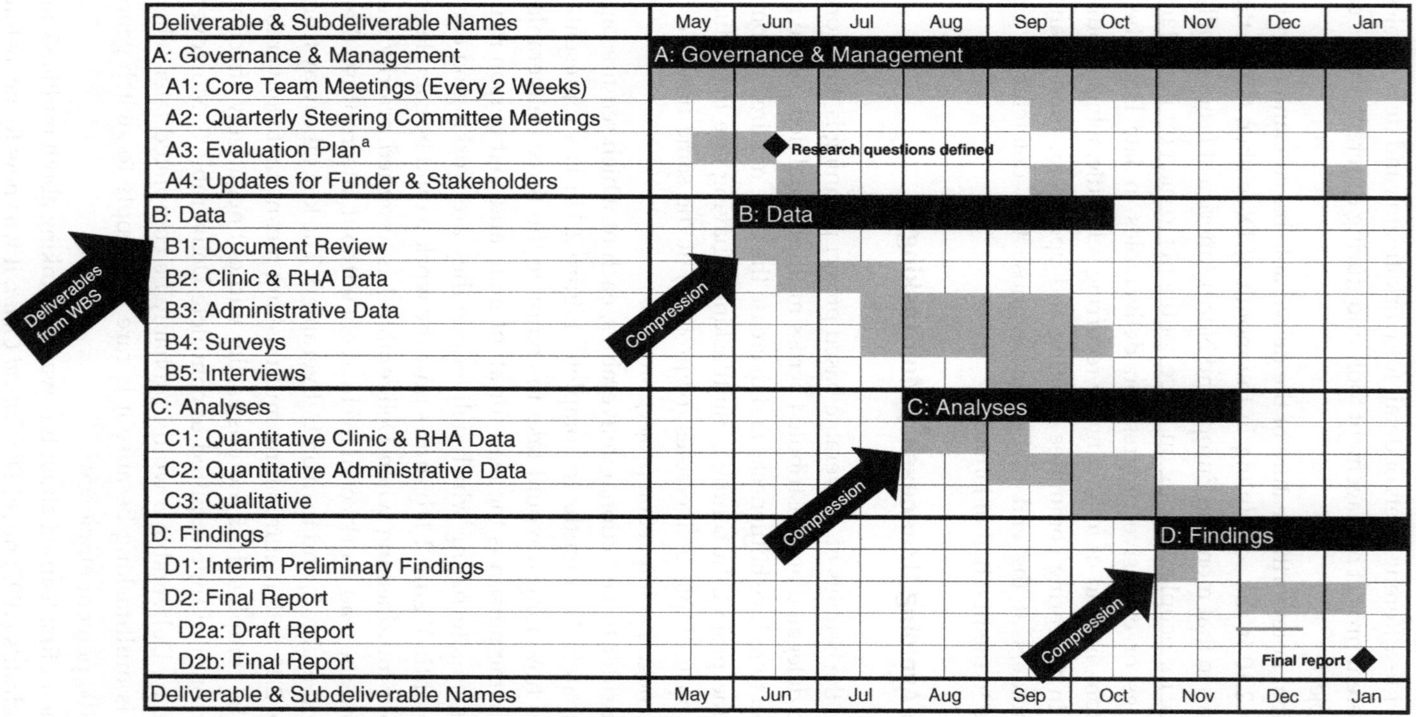

Deliverable & Subdeliverable Names	May	Jun	Jul	Aug	Sep	Oct	Nov	Dec	Jan
A: Governance & Management									
A1: Core Team Meetings (Every 2 Weeks)									
A2: Quarterly Steering Committee Meetings									
A3: Evaluation Plan[a]									
A4: Updates for Funder & Stakeholders									
B: Data									
B1: Document Review									
B2: Clinic & RHA Data									
B3: Administrative Data									
B4: Surveys									
B5: Interviews									
C: Analyses									
C1: Quantitative Clinic & RHA Data									
C2: Quantitative Administrative Data									
C3: Qualitative									
D: Findings									
D1: Interim Preliminary Findings									
D2: Final Report									
D2a: Draft Report									
D2b: Final Report									
Deliverable & Subdeliverable Names	May	Jun	Jul	Aug	Sep	Oct	Nov	Dec	Jan

Chart labels: A: Governance & Management — Research questions defined; B: Data; C: Analyses; D: Findings; Final report; Compression; Deliverables from WBS.

Figure 2.10. Deliverable-Based Gantt Chart for a Fictional Seniors' Health Clinics Evaluation Project

[a] The evaluation plan includes A3a: Logic Model, A3b: Research Questions, A3c: Inventory of Data Sources, A3d: Description of Methods, A3e: Survey Questionnaire, and A3f: Interview Guide & Schedule.

that, multitasking had always been presented to me as a valuable and desirable skill. Goldratt's message, though, is that avoidable multitasking is equivalent to sacrificing early completion dates in favor of less important work.

In practice, it is hard, if not impossible, to deny requests that would take a small amount of time, and few of us can live and work as represented in Figure 2.11b all the time. However, to the extent

> ## LEADERSHIP ADVICE CROSSWALK
>
> ### 2.4. KNOW WHEN TO SAY NO
> Without being aware of each other's views, Colleen Flood, Barbara Sherwood Lollar, Sharon Straus, Stefaan Verhulst, and Rich Zemel all provided advice about saying no to some things or, put another way, only saying yes to the right things. As tempting as it might be to join new initiatives, these leaders emphasized that saying yes to everything would unavoidably affect the progress or quality of the work that is most important to them.

that you can and when it is in your control, Goldratt's message is that you should avoid multitasking. So, if you are asked to take on some new work that would require significant effort, and you already have a full workload, instead of automatically agreeing to take it on, you should let the requestor know whether and how the new work will delay other deliverables so you can decide together what to prioritize.

A final point related to scheduling is that, depending on the funder, the possibility of extensions might serve as a disincentive to schedule compression. Although it is true that you may want or need to use

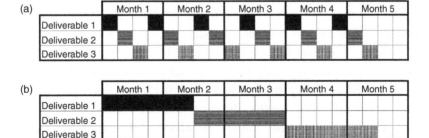

Figure 2.11. Downside of Multitasking: (a) with Multitasking, All Three Deliverables Are Completed within 4 to 4.5 Months; (b) without Multitasking, Priority Deliverable 1 Is Completed 2.5 Months Earlier, and Deliverable 3 Is Not Finished Any Later

research funder extensions under some circumstances, you probably do not want to make a habit of doing so. Even if extensions are possible, there is an opportunity cost to using them in the long term. Research project teams need to consider all the things that they will not start, or work on, if research projects drag on. So, it is best to plan to complete research projects within funded periods whenever possible and use extensions strategically and only when necessary.

2.3 DELIVERABLE-BASED BUDGET

2.3.1 The Budget as a Tool to Ensure Sufficient Funding for All Deliverables

Some group or organization has decided to invest in your research project because they believe in the results that the research project team can produce. Generally, research funders do not want to receive money back from funding recipients, but they may not have the flexibility to allow you to carry funds into future years or move them to other projects. Good research project budget management is how the research project team does its part to transform funders' available research investment dollars into new knowledge, products, and services.

The budget is the document that presents and allocates the resources required to complete the project. For research projects, a WBS, a deliverable-based schedule, historical information or advice from people who have been involved in similar research projects, and research funder requirements are often sufficient to develop a useful budget with the necessary level of detail.

Research funders all have rules regarding eligible and ineligible expenses and will typically require a budget that includes categories such as personnel (broken down to show salary and compensation for research staff, faculty, students, and non-students), supplies and services, equipment, and travel. Those budget categories are established to ensure that research project teams are financially accountable and to prevent the misuse of funds. For example, funders may set limits on how much funding can be used for travel or consultants.

However, simple planning and reporting based on funder budget categories does not help a research project team with budget management. For example, knowing that 70 percent of research project's budget is allocated to personnel does not tell the team anything about which people in which locations are funded to do what work. For effective research budget management, teams need some breakdown of the high-level information provided under funder budget categories. Breaking the budget down by deliverables offers several benefits. Foremost, if you have used the deliverables from a WBS as the foundation for your budget, you know the budget will be complete. This does not necessarily mean that every deliverable will have its own budget line, but it does prompt you to think about the costs for all deliverables and, at a minimum, plan for deliverables that have unique or atypically large costs.

To illustrate this point, the budget for the fictional pollution research project highlights significant costs for the drone that will be used to collect air samples and other unique costs associated with the drone, such as coding support and programming consultants (see Table 2.1). Most of the other project costs for the pollution monitoring project in Table 2.1 are grouped together under Workstream A: Governance & Management and explained in budget notes. This is okay. Research funders generally allow some movement of funds between budget lines without prior approval provided they are within specified percentage limits. It is often a good idea to combine costs into higher-level budget lines because that provides more flexibility during project implementation. For example, if up to 10 percent of the amount in a budget line can be reallocated to other project expenses, it is much more helpful for a research project team to have the flexibility to move and reallocate 10 percent of $100,000 than 10 percent of $5,000. This is not a matter of working around funder requirements. Research project teams should always provide their funders with whatever budget breakdown the funder's rules require, but by not going further than the funder's required level of detail and breakdown, teams will have more flexibility to use funds in ways that make sense during project implementation.

As long as your budget covers all the work and all the deliverables, it can be considered complete. If your funder does not require you to have multiple rows with zero amounts, feel free to delete those

Table 2.1. Deliverable-Based Budget for a Fictional Pollution Research Project

Workstream and Deliverable Name	Year, $	
	1	2
A: Governance & Management[a]	104,500	120,000
Personnel costs[b]	96,500	107,000
Materials costs	5,000	5,000
Travel costs	3,000	8,000
B: Data	45,500	5,000
B1: Purchased drone[c]	30,000	–
B2: Code for drone air sample capture[d]	10,000	–
B4: Permits	500	–
B6: Full-scale data[e]	5,000	5,000
C: Analyses[f]	–	10,000
D: Knowledge mobilization[g]	–	15,000
Total	150,000	150,000

Note: Dashes indicate no budget allocation.

[a] Includes all core costs for the project, including staff time, student compensation, materials, teleconference costs, travel costs associated with sampling, and publication costs; consultant and specialist services costs are excluded from this line and presented below for specific deliverables.

[b] Includes standard host institution benefits and annual compensation increases where applicable.

[c] Estimate $5,000 for 3 drones, $25,000 for 2 air samplers

[d] Budget for specialist and consultant services related to programming drone.

[e] Budget for rented server space.

[f] Statistician fee.

[g] Budget for open access publication, conference registration, and conference-related travel.

from your budget table. As with all project management documents, the research project team, stakeholders, and partners are more likely to read and process the information provided to them if documents are short.

If a research project team does contract out research, the budget may need to be more detailed. The deliverable-based budget table for the fictional seniors' health clinics evaluation (Table 2.2) is an example in which every deliverable line has its own budget allocation. However, instead of expressing personnel time in terms of funds consumed, the budget in Table 2.2 emphasizes the hours that a research associate and other contributors will put toward the project and has a footnote specifying different hourly rates. An advantage of the detailed deliverable-based presentation in Table 2.2 is that it easy to see

Table 2.2. Deliverable-Based Budget for a Fictional Seniors' Health Clinics Evaluation Project

Workstream and Deliverable Name	Research Associate Hours[a]	Other Hours[b]	Other, $	Total, $
A: Governance & management	68	236	4,500	32,400
A1: Core team meetings every 2 weeks (18 total)	36	144	–	16,200
A2: Quarterly steering committee meetings (3 total)	20	20	4,500[c]	9,000
A3: Evaluation plan	4	40	–	3,600
A4: Updates for funder & stakeholders (3 total)	8	32	–	3,600
B: Data	36	132	10,550	25,850
B1: Document review	8	32	–	3,600
B2: Clinic & RHA data	8	48	–	4,800
B3: Administrative data	4	12	10,000[d]	11,500
B4: Surveys	8	16	150[e]	2,550
B5: Interviews (8 total)	8	24	400[f]	3,400
C: Analyses	40	156	5,000	22,700
C1: Quantitative clinic & RHA data	16	72	–	7,800
C2: Quantitative administrative data	8	24	5,000[g]	8,000
C3: Qualitative	16	60	–	6,900
D: Findings	24	60	400	8,500
D1: Interim preliminary findings	8	24	–	3,000
D2: Final report	16	36	400[h]	5,500
Total				89,450

Notes: Dashes indicate no funds allocated. RHA = regional health authority.
[a] Senior research associate rate is $150/hour.
[b] Other research project team staff rate is $75/hour.
[c] Includes meeting room booking and lunch for steering committee meetings.
[d] Dataset creation and data access costs for administrative data.
[e] License for premium online survey tool with data security.
[f] Honorariums of $50 for each interviewee.
[g] Consultant fees for advice on administrative data analyses.
[h] Graphic designer fees for final report.

how much of the project funds are directed to different deliverables (e.g., data and analyses vs. meetings), which provides an opportunity to confirm that funds are allocated to funder and stakeholder priorities (see Section 2.4, "Involving Stakeholders in Project Planning").

At the other end of the spectrum, you may have research projects that need only the time of research staff and students who are already funded. In those cases, you might not need a deliverable-based budget table at all. It may be sufficient to have a budget section that states "Work will be performed by existing salaried staff and students with departmental compensation," perhaps with a line or two about any non-staff expenses, such as "Up to $1,000, taken from existing available departmental budget, for refreshments at staff training sessions."

2.3.2 Estimating the Costs for Common Research Budget Lines

Tables 2.1 and 2.2 both reflect the fact that, for most research projects, personnel costs are one of the largest, if not the single largest, cost line. This is actually good news when it comes to accurate research project budget planning, because in almost all cases you can use established compensation ranges for staff, fellows, and students to build the majority of your budget. Developing the total budget for personnel then becomes a simple calculation based on the estimated number of different kinds of full-time equivalents that you will need to complete the deliverables, using the WBS, expert judgment, and historical information.

When thinking about how many people you will need to complete the project deliverables, be realistic and try to plan for ways in which you can have continuous employment for people. With the exception of staff who have specialized skills that they contribute to many projects for short periods of time (e.g., expertise related to intellectual property, computer code development, statistical analyses, procurement), most people working on your project are going to be seeking continuous project work as opposed to something that offers them only a few weeks or months of work at a time. If you do not have sufficient funds to bring

LEADERSHIP ADVICE CROSSWALK

2.5. THE BUDGET FOLLOWS THE WORK

Steve Farber emphasized that for large research projects that involve investigators at multiple locations, most of the budget will go toward funding students and staff at other organizations. The organization of the lead principal investigator does receive more funding than other organizations, but only because it hosts a small number of staff who are responsible for coordination and bringing everything together.

people on full time for the duration of the project, the second-best approach is often to offer part-time continuous employment or continuous work spread across multiple projects to provide income security. Additionally, or alternatively, you could offer employment that starts several months after the project begins or finishes before the project ends.

Another practical tip is to avoid planning for the full staff and student complement from the very start to the end date of your project. Most research projects ramp up the number of research project team members over several months, and certain research project deliverables often do not require personnel to be assigned to them until months or years after the project starts.

When developing your research personnel budget, it is also important to be realistic about what you will be asking individuals to accomplish, whether they work full or part time. This means avoiding plans that would have the same person multitasking on multiple deliverables at the same time and taking research project team members' other commitments into account (e.g., acknowledging that first-year graduate students will typically spend a lot of their time on coursework and may also have tutorial assistant responsibilities). Also keep in mind that funders may require or prefer that trainees, as opposed to staff or consultants, perform the work described in research proposals.

Another big budget line for many research projects is equipment. As is the case for personnel budget estimating, resources are available to help you get an accurate estimate of equipment costs. In the case of routine research equipment, such as laptop computers and field supplies, your department should have some historical information about unit costs. If you are purchasing a new, large piece of equipment, vendors are your best source of information, combined with information about discounts or donations your organization has benefited from in the past.

Research project budgets may also include significant funds for in-person meetings. Between accommodation, room rental, and food costs, in-person meetings can cost well over $1,000 per person even before flights and ground travel are included. For international research project teams, a single in-person meeting can cost tens of thousands of dollars. The cost of in-person meetings can be calculated by estimating the number of attendees and searching the internet for information on flight, hotel, and meal costs, being careful not to assume that the lowest-cost options will always be available when it comes time for you to expend funds.

Although the cost of in-person meetings can be high relative to other research project costs, that does not mean the research project team should avoid including them in the budget. Restrictions on travel and in-person gatherings during the coronavirus pandemic showed that much of the work of research project teams can be done remotely while also making research project teams acutely aware of what is lost when there is no in-person interaction at all. Although web meetings are useful for short, touch-base meetings, and less costly and more environmentally friendly than in-person meetings, they have their limits. For example, many people find consecutive hours of web meetings tiring, and it is very hard for people who only meet virtually to realize the benefits of the small interactions that happen between individuals and agenda items when people meet in person. Generative dialogue, especially dialogue that requires hours or days to come to fruition, is very hard to do remotely, and it is also hard to build trust and relationships when all you can see is a small screen with an image of someone's face. There is no single right answer when it comes to how much of the project budget should be invested in in-person meetings, but, given their cost, it is important that projects that include them do so with full knowledge of the budget trade-offs they are making (e.g., in some cases, funding fewer students or staff members so that funds can be used for an in-person meeting).

Because the cost of large equipment and in-person meetings can be very high and have a large impact on budget funds available for other deliverables, you might want to put extra effort into developing accurate estimates for them. The simple technique of parametric estimating (Figure 2.12) allows you to calculate an estimate of your deliverable cost using a weighted combination of the median cost (i.e., most common

> **LEADERSHIP ADVICE CROSSWALK**
>
> **2.6. IN-PERSON MEETINGS HAVE UNIQUE VALUE**
>
> Steve Farber and Kim McGrail each spoke about why in-person meetings are essential for topics that require hours of dialogue and for building trust and human connections among research project team members.

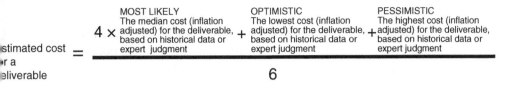

Figure 2.12. Parametric Estimate of Deliverable Costs

cost), the lowest (most optimistic) cost, and the highest (most pessimistic) cost. For each of the three values, you can use historical data from similar projects, expert judgment (i.e., the advice of someone who would be in a position to know based on their past experience), or both, taking care to adjust for inflation if the data or historical information are not current. Parametric estimating can be a fast and practical way to increase budget estimate accuracy, rather than defaulting to an average cost or an overly pessimistic or overly optimistic cost estimate.

For many research project teams, personnel, equipment, and in-person meetings will constitute 80 percent or more of the project budget. But budgeting does not stop with those three categories. For completeness, the team should also consider open access publication costs (typically thousands of dollars per publication), ongoing software costs (e.g., web meeting applications, research software licenses), and basic supplies and services for the research project team (e.g., printing costs, stationery, postal and courier charges). These small costs will not make or break a research project, but you do want to include them in your budget, using historical data, expert advice from someone who has run similar projects in the past, or both to make sure that they do not end up consuming funds you had planned to use for other purposes.

2.3.3 Steps for Developing a Deliverable-Based Budget for a Research Project

The general steps to establish a research project deliverable-based budget are as follows:

1 Make note of any funder requirements and key constraints. For example, competitions for research funding often include lists of

eligible and ineligible expenses and annual and total budget maximum and minimum values. If you know your project includes expenses that are ineligible for one funder, it may still be possible to apply for funding as long as you are able to identify alternative funding for those expenses (e.g., your institution, a foundation, or a private-sector partner).

2 Estimate the cost for each deliverable, including ongoing costs (such as the number of staff or students) and one-time costs (such as equipment purchases and in-person meetings). As noted in Section 2.3.2, "Estimating the Costs for Common Research Budget Lines," for personnel costs, make sure that the resources you have allocated are realistic and account for the fact that some research project team members may have other commitments that will prevent them from working on the project full time. When allocating personnel to deliverables, aim for full-time continuous employment, and do not automatically plan for every research project team member to be funded from the first day to the last day of the project.

3 Where applicable, check that the total eligible project costs are within the fundable range. If the budget is too high, work with the team and project stakeholders on ways to decrease the project scope and budget. This is one of the strengths of deliverable-based scheduling: it allows you to consider and make informed trade-offs regarding the deliverables that will be funded or cut.

4 For multiyear projects, once the costs for each deliverable have been established, use the deliverable-based Gantt chart to determine how these costs will be distributed across the funded years. If necessary to stay within the funder's annual limit, move non-time-constrained expenses forward or backward in time to level the budget. For this task, large one-time, non-time-constrained costs can be very helpful. For example, the ability to prepay for rooms and flights, potentially with associated discounts, can free up funds and create budget flexibility. For large purchases, be sure to include time to follow your organization's procurement policies. Research institutions often require time-consuming competitive processes when purchases exceed thresholds, for example, $25,000. For that reason, it is a good idea to obtain or create a document that summarizes procurement rules, restrictions, and approximate timelines at your organization.

5 If possible, build in some contingency funds. You can think of these as the budget equivalent of buffer in the schedule. Non-research project budgets typically have contingency funding of 5 to 10 percent of the total budget, but research funders rarely allow large amounts of unallocated funding. In those cases, you should, at a minimum, have information in the background about the deliverables you will cut or decrease the scope for to keep the project within budget if some costs increase for reasons beyond your control. For example, your research project budget might begin with a plan to create a $10,000 website but decrease the allocation to a $5,000 website with fewer pages and features if funds need to be shifted to another deliverable. Additionally, you can create budget room by holding off on recruiting and assigning all funded personnel until you have a sense of project progress and risks.

6 As a final step, create a version of the budget that presents cost information for each funder category by funding year. In this budget, maintain as much flexibility as the funder allows, for example, presenting the highest-level categories and aggregation that the funder will accept. This is not about hiding information from your funders; it is about increasing the likelihood that you will be able to move funds and make adjustments to your project in response to its natural evolution without breaking any of the funder's rules.

2.4 INVOLVING STAKEHOLDERS IN PROJECT PLANNING

In literal terms, a project stakeholder is any person or group that will be affected by a project, including the members of a research project team. However, in practice, the term "stakeholder engagement" is usually focused on how you will engage and involve people external to the research project team who might contribute, benefit, or, in some cases, be harmed or burdened by the research.

For decades, funders of applied research have required researchers to work with decision makers, including companies and government departments. These stakeholders are often called "knowledge users" because they are positioned to put the knowledge generated by research into action (CIHR, 2016). More recently, increased attention has been paid to involving people who bring in the perspective of the intended beneficiaries of the project, which can include people who would be affected by the goods, services, processes, or policies that are developed by the project, regardless of whether those people have decision-making authority.

Sometimes research project teams are established to include these external stakeholders as research project team members who are actively involved in designing, conducting, and disseminating the research. For example, the United States' Patient-Centered Outcomes Research Institute (n.d.) and Canada's Strategy for Patient-Oriented Research (CIHR, n.d.) are examples of national-scale research initiatives that require the deep involvement of patients, not as research subjects, but as codevelopers and contributors to the research project team. In other cases, external stakeholders are treated as partners who are not part of the research project team but who have defined roles in funding, designing, and conducting the research or in disseminating research findings. Some external stakeholders influence research projects via consultation at specific points in time or by providing advice on specific deliverables. Regardless of the depth of stakeholder involvement, these are all examples of efforts to bring outside perspectives into research projects to strengthen research outputs.

The guidance presented earlier for developing your WBS, schedule, and budget (Sections 2.1, 2.2, and 2.3) refers to involving stakeholders. That advice is most obviously applicable to research that is directed toward some purpose, that is, applied research or experimental development, but it is also true that basic research is more likely to have an impact if it addresses a gap that stakeholders in the field agree is important. Involving stakeholders in planning does not mean developing materials to the point at which they are almost complete and then asking for stakeholders' endorsement. Stakeholder involvement usually has the highest impact and is most beneficial when research knowledge users, intended beneficiaries, and other stakeholders are involved in the research project from the very beginning (i.e., when scope and research question are being defined). External stakeholders can provide critical information about the overlap between what the research project team has the capacity to do and what stakeholders need or would find useful or interesting.

Therefore, when developing a new research grant application, it is important to get advice and direct feedback from stakeholders about the proposed work early in the process. In doing so, you may learn of tweaks and small suggestions that would make the project more useful and interesting from the stakeholder's perspective, but you should also be open to advice that can change the project in major ways. Your stakeholders know their own problems and opportunities best. They also know about existing processes, tools, and products that might support or integrate with the new research to amplify its impact.

Deep understanding of stakeholder interests comes through relationships that build trust. Put yourself in the stakeholder's shoes and think about the circum-

LEADERSHIP ADVICE CROSSWALK

2.7. INVOLVE EXTERNAL STAKEHOLDERS

Many research leaders spoke about the importance of involving external stakeholders in the early stages of research planning and the role of the research leader in building bridges between disciplines and sectors. For example, Steve Farber and Stefaan Verhulst described new research initiatives that were codeveloped with stakeholders, David Wolfe reflected on how deeper involvement of stakeholders earlier might have prevented problems during project implementation, and Aled Edwards focused his interview on understanding stakeholders' culture. However, research leaders also had some cautionary words of advice about stakeholder involvement. Jutta Treviranus emphasized the need to take care when working with stakeholders who may not be familiar with how rare it is to get research funding on the first try, and Arjumand Siddiqi spoke about important topics that should be studied for which stakeholder involvement may not be practical or possible.

stances under which you would trust an outside group to perform research based on data about you (particularly if the data quality for the research is not proven) or the extent to which you would be willing to change the course of action for your organization or your community on the basis of a research study performed by people who live very different lives than yours. Stakeholder trust in research is earned over time. This does not mean you should hesitate to engage with a new stakeholder, but in practical terms it does mean that you will often start a new relationship with a stakeholder with a relatively small-scale collaboration that demonstrates the value of your research, and your trustworthiness, and build the relationship over time.

Over the past two decades, research projects and organizations have become more international and interdisciplinary, with deeper involvement of diverse stakeholders and knowledge users. That trend is expected to increase as research contributes to global opportunities, such as clean energy and more personalized medicine, and challenges such as climate change, the environmental impact of human society, infectious diseases, and social inequalities. So, it is very important to get stakeholder engagement right.

Research has a role to play in addressing the world's major challenges, including inequities in society. To do that, the perspectives of the groups who have historically been marginalized or colonized are important. Resources other than this handbook provide guidance regarding who should be involved and in what ways for research to be relevant and ethical for First Nations, Inuit, and Métis peoples, Black communities, people with disabilities, and other historically marginalized or colonized communities. Here, I just note that much of the spirit of the emerging guidance focuses on having research project teams acknowledge that context is critical for the design, conduct, interpretation, and dissemination of research. From that perspective, the recent focus on increasing inclusivity, diversity, and equity in research, along with efforts to make research accessible for people with disabilities, can be understood as a prompt for researchers to think about the limits of their own knowledge and experiences. It is about asking questions such as "Does the team understand the space we are exploring enough to be sure that our research will produce a benefit, and if not, who should be involved, and in what ways, to increase the likelihood that our research will be helpful and useful and not lead to unintended harm?" In some cases, questions such as these may lead

LEADERSHIP ADVICE CROSSWALK

2.8. EQUITY IN RESEARCH
Many research leaders spoke about amplifying voices that have not been represented in research and increasing equity in research at the project, organization, sector, or system level (e.g., see, Elspeth Brown, Beth Coleman, Kim McGrail, Michael Schull, Arjumand Siddiqi, Sharon Straus, Jutta Treviranus, and Stefaan Verhulst).

to the conclusion that certain research should not happen unless it is community led or co-led.

2.5 TRIPLE CONSTRAINT OF SCOPE, TIME, AND COST

There is nothing magic about project management. It will not transform a project with an unrealistic scope into something that can be accomplished or allow you to stretch an insufficient budget to cover all project costs. But project management for research has concrete benefits, including that it

- helps the research project team articulate and plan for complete scope;
- increases the efficiency of project work via formal communications and a common understanding of the deliverables and who is responsible for them;
- enables coordinated effort through a shared understanding of dependencies and schedule constraints;
- drives progress by establishing a timeline (and reporting progress against it);
- can decrease unnecessary multitasking, leading to earlier completion dates for priority deliverables; and
- helps the team understand its budget needs and identify when changes to budget allocation need to be made.

The triple constraint of project management refers to fact that the scope, time, and cost of a project are related. It is easy to understand that someone building a house cannot double its size without increasing the schedule and budget. This is also true for research projects, even if they are much less certain and defined. Using the deliverables from the WBS to create your Gantt chart and budget has the benefit of creating a common thread among the three elements of the triple constraint, which allows teams to make informed trade-offs during project planning and implementation (Figure 2.13).

The triple constraint prompts the team to ask planning questions, such as "Do we have enough funding and time to complete our desired scope?" "Is it worth having this many meetings?" "What might we do with the funds and time if we don't hold an international

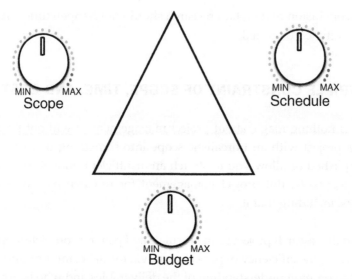

Figure 2.13. Scope, Schedule, and Budget Are Related through the Triple Constraint

in-person summit?" and "Which deliverables are most important to our stakeholders, and how can we ensure that they are fully resourced and completed on time?" At the planning stage, fulfilling the triple constraint means that your project scope, schedule, and budget will be aligned, interrelated, and realistic.

Understanding the budget and schedule requirements at a deliverable level can also help the team with modular grant application development. For example, a team with a high-level $500,000 2-year plan with a breakdown of the schedule and budget requirements for each deliverable would be well positioned to divide its scope, schedule, and budget to prepare a scaled-down grant application if they see an opportunity to begin the work by applying for funding in a call for proposals that has a $250,000 budget maximum.

The triple constraint is even more important to consider during the implementation phase of projects. You need to understand the triple constraint to make adjustments and informed trade-offs if your project needs to change or is threatened by external factors. Because scope, schedule, and budget are connected, it is rare for a single dial in Figure 2.13 to move independently. Usually, if you increase the scope of your research by 30 percent, the schedule, the budget, or both will have to increase as well. An exception to this may be if some of your planning assumptions prove to be false. For example, if you underestimated the resources and time required to complete your project and there is no possibility of finding more, you will need to dial down the scope while keeping

> **LEADERSHIP ADVICE CROSSWALK**
>
> **2.9. PLANS MUST CHANGE IF THERE ARE MAJOR SCOPE INCREASES**
>
> Steini Brown's realization that he could not absorb project scope increases with the existing budget and resources is an example of how the triple constraint comes into play during project implementation.

the budget and schedule at the maximum allowed by your funding agreement.

Simultaneous consideration of the triple constraint is also essential for research project teams to understand project progress during project implementation. Consider a team that is 1 year into a 2-year project and has consumed half of its budget. This could be bad news (if the team has used half the time and money but only completed one-quarter of its scope), good news (if the team is on track to produce all deliverables using the forecasted amount of time and money), or great news (if the team has completed three-quarters of the project's scope with half the time and money). The point is that you need to simultaneously consider scope, schedule, and budget to understand how your project is progressing during implementation.

Transitioning from Research Project Planning to Implementation

3.1 PROGRESSIVE AND ITERATIVE ELABORATION OF PROJECT DETAILS

As your research project progresses from early planning into implementation, you will articulate more details about it. Some of the detailed information will be prepared and managed by the research project team members who are leads for specific deliverables in documents that contain a lot of detail (e.g., study protocols, ethics submissions, permit applications). The details of the documents that a subset of team members will use are not the focus of this handbook; however, there are some topics – beyond scope, schedule, and budget planning – that the entire research project team can benefit from knowing about.

In this section, I present three topics that often fall into that category: risk management, roles and responsibilities, and project governance. Depending on

---

LEADERSHIP ADVICE CROSSWALK

3.1. YOUR RESEARCH PLAN SHOULD NOT BE RIGID

Lorna MacDonald, Kim McGrail, Molly Shoichet, Jutta Treviranus, and Stefaan Verhulst all spoke about how research leaders need to adapt versus adhere rigidly to a predefined plan. Research projects can and should change as the research project team learns new things and the context in which they operate changes.

the requirements of the research funding competition process, your research project team may need to describe its approach to these three topics as part of a research proposal or grant application, or they may hold off on working on them until after project funding is secured. However, even if your funder does not require it, this information can also help strengthen a grant application (see Section 3.5, "Using Project Management to Strengthen Grant Applications"), and it is a good idea to at least consider putting in writing some things related to risks, roles and responsibilities, and governance before project implementation starts.

3.2 PROCESSES TO IDENTIFY AND MANAGE RISKS

3.2.1 Distinguishing Risks from Issues and Opportunities

A *project risk* is any uncertain event or condition that, if it does occur, would have a positive or negative effect on the project. Notably, although most people use the word "risk" to describe something that is negative, in project management risks can be positive, too. The key characteristic of a risk in project management is that it has not yet occurred or been realized. In other words, if you know something will occur, or something has occurred, it is not a risk – it is either an issue (a negative risk that has been realized) or an opportunity (a positive risk that has been realized). For example, the possibility of a funder withdrawing is a negative risk for a project, but if a funder has already withdrawn and the project does not have enough funding to be completed, that is not a risk, it is an issue.

When a research project faces a concrete issue or opportunity, the team will invest whatever time and resources are needed to address it. In contrast, research project risk management is mostly about up-front thinking and low-resource activities to decrease the likelihood of important negative risks occurring and the impacts if negative risks are realized, plus some thinking about how to increase the chances that the project will realize benefits from positive risks.

3.2.2 Identifying, Prioritizing, and Responding to Negative Risks for Research

A *negative risk management plan* is a project management tool used to identify the most important negative risks for your research project and risk responses to them (see Table 3.1 for examples). The process to populate the tool begins with the identification of a group of people who will, collectively, have knowledge about a range of negative risks for the project. For example, you may want to include all the leads for work breakdown structure (WBS) deliverables plus people who have specialized knowledge about legal, funding, cybersecurity, and other risks.

It is often helpful to use a facilitated process and in-person meetings to brainstorm, prioritize, and develop responses for negative risks, according to the following steps:

1 Start the process by communicating the difference between a negative risk and an issue to ensure all participants understand the objectives of the process. It may help to present negative risks as the "X" in the statement "If X happens, it will be bad for the project." This can help the team identify specific negative risks with actionable risk responses.
2 For a few minutes, have each person brainstorm and write down negative risks that might be important for the project. Prompt participants to record some risks that may be unlikely but would have high negative impact if they were realized, because those risks may not be top of mind as a result of recency or frequency bias. It can also be helpful to present participants with the project WBS and ask them to think about the workstreams and deliverables with the highest inherent negative risks.
3 When individual brainstorming has been completed, have participants work in pairs or small groups to identify four to seven negative risks that might be important to develop responses for. Ask them to consider both likelihood – the chances that the risk will happen – and impact – the effect if the risk does happen. For research projects that are well defined, it may be possible to assign quantitative risk scores, but more typically academic research

Table 3.1. Example Negative Risk Management Plan

Negative Risk	Likelihood	Impact if Realized	Response
1. Non-responsive partner	Medium high	Very high	• Tailor communications format and frequency to partner's preferences. • Develop relationships with people at multiple levels within partner organization.
2. Insufficient data	Medium	High	• Engage statisticians in study design to ensure that it has enough power. • Identify primary outcomes that can be assessed even if the data are insufficient to assess secondary outcomes.
3. Staff member leaves	Medium	Medium	• Reserve their last 2 weeks for them to transfer their knowledge and documents to other team members. • Offer a flexible work environment that makes it less likely people will leave for another job.
4. Delayed start of funding results in insufficient time to complete project	Medium	Medium	• Start work on ethics and regulatory approvals before funding starts. • Plan to ask for a 1-year extension if needed.
5. Funder withdraws	Low	High	• Tailor communications format and frequency to funder's preferences. • Identify other potential funders to reach out to if there are signals that a funder may withdraw.

project risks will have qualitative and relative scores (e.g., very high, high, medium-high). This is okay. For innovative research projects that have uncertainty related to the deliverables, schedule, and budget, it is unlikely that you can quantify risks with meaningful precision, but it is still important to distinguish between negative risks that have high likelihood or the potential for high impact and negative risks that will not have much of an effect on the project if they are realized. Be sure to allow time for discussion in pairs or small groups. It may be the case that only one or two team members have knowledge of specific important risks, such as those related to cybersecurity, and you do not want the important minority inputs to be excluded or outvoted without due consideration.

4 After the pairs or small groups have identified their top four to
   seven negative risks, reconvene the whole group (possibly in a
   separate second meeting) to identify a small number of key risks
   that the team will invest some resources in identifying responses
   to. As negative risks are identified, the natural inclination may
   be to develop responses for many, if not all, of them. For research
   projects, this is usually not realistic. Research projects do not exist
   to manage risks; they exist to produce new knowledge, products,
   and services. For this reason, you may want to use voting or a
   consensus-building method to identify the top four to seven negative risks for the project as a whole. All of the risks that the participants identify as being potentially important can be captured in a
   "risk registry," but risk responses should only be developed for the
   top negative risks.
5 Simply knowing what the top negative risks are will not help
   the project. Risk responses need to be developed for them.
   Practically speaking, there are four main options for negative
   risk responses:
   ° Avoid – This means changing your project plan so that the
     negative risk is no longer a possibility. For example, if your
     research plan includes fieldwork that has the potential to be
     dangerous because of local climate change or political in-
     stability, you might change your plan to do the fieldwork at
     another site. Avoiding a risk always has a cost in that it means
     you will no longer be implementing the project you initially
     envisioned. Avoiding one risk may also introduce other new
     risks. However, if the combined likelihood and impact of a
     negative risk is perceived to be an unacceptable threat to your
     project, risk avoidance may be the best course of action.
   ° Mitigate – This means investing small amounts of time and
     resources in responses that will decrease either the likelihood
     of a negative risk occurring or the impact if the negative risk
     is realized. For example, if you are concerned that you will
     not have enough study participants, you might invest time
     in working with community groups to help with recruit-
     ment and decrease the likelihood of the risk being realized.
     Alternatively or additionally, to decrease the impact of that
     negative risk, you might involve a statistician in the study

design to make sure that you have enough power to generate conclusive results for your primary outcome, even if you do not have enough participants to assess all the outcomes of interest.

  ° Transfer – This means shifting the risk to another person, group, or organization that is in a better position to manage the risk. The classic example of risk transfer for a non-research project is the purchase of insurance in response to risks related to theft, fire, illness, and so forth. Insurance may also be an appropriate risk response for research project teams in some cases, but research project teams might more typically transfer the risk that the team does not have sufficient experience or time to complete a deliverable by partnering with another group or paying for an experienced consultant to work on the deliverable.

  ° Accept – It is unlikely that you will choose this response for any of your top negative risks, but it is included because it is the response that research project teams apply to most of the negative risks that they identify. Accepting a risk does not mean denying its existence. If the negative risk is realized and becomes an issue, the research project team will deal with it. Accepting a risk means that the team will not invest any time or resources in mitigating, avoiding, or transferring it.

When these five steps were followed in 15 different risk management sessions, the most common risks across sessions were related to funding, team instability, unreliable partners, study participant recruitment, and data access, in approximately that order (Paprica, 2021). Example risk responses for the top three negative risks from those sessions are presented in Box 3.1.

There is no single right set of risk responses. As illustrated in Figure 3.1, research project teams are most likely to accept negative risks that have low likelihood and low impact and avoid or transfer negative risks that have high likelihood or high impact. Negative risks in the middle are more likely to be mitigated. The specific choices for risk responses depend on the risk tolerance of individuals and the research project team, both of which can vary depending

BOX 3.1. EXAMPLES OF NEGATIVE RISKS AND RESPONSES TO THEM

Possible responses to the risk that a team member will leave the project:

- Mitigate impact: If someone is leaving, reserve their last 2 weeks for them to transfer their knowledge and documents to other team members versus having them work on deliverables until their very last day of work.
- Mitigate likelihood: Offer a flexible work environment that makes it less likely that people will leave for another job.
- Mitigate impact: Require team members with highly specialized skills to train or mentor at least one other person on the team.
- Accept: Understand that people who are just starting out in their careers often move every 2 to 3 years, and expect some people to leave the team during the project.

Possible responses to the risk that a funder will withdraw from the project:

- Mitigate likelihood: Incorporate and highlight milestones and deliverables that clearly and obviously align with the funder's preferences and needs.
- Mitigate impact: Proactively identify the deliverables that will be delayed, cut, or partially reduced if negative risks related to funding are realized.
- Mitigate likelihood: Build and maintain strong personal relationships with the funder.
- Mitigate impact: Invest time and resources in identifying additional alternative funders.

Possible responses to the risk that a stakeholder knowledge user will stop participating in the project:

- Mitigate likelihood: Set up mechanisms to bring in the stakeholder's advice, for example, 15-minute one-on-one briefings that fit into the stakeholder's schedule.
- Mitigate impact: Develop relationships with multiple people in the stakeholder's organization, for example, people who report to your knowledge user or peers of the stakeholder.
- Mitigate likelihood: Develop tailored communications material that focuses on the relevance of the project to the stakeholder and their organization's strategic priorities.

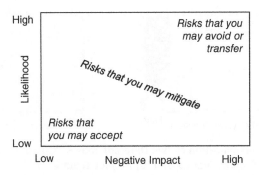

Figure 3.1. Relationship between Risk Responses and the Likelihood and Impact of Negative Risks

on the context. Sometimes research project teams with low resources have no choice but to accept negative risks because actively monitoring and developing responses to risks always takes more resources than accepting them.

Figure 3.2 is presented to highlight this variation in risk tolerance. At first glance, it might appear that Figure 3.2a represents a more risk-tolerant team or organization than Figure 3.2b because Figure 3.2a indicates that many negative risks are accepted, including some with medium-high potential impact. Closer inspection of Figure 3.2a, though, reveals a low tolerance for risks that would have a high negative impact even when they have medium to low likelihood. This can happen with research project teams. Sometimes an individual's or team's prior experience with a negative risk that was realized makes them unwilling to accept similar risks for a new project. That is okay. As with all project management, the research project team should use whatever risk management approach is right for them and their unique project and circumstances.

3.2.3 Positive Risk Management

As noted earlier, project risks are not always negative. There are also positive risks, which are also known as potential opportunities, and you do not want them to pass your project by. Examples of positive risks for research projects include when applications to multiple funders for similar work are successful, a new finding or deliverable produced by an external group benefits your project (e.g., a systematic

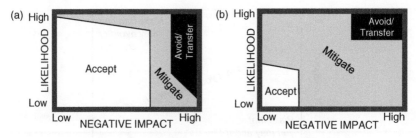

Figure 3.2. Representation of Two Different Teams' Negative Risk Tolerance: (a) Project Team 1 and (b) Project Team 2

review performed by others eliminates the need for you to do comprehensive literature review), new partners want to join the project, geographically dispersed team members are brought together by an external event such as a conference, procurement takes less money or time than forecast, or unexpected funds become available.

To identify your project's top positive risks, follow steps similar to those described for negative risks, except choose from the following mirror-image responses for positive risks:

- Exploit – Change the plan so that the positive risk becomes an opportunity that the project benefits from.
- Enhance – Change or adjust your plan to increase the likelihood of a positive risk being realized or to increase the impact if it is realized.
- Share – Partner with others so that you are in a better position to realize benefits from the positive risk if it becomes a real opportunity.
- Accept – Do not actively invest any resources in increasing the likelihood or impact of the positive risk, but know that you can still realize benefits if opportunity knocks.

Box 3.2 presents examples of some potential positive risk responses.

3.2.4 Research Project Risk Management Plan

As with all project management information, your work on risks needs to be shared with and used by the research project team and

BOX 3.2. EXAMPLES OF POSITIVE RISKS AND RESPONSES TO THEM

* Exploit
    ° You are told that you can receive an additional $60,000 if you complete a particular milestone 6 months earlier than planned; you change the project plan so that the milestone is completed earlier, ensuring you will receive the additional funds.
* Enhance
    ° You hear that a funder may (or may not) have surplus year-end funds available; you create a list of new deliverables that the funds could be invested in and share it with the funder to increase the likelihood they will invest surplus funds in your project.
    ° Maintain a short list of enhancements or new activities you will invest in if a large piece of equipment is procured for a lower amount than was planned for.
* Share
    ° You have submitted two $1 million grant applications with similar scope to two different research funders. You do not have the capacity (team, materials, space) to perform $2 million of research if both of the applications are awarded funding, so you reach out to another lab that does related work to see whether they would be interested in partnering to develop a complementary proposal with $1 million of related scope for the funders' consideration if both funders award $1 million to your proposal.

project stakeholders for it to have a benefit. A full research project risk management plan will typically be between one and three pages long. It will often include the following:

1 A negative risks table that includes the top negative risks and the likelihood, impact, and risk response for each (e.g., see Table 3.1). There is no hard-and-fast rule about how many negative risks to include, but practically speaking, if you include more than seven negative risks, you may find it challenging to actually implement the risk responses that your plan commits you to.

2 Bullet points or short blocks of text with key positive risks and responses for them. Again, there is no correct number of positive risks to include, but it is a good idea to challenge your team to identify at least one or two positive risks and responses. Otherwise, important potential opportunities might pass right by the project with the research project team unaware of them.

3 A description of the process and individuals involved in identifying and prioritizing risks and developing responses. This is important because the negative and positive risks that you identify will depend on the knowledge of the people who contributed to the development of the risk management plan. For example, if you do not include anybody with legal, cybersecurity, or finance management skills, risks related to those topics might not make it into your risk management plan, even if they are important. That is okay. Projects do not exist to manage risks, and there is a practical limit to how much effort you can put into identifying them. However, including a list of the people and roles that contributed to developing the risk plan can help the team understand its origin and limitations.

4 A commitment about when risks will be revisited. It often makes sense to revisit risk quarterly in the first and final years of a major initiative and once or twice per year in other years. It is important to revisit the risk management plan with some regularity because the risks for your project are likely to change as the project progresses and as a result of external factors (e.g., the negative risk of an insufficient budget could change on the basis of foreign exchange rates).

5 It is a good idea to include an appendix or direct people to a risk registry that includes all the risks that were brainstormed, including those for which no response was developed. Including the risk registry is a good way to kick-start the process when you revisit risks because it allows you to build on previous brainstorming instead of starting from scratch.

By keeping your risk management plan short and helpful, you will be prepared to act in a coordinated and informed way if negative risks are realized and positioned to take advantage of potential opportunities.

3.3 ROLES AND RESPONSIBILITIES

3.3.1 Importance of Understanding Who Will Do What on the Research Project Team

An informal rule of thumb in project management is that 80 percent of its value comes from getting the scope and roles and responsibilities right. This may be even more true for research projects than for non-research projects because so much of a research project's success depends on the contributions of individual research project team members. People who prepare research grant applications implicitly acknowledge the importance of roles and responsibilities when they develop proposals with large, and often interdisciplinary, teams. The challenge is that, in the absence of project management tools, it can be hard to know whether individual named team members are involved as occasional advisors or as major contributors.

It is a best practice in project management to identify a single lead for each deliverable. This does not mean that you cannot have democratic processes and distributed leadership across the project, but in the absence of a single lead for each deliverable, there is always the risk that work will slip through the cracks (because every co-lead assumed another co-lead was doing the work) or that work will be duplicated (because multiple co-leads all assumed that they were responsible for the work). Of the two risks, duplication can do the most damage because it can create conflict within the research project team. As discussed later in Section 3.3.5, "The RACI as a Tool to Define Multiple Roles," having one lead for each deliverable does not mean that others do not or cannot contribute to it.

Depending on the complexity of your project and the needs of the research project team, the approach to defining roles and responsibilities can be very light-touch or more detailed. As always, the team should start with the low-effort tools and processes and add more only when doing so adds value and is worth the investment of time.

3.3.2 Work Breakdown Structure with the Leads' Initials as a Tool for Identifying Workstream and Deliverable Leads

Often in research project grant applications, and definitely by the time you move into project implementation, you need to determine

3.2. DISTRIBUTE LEADERSHIP

Many research leaders emphasized that the research leader should not try to take on all of the work themselves because the best research teams are those that mobilize people with complementary skills (e.g., see Elspeth Brown, Beth Coleman, Aled Edwards, Colleen Flood, Molly Shoichet, and Mohamad Tavakoli-Targhi). The research leaders also noted that distributing or delegating work, then getting out of the way and supporting people was professionally gratifying, more efficient than trying to do everything themselves, and led to better research outputs (e.g., see Steini Brown, Lorna MacDonald, Michael Schull, Zaïna Soré, and David Wolfe).

who will be the lead for different elements of the project. It might be tempting to think of the principal investigator, senior scientist, or, in some cases, the responsible graduate student as the lead for everything, but doing so often creates bottlenecks and nullifies the benefit of project management and the diversity of research project team members' expertise.

Project management is a discipline that helps bring together the expertise and capabilities of multiple people to create something – knowledge, a product, or a service – that no single person could create on their own. Assigning leads to each of the deliverables and workstreams by adding their initials to the WBS is a simple way to distribute the work of the project across multiple qualified individuals (see Figure 3.3).

A couple things are worth noting about the lead initials on the WBS in Figure 3.3. Within the hierarchy, it is usually the case that the lead for the whole project is also the lead for at least one of the workstreams. Similarly, the lead for each workstream is also often the lead for at least one of the deliverables under it. This is not a hard-and-fast rule, but because the workstream lead role is assigned on the basis of the person's expertise, it would be unusual to have someone leading a workstream who was not also a natural fit for at least one of the deliverables under it. An alternative, deliberately not shown in Figure 3.3, would be to have the workstreams co-led by all the deliverable leads working on it (or to have the project co-led by all the workstream leads). Because having shared leadership for workstreams, or deliverables, creates risk for a project, it is not shown in Figure 3.3.

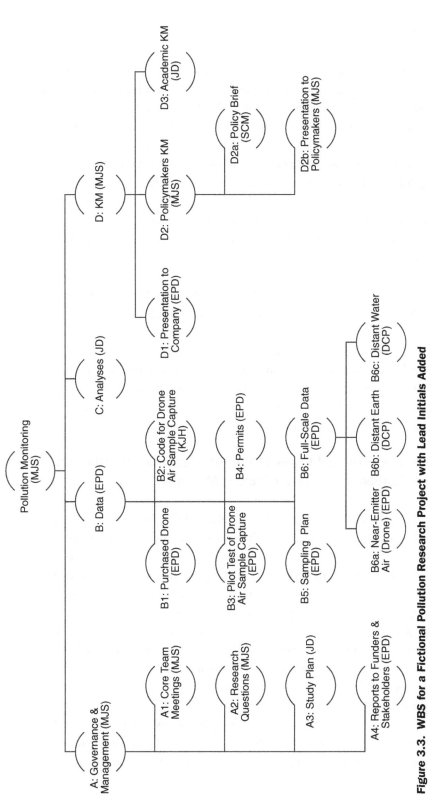

Figure 3.3. WBS for a Fictional Pollution Research Project with Lead Initials Added

Notes: KM = knowledge mobilization; WBS = work breakdown structure.

"Deliverable lead" is not a term that has a universally accepted definition, but it is often understood to refer to the most senior person who works on a deliverable most weeks. The deliverable lead would be the person to whom the team would pose questions about the deliverable or want in the room if a stakeholder had questions about the deliverable. The deliverable lead could be a senior person such as the principal investigator or someone who is earlier in their career, such as an early career researcher, postdoctoral fellow, student, or entry-level staff person. As long as a person has the skills and capacity to do the work or sufficient support from people with more experience, they can be a deliverable lead.

One of the beneficial features of the WBS is that you can intentionally break deliverables down to the point at which you have subdeliverables that provide leadership opportunities for people who are earlier in their careers. For example, Workstream D: KM is led by MJS, but EPD is identified as the lead for Deliverable D1: Presentation to Company and SCM as the lead for Deliverable D2a: Policy Brief. This could be a way to provide trainees EPD and SCM with an opportunity to increase their skills, and build their résumés, by being able to claim genuine leadership of those two relatively straightforward deliverables, particularly if MJS provides them with mentoring and support.

3.3.3 Intertwined Roles of the Principal Investigator and the Academic Research Project Manager

The principal investigator is understood to be the person who leads and is accountable for a research project as a whole, but that does not mean that they should be the named lead for every workstream and deliverable. Projects are performed to bring together the skills and expertise of multiple contributors. How the principal investigator mobilizes people depends on their personal style, and there is no right or wrong approach. A research leader could achieve success by being the lead executor and principal controller of a comprehensive plan, by leading from behind and following the paths that other research project team members set out, or by adopting a practice somewhere between those approaches.

For non-academic research projects, the project manager is understood to be the person who is the lead for project planning (including scoping), project implementation (including monitoring and controlling the project), and project closure. Academic research project teams may not have anyone who has the title "project manager." Sometimes this is because the person responsible for project management has some other title (e.g., program administrator, executive director, research coordinator, research director), sometimes it is because the principal investigator takes on project management responsibilities themselves, and sometimes it is because project management responsibilities are divided and delegated to multiple people.

> **LEADERSHIP ADVICE CROSSWALK**
>
> **3.3. ACCOUNTABILITY AND THE DISTRIBUTION OF WORK**
> Lorna MacDonald and Michael Schull both emphasized that the research leader is the person who is accountable for the research, but that does not mean that they do all the research work themselves. Research leaders described different approaches to distributing the work. For example, David Wolfe's approach involved memorandums of understanding that delegated work to subteams, whereas Elspeth Brown and Kim McGrail emphasized leading from behind. Lorna MacDonald spoke about the need to find a balance between keeping the work true to her personal vision and distributing leadership.

For academic research projects, it is very hard, if not impossible, for anyone who is not the principal investigator to lead all aspects of the work, because a lot of academic research project leadership requires deep subject matter knowledge of the research topic. Consequently, when a research team does include a project manager (or equivalent), that person usually supports the principal investigator and provides coordination, as opposed to being an authoritative leader or decision maker within the team.

Regardless of whether there is someone in a full-time project management position or not, and regardless of how much power and authority the people performing project management functions have, it is important that they focus their efforts on tools and processes that provide clear benefits to the project team and project.

Overall, principal investigators and academic research project teams tend to value project managers (or equivalents) who can bring the right amount of structure and process to research projects – that is, the tools and processes that are helpful without constraining or hampering inquiry and innovation. The last thing that most principal investigators or research project team members want is a project manager who enters the scene with a bunch of documentation for other team members to complete, especially if the team was doing well in terms of achieving its research goals and milestones before the project manager arrived. I have seen several experienced project managers struggle as they try to bring standard tools and processes into academic research environments. I also know principal investigators who have been frustrated by formally trained project managers whom they perceive to be pushing project management documentation that does not add value. So, the most important skill for academic research project managers to have is the ability to select, adapt, and implement project management tools and processes that are actually helpful to the research project and the rest of the team. Figure 1.4 and Box 1.7 provide some guidance about which tools and processes are generally helpful in different situations, but skilled project managers will use their own judgment and feedback from their team members when deciding which project management tools and processes to apply to academic research projects.

In academic research environments, interpersonal skills, including the ability to communicate well with, and influence, diverse team members and stakeholders, are as important as project management skills for both the principal investigator and the project manager. Part of this is understanding which project management tools and processes everyone needs to see and contribute to and which ones might be useful for just the project manager or a subset of the team members. However, research project communications skills are much more than curating project management documentation. Principal investigators and academic research

LEADERSHIP ADVICE CROSSWALK

3.4. PROJECT MANAGEMENT SKILLS WITHIN THE TEAM

Elspeth Brown, Beth Coleman, Steve Farber, Lorna MacDonald, Kim McGrail, and David Wolfe all spoke about what a big difference it made to have people with project management skills on their teams. When other team members take on tasks related to project management (and do them very well), it frees up the principal investigator's time to focus on leading the research, building the team's capacity, and partnerships.

project managers need to be able to listen to and really understand the advice and needs of the principal investigator and others in order to bring people together, including team members from different disciplines and with different levels of experience.

Because academic research project teams need to be able to secure external funding to perform work, they benefit when principal investigators and research project managers have the skills to prepare strong grant applications. Regardless of the title of the person doing the project management work, they are usually the ones who are also tasked with preparing budgets and schedules in grant applications. Often, they also do the actual writing of the first draft of the grant application, which the principal investigator and other research team members review and refine. Academic research project managers will be best at that task if they listen to the details of what is important to the principal investigator, stakeholders, and research project team members who are leading various elements of the grant application, and if they have the ability to quickly come up with options for scope, schedule, and budget combinations that are feasible and aligned with the priorities of whichever research funder they are applying to.

3.3.4 Core Team

In this handbook, I have deliberately used the term "research project team" in an open way because the guidance that the book presents applies no matter what form the team takes. Depending on the size and complexity of the project, the team can be two or three people who work in the same physical space, or tens of people distributed across multiple countries. Sometimes the research project team for a graduate student's research project, or for a small project, is really just one person and their advisors (see Box 3.3).

If the research project team is large, or if the team includes some people who do not work on the project full time, it often works to the project's advantage to define one or more core teams. A *core team* consists of the people who do project work regularly (e.g., do some work on project deliverables most weeks). The core team brings together people with complementary skills who work together to deliver the project and often includes

- the principal investigator (or their delegate),
- the project manager (or whatever title applies to the person who does the project management work),
- leads for workstreams and deliverables, and
- people who are not the designated lead for anything but do project work (e.g., students and research support staff).

Sometimes the core team includes stakeholders such as knowledge user partners who participate in all meetings, but more typically these kinds of contributors would be considered part of the broader research project team that meets less frequently (see Figure 3.4).

Core team meetings are the most frequent of all project meetings, usually occurring monthly or every 2 weeks, and sometimes more frequently. People who are not members of the core team may participate in core team meetings at key points of the project (e.g., a procurement expert might participate immediately before and during procurement of large equipment) or for key decisions, but they would not usually attend all core team meetings.

BOX 3.3. WHEN THE RESEARCH PROJECT TEAM CONSISTS OF ONE PERSON

Project management tools and processes are designed to help teams of people work together in a coordinated and productive way, but they can also be adapted and add value even when the research project team consists of a single person.

In terms of the specific tools and process to apply when working on a project alone, many people find that the WBS helps clarify their own thinking, so it is often the best tool to start with. From there, you might want to consider whether or how a deliverable-based Gantt chart or tracking sheet to capture project information would add value. These three pages, which I sometimes refer to as "three-page project management" (see Figure 1.4), are presented for a fictional project in Appendix D, "Three Pages for Planning and Managing a Fictional Seniors' Health Clinics Evaluation Project."

When using project management tools for a team of one, plan on having fewer meetings and focus on the content as opposed to the formatting of project management tools unless advisors or other stakeholders want to see them.

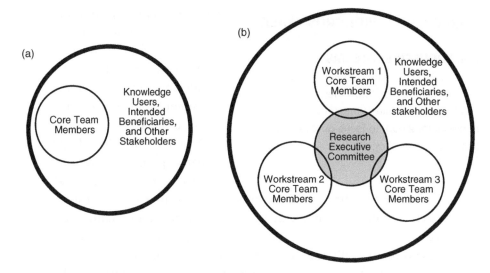

Figure 3.4. Relationship among the Research Project Team, Core Team or Teams, and Research Executive Committee: (a) Research Project Team and (b) Research Project Team for Large Projects

Ideally, the core team will be no more than 10 people, and preferably consist of 7 or fewer individuals. The more people you have on the core team, the harder it is to schedule meetings and have effective, free-flowing communication. To illustrate this point, consider how many 2-person relationships would be needed as the core team size increases. A 5-person team has 10 2-person relationships, a 7-person team has 21, and a 10-person team has 45. Even though you will have ways for team members to work together as a group, if you really want people to get to know and trust each other, small groups are better. For that reason, if you have 10 or more people who work on the project most weeks, you may find it helpful to divide the group so that there are different core teams for different elements of the project. Ideally, the WBS will be organized in such a way that each core team maps to its own workstreams or deliverables. For example, if you have a project with teams in multiple countries, you might organize the WBS so that each country has its own workstream and distinct deliverables for data collection, analyses, findings, and so forth. Alternatively, it may be possible to divide the project into natural phases with different core teams for each phase.

LEADERSHIP ADVICE CROSSWALK

3.5. FOCUSED SUBTEAMS
Lorna MacDonald and Michael Schull provided examples of how they established multiple teams (or subteams of the larger group) to focus on different aspects of work they led.

For example, if your research involves the procurement and installation of a new piece of equipment, you might have a different core team for the procurement than you have for the installation.

Another thing that large research project teams may want to consider, regardless of whether they have multiple core teams, is the creation of a research executive committee that serves as the decision-making body (see Figure 3.4 and Box 3.4). Although it might seem less controversial and more egalitarian to say that the core team, or the entire research project team, makes decisions together, it is important to be honest and accurate about how decisions are actually made. For example, if someone on the research project team is not a deliverable lead and has not been actively engaged in the project for months, how much say would they really have in an important project decision? The same may be true for new staff or students on the core team who are just beginning their careers. For those reasons, your project documentation should be clear about the minimum set of people who need to be involved for decisions to be valid, noting that nothing prevents you from involving additional people for specific decisions, including students, new staff, subject matter experts, and external stakeholders.

BOX 3.4. RESEARCH EXECUTIVE COMMITTEES FOR LARGE PROJECTS AND INITIATIVES
Large projects and research initiatives often benefit from the establishment of a research executive committee to make decisions. Typically, the research executive committee includes the principal investigator, who serves as the chair, as well as the workstream leads and project manager (or whatever title applies to the person performing project management functions).

Having a defined research executive committee allows teams to realize the benefits of having multiple people contribute to decisions while keeping meeting scheduling feasible. It also means that you have a relatively small group of people to convene if a time-sensitive decision must be made.

Nothing prevents the team from involving people outside the research executive committee in decisions, but it is good to establish the minimum set of individuals who will be involved before a decision needs to be made, particularly if you need to make a decision that is contentious in some way (see also Box 3.6, "Examples of Potentially Contentious Research Project Decisions," in Section 3.4.2, "Decision-Making Processes").

If the research executive committee is more than four people, some teams will authorize a subset of the research executive committee members to make routine decisions, such as releasing the planned budget on schedule or paying for external services within a defined budget threshold.

3.3.5 The RACI as a Tool to Define Multiple Roles

If you want to, or need to, go beyond identifying deliverable leads on the work breakdown structure (WBS), the RACI is the tool for you. There is some variation in what people consider the acronym RACI to stand for, but a definition that is probably the most intuitive for academic research project teams is as follows:

- **Resource**: does the work
- **Approver**: approves and is accountable for the work
- **Consulted**: provides council for and input to the work
- **Informed**: is kept informed of the work

The RACI is easy to apply to research projects. Simply create a table that has the deliverables from the WBS (and subdeliverables, when applicable) in the first column, followed by a column for each of the four RACI categories (Table 3.2). There are a few points to note when using the RACI for research projects. For Resource, you want to avoid

Table 3.2. Example of a Partially Completed RACI for a Generic Research Project

Deliverable	Resource(s)	Approver	Consulted	Informed
A: Governance & management	EPD	MJS[a]	Stakeholders	Funders
A1: Core team meetings	EPD	MJS[a]		
A2: Research questions	EPD	MJS[a] and research executive committee	Stakeholders	Funders
A3: Study plan	EPD, JD[a]	MJS	Stakeholders	Funders
A4: Reports for funders & stakeholders	EPD,[a] JD	MJS	Funders and stakeholders	Entire research project team
B: Data	EPD, JD	EPD[†]		Stakeholders
C: Analyses	EPD, SCM, JD[a]	MJS		Funders and stakeholders
D: Knowledge mobilization	EPD, SCM, JD	MJS[a]	Stakeholders	Funders and stakeholders

Note: See also Appendices E and F for example deliverable-based RACI charts.
[a] Deliverable or workstream lead.

shared responsibility when possible. Sometimes you can do this by breaking a deliverable down into subdeliverables with one resource each, but that is not always natural or possible. In those cases, you may have more than one person's name, or initials, in the resource categories for some deliverables.

You may notice that the letters for RACI do not identify an obvious deliverable lead (see Section 3.3.2). If the same individual is the Resource and Approver for a deliverable, they will also be the lead for that deliverable. Footnotes can be added to the RACI to clarify who is the deliverable lead when multiple people have Resource or Approver roles for a deliverable.

For A: Approver, at a minimum, the deliverable lead should be included. "A: Approver" means that a person has veto power regarding whether a deliverable is deemed to be complete and over any plans and investment related to the deliverable. Some deliverables may have one person who is both R: Resource and A: Approver. That is okay for small and straightforward deliverables; however, it is usually best to have someone other than the R: Resource to approve major project deliverables that are going to be seen by people outside of the core team. For deliverables that affect the whole project, such as the research questions, you will always want the principal investigator as A: Approver, either on their own or by having the research executive committee named under A: Approver.

It is also possible that some deliverables will have the research executive committee plus one or two other named individuals (e.g., because they are subject matter experts) as A: Approver. Although it may be tempting to include many, or even all, team members as A: Approver, there are two reasons to think carefully about doing that. First, it may be the case that not everyone wants to be involved in all decisions. For example, if someone does not have the time to review or expertise related to a deliverable, they may prefer not to be included as A: Approver for it. Second, if you put in writing that a person has a role in approving a deliverable, and the person is not available for some reason, you may have boxed yourself in in terms of your ability to call the deliverable complete. For that reason, it may be better to include people who are not essential to the approvals process under C: Consulted.

For the "C" in RACI to be meaningful, the people who are consulted need to be provided with enough time and information to provide advice. The main difference between C: Consulted and A: Approver is that work on deliverables can go forward even if the people consulted do not agree that a deliverable has been completed or agree on the proposed course of action for it. However, in practice the line between C: Consulted and A: Approver can become blurred. For example, if many (or most) of the people you consult with do not agree that a deliverable has been completed, or do not agree with the planned course of action for it, it can be hard for the approvers to justify going forward. In those cases, the people under C: Consulted would have a role to play in helping the team identify preferable options based on the deficiencies they perceive. The people or groups with a C: Consulted role are identified based on their potential to strengthen the deliverables and project as a whole, and your process needs to provide them with the opportunity to do that.

The final category, I: Informed, is sometimes referred to as the for-your-information (FYI) category. It identifies the people and groups who will receive information about, or copies of, deliverables, often after the fact. For example, your funder may receive a copy of the research questions without having any role in establishing them. Apart from potential concerns about confidentiality, there is no limit on how many people or groups are identified as I: Informed. Including more people and groups as I: Informed will not slow your project down because people who are informed do not affect the rate at which project work is completed. What is important is to share your FYI items in a coordinated manner; otherwise they may get lost in emails, or you may inadvertently forget to share information with some I: Informed people or groups who expect to receive it.

As with the WBS and the Gantt chart, the RACI is often held up as a very important and useful project management tool. Referring back to Table 3.2, the deliverable-based RACI immediately clarifies who is involved in the production each deliverable and in what way. The RACI conveys a lot of information and can be particularly helpful in grant applications when you have a large team and need to demonstrate meaningful roles and contributions for all the contributors in a small amount of space.

LEADERSHIP ADVICE CROSSWALK

3.6. BUILDING OTHERS' CAPACITY

Many research leaders spoke about the privilege and responsibility that they associated with mentoring and building the capacity of students and early career researchers (e.g., see Elspeth Brown, Aled Edwards, Arjumand Siddiqi, Molly Shoichet, Sharon Straus, Mohamad Tavakoli-Targhi, and Rich Zemel). Often, their advice emphasized optimistic and supportive styles and human connections. Many research leaders made a point of speaking about people who are earlier in their careers as colleagues, not as subordinates, and noted how rewarding it was for them to play a role in developing the next generation of researchers.

3.3.6 Building Capacity across the Research Project Team

One of the ways in which academic research projects often differ from non-academic projects is that they have the dual objectives of conducting research and building capacity. It is understood that graduate students, postdoctoral fellows, and early career researchers will all be learning and developing skills as the project progresses and, by extension, that they may not have all the skills and knowledge they need to make their contributions when the project starts.

The WBS in Figure 2.3 presents some deliverables specifically focused on training and capacity building: F1: Trainee-Led Lunch & Learns, F2: Mentoring Program, and F3: Journal Club. These are deliverables that are often good to include, but they by

> **LEADERSHIP ADVICE CROSSWALK**
>
> **3.7. LEADERS ARE ALSO LEARNERS**
> Several research leaders emphasized the fact that the research leader is also a learner (e.g., see Elspeth Brown, Steini Brown, Kim McGrail, and Michael Schull)

no means cover all the things that research project teams and research leader can or should do to build capacity in their teams.

Motivated, in part, by the surplus of PhD graduates relative to the number of available academic positions, the Canadian Health Services and Policy Research Alliance led a Canada-wide process focused on modernizing the content of graduate student training. This led to the identification of enriched core competencies for PhD training to give graduates the skills they need to work in academic and non-academic careers (CHSPRA, 2015; CIHR, 2017). Six of the 10 competencies identified by CHSPRA and CIHR focused on professional skills (see Box 3.5; CIHR, 2017).

Although the focus of the CHSPRA Working Group on Training was on PhD graduate students in health policy research, the professional attributes and competencies have been included in this handbook with the permission of the co-chairs of the CHSPRA Working Group on Training because they can also serve as prompts for readers to think about in terms of personal and team member development (see Box 3.5).

How to go about building these and other attributes and competencies in others is a topic that has been the subject of many books and academic articles, including several by Sharon Straus (Sambunjak et al., 2006; Straus & Sacket, 2013), one of the research leaders who graciously agreed to be interviewed for this handbook. In their interviews, multiple research leaders spoke about the fact that all research team members, including themselves, are constantly learning and developing their skills.

Full coverage of mentoring and capacity building is beyond the scope of this handbook; however, I share one piece of advice that I received in 2007 because it has been very helpful to me: When you

---

BOX 3.5. PROFESSIONAL ATTRIBUTES AND COMPETENCIES

- **Leadership, mentorship, and collaboration** – the ability to lead, organize, and support team members from various backgrounds to work together to achieve a specific outcome
- **Project management** – the ability to organize and coordinate all stages of a project in an academic or non-academic environment, from scoping through to knowledge translation and extension.
- **Interdisciplinary work** – the ability to effectively use, and to combine when appropriate, methods and insights from multiple academic disciplines
- **Knowledge mobilization, communication, and brokerage** – the ability to use multiple methods of communication and to communicate appropriately with different kinds of audiences
- **Networking** – the ability to develop and maintain productive relationships within and outside of academia
- **Dialogue and negotiation** – the ability to work toward win–win outcomes and value-added results, including understanding other perspectives and how to respond to them
- **Change management and implementation** – the ability to plan, manage, and implement change, including to communicate a clear vision for change, to lead people and organizations through change, to manage and implement successful transitions, and to evaluate and report on change.

Source: Canadian Institutes of Health Research (2017).

---

are mentoring or supervising someone, and they come to you to discuss a decision or proposed course of action, it is a good idea to find out the following before you start speaking:

- Have they come to you because they do not know where to begin and are looking for ideas and direction?
- Have they come to you because they have a partially developed plan and are seeking your advice to improve it?
- Have they come to you because they have what they believe to be a fully developed plan that they want to discuss with you before they implement it?

I like these questions because (a) they help ensure that I do not inadvertently take a leadership opportunity away from someone who is ready for it and (b) I think they apply to everyone, including me. Whether it is a graduate student supporting a peer or someone with decades of experience starting a new project, everyone in research is learning all the time. Finding out the answers to these questions, directly or indirectly, is one of the ways to provide space and opportunity for that learning.

3.4 DECISION MAKING, GOVERNANCE, AND OVERSIGHT

3.4.1 Research Project Governance

There is a lot of variation in the ways the term "governance" is used when it comes to academic research. In some cases, the focus is research systems, and governance describes how funders make decisions about what research to fund and how they evaluate the investments they have made. The governance content of this handbook is more narrowly focused on how and by whom decisions are made in teams that perform research.

Project-level governance is particularly important for academic research because research's inherent uncertainty means that plans for it can change in big ways during project implementation. In addition, as funders are investing in larger and more multidisciplinary projects, there is more focus on the effective governance of large grants, with some research funders requiring descriptions of governance in grant applications (see, e.g., Canada, National Centres of Excellence, 2018; Innovation, Science and Economic Development Canada, 2022).

Research decision making can include both governance bodies, which have an oversight or advisory function, and management bodies, which do the work (see Figure 3.5). To understand the difference

> **LEADERSHIP ADVICE CROSSWALK**
>
> **3.8. BE PREPARED TO MAKE DECISIONS**
> Kim McGrail spoke about the need to balance consensus-focused approaches with the reality that somebody has to be in charge, and the fact that sometimes the research leader will be the final arbiter.

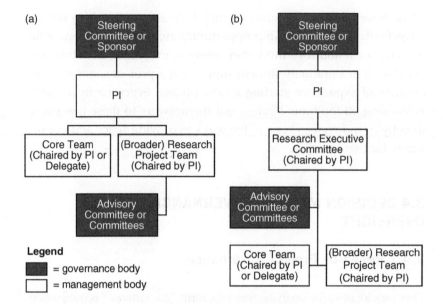

Figure 3.5. Examples of Hierarchy in Research Project Governance and Management: (a) Regular Research Project and (b) Large Research Project
Note: PI = principal investigator.

between governance and management, it may help to draw parallels with the corporate structure of organizations:

- **Corporate governance** is the responsibility of boards of directors, who provide strategic direction and are legally accountable for the corporation.
- **Corporate management** is the responsibility of the chief executive officer and management team, who are responsible for planning and managing operations and report to the board of directors.

Many current approaches to research are intentionally non-hierarchical, but, in my view, a defined hierarchy is needed to provide clarity about governance (e.g., see Figure 3.5). This does not mean that the contributions of individuals and teams lower in the hierarchy are devalued or ignored, but it does provide accountability, a clear path for decisions to be made even if consensus cannot be achieved, and a way for the project to benefit from external expertise and advice.

The management bodies in Figure 3.5 – the principal investigator, research executive committee, and core team – have already been discussed in Section 3.3, "Roles and Responsibilities." Figure 3.5 also identifies three different governance bodies – the steering committee, the sponsor, and the advisory committee or committees – each of which is discussed in brief, beginning with the sponsor.

The sponsor role is usually held by a senior person who is not on the project team but within the organization. If the term "sponsor" has the potential to be confused with "funder" in your organization (e.g., for industry-sponsored research), you should feel free to use some other term that makes sense in your environment, such as "executive project advisor."

The sponsor serves as a champion or advocate for the project and, in some cases, is accountable for the project. The sponsor makes strategic contributions to the project and does not perform day-to-day project activities. For example, a sponsor for an academic research project might

- confirm the scope of work and advise on potential changes to scope (e.g., approve decreased scope in response to schedule or budget deficits),
- help identify and secure additional financial or other resources if opportunities or risks mean that the project requires additional resources to succeed,
- provide advice or direction when the principal investigator needs assistance in making decisions or managing risks and opportunities,
- support the project in internal politics, and
- approve or make decisions that are beyond the capacity or authority of the principal investigator, research executive committee, or research project team.

Generally, the more senior the sponsor is within an organization, the higher the probability of project success. This is because having that one senior-level individual associated with the project can provide a way forward in cases in which the principal investigator or research project team hits a barrier that they cannot overcome or a decision they cannot make.

Even if your project is small, it is a good idea to secure a senior person to serve as sponsor for your project. For academic research projects, the sponsor might be the dean, vice dean, or a professor emeritus. If you do have a sponsor, be sure to provide them with updates using their preferred format and mechanism. This could be 15-minute briefings each month or written reports, depending on the sponsor's preference. They might prefer the opportunity to ask questions as opposed to having information presented to them in writing. Whatever communications approach you use, be sure to keep the sponsor updated regularly, not just when you need their help. You want the sponsor to view the project in a positive light, not as a source of problems.

The second governance body shown in Figure 3.5 is the steering committee. As the name implies, steering committees steer or direct a project. They have a strategic oversight function, similar to how a board of directors provides strategic oversight and direction for a corporation. In the same way as you would select individuals with relevant, diverse, and complementary skills and competencies for the board of directors of a corporation, so too should you select individuals for your research steering committee. Steering committees often have responsibilities similar to those of the sponsor, except that, instead of one person, a group of people provides strategic direction and advice. There is no right number of members for governance committees, but they typically have at least 5 members and as many as 12 to 15 members to ensure that they are big enough to bring in different perspectives and expertise but not so big that scheduling meetings that all members can attend becomes unworkable.

The principal investigator usually attends steering committee meetings but typically does not chair them. The whole point of a steering committee is to have a group of people who can provide strategic direction from a distance. If you have the principal investigator as chair of the steering committee, or even as a member who votes or contributes to its decision making, the principal investigator will naturally lean toward supporting the ongoing work and plans of the core team and research executive committee because the principal investigator is one of the people who helped establish those plans. If the steering committee is going to make a difference in the governance of the project, it should provide advice and directions that are different from what the principal investigator and research project team would have come up with in the absence of a steering committee. For that reason, it is best practice to have the principal investigator attend steering committee meetings as someone who presents information, observes discussions, and answers questions but does not vote.

The last governance body shown in Figure 3.5 is the advisory committee. As the name implies, advisory committees provide advice as opposed to steering the project or making decisions. However, just like people who fall under Consulted on the RACI, you seek advice from your advisory committee on the basis of their expertise and knowledge, and if all members of an advisory committee oppose a planned course of action, it is probably time to change your plan (see Section 3.3.5, "The RACI as a Tool to Define Multiple Roles"). Because advisory committees provide advice rather than make decisions, you do not have to bring together a group of people who will come to consensus. In fact, it may help the project and research project team more to have an advisory committee made up of a diverse group of people who consistently bring in different perspectives and rarely, or never, agree. For large scientific projects, it is common to have a scientific advisory committee composed of scientists who are not involved in the project but are experts on related topics. Increasingly, projects also have at least one advisory committee to bring in the perspectives of knowledge users and the intended project beneficiaries (e.g., patients, clients, members of society).

3.4.2 Decision-Making Processes

Because some research project decisions can be contentious (see Box 3.6), it is best practice to establish decision-making processes and roles before there is a need to make a decision. Otherwise, people might perceive that the process and people involved were deliberately selected to steer the decision in a particular direction.

When it comes to the process used for decision making, voting is often the first thing that comes to mind, but it is not usually the best first approach for research project decisions. By design, research project teams bring together people with complementary skills and knowledge, sometimes from different disciplines. If you immediately

> **BOX 3.6. EXAMPLES OF POTENTIALLY CONTENTIOUS RESEARCH PROJECT DECISIONS**
>
> - Who or which deliverable gets a decrease in budget when unavoidable fixed costs increase or the budget is cut
> - A partner organization or researcher needs to be taken off the project because they are not contributing
> - Assignment of intellectual property rights (i.e., what percentage to whom)
> - Authorship assignments (first author, last author, second author), particularly when the team is large
> - The project must be terminated (e.g., because the research is found to be harmful, not feasible, or no longer worth conducting).

(or always) use voting to make decisions, you may overwhelm important minority views and lose the power of that diversity. For that reason, a better approach to decision making is often to strive for consensus and allow time for the planned course of action to be modified to integrate advice from the research project team (Box 3.7).

Good decisions start with giving the people involved advance notice, relevant materials, and time for synchronous discussion. This is how you will ensure that the final decision has benefited from the expertise of different people. Ideally, consensus will emerge from the discussion. In some cases, people might abstain, for example, because they do not feel they know enough to contribute, and that is okay. Consensus does not have to mean that everybody endorses a decision; it can also mean that everyone who did not abstain supported the planned course of action.

If it is not possible to achieve consensus, and if you have or can make the time, the best next step is to see whether the proposed item can be modified to incorporate the suggestions and ideas that came out during the discussion. If you still cannot achieve consensus within the time available, you then have a choice between escalating the decision or voting (see Box 3.7). The first option means that you take the decision away from the team and ask the principal investigator, sponsor, or steering committee to

BOX 3.7. TWO COMMON OPTIONS FOR CONSENSUS-BASED DECISION MAKING FOR RESEARCH

Option 1 – Aim for Consensus, Resolve by Escalation If Needed	Option 2 – Aim for Consensus, Resolve by Simple Majority Vote If Needed
• Provide advance notice that a decision will be made, along with relevant materials, ideally 1 week before the decision and at least 1 full day before the decision.	
• Allow time for discussion, and strive to make decisions by consensus, that is, decisions that no member indicates dissent for, noting that abstaining does not count as dissent.	
• If there is no consensus, and when time allows, the member presenting the item modifies it, within the time frame specified by the chair, making changes that increase the likelihood that consensus can be achieved.	
• If consensus cannot be achieved within the specified time frame, the decision will be made by a higher-authority body or individual, e.g., the principal investigator, sponsor, or steering committee.	• If consensus cannot be achieved within the time frame specified by the chair, the decision will be made by majority vote (i.e., a decision will be made if more than 50% of the members contributing to quorum vote to support it).
	• In cases in which there is a tie, input will be sought from members who were not present when the vote was taken, within a time frame specified by the chair.
	• In cases in which there is a tie after votes have been counted from all members available in the specified time frame, the decision will be made by a higher-authority body or individual (e.g., the principal investigator, sponsor, or steering committee).

make it. This can be a good option if the decision is a strategic one, with pros and cons on each side, as opposed to one that has any single correct answer.

The other option is voting. If you do vote, you want to keep the rules as simple as possible. This usually means that a simple majority makes the decision, but you can also bring in other rules, such as not making a decision until you have received votes from team members who were unable to be present at the meeting.

3.4.3 Bringing Governance and Management Together

All project governance and management bodies should have terms of reference that spell out their roles and responsibilities (e.g., see Box 3.8). As with everything in light-touch project management, you want your terms-of-reference documents to be only as long and detailed as they need to be, because people are more likely to read and process short documents. You can think of the terms of reference as containing the key information that you would want to know if someone were asking you to join a committee, such as the committee's purpose, role, authority, time commitment, and so forth. For the same reasons that you want to identify one, and only one, deliverable lead (see Section 3.3.1), it is best practice to have a single chair for each committee. Having a single chair means that there will be no ambiguity in terms of who is in charge and less likelihood that the work associated with leading the committee will be duplicated or slip through the cracks. However, some committees do identify a vice-chair (or deputy chair) to distribute the chair's responsibilities and so a specific person is identified in cases in which the chair is absent or unable to participate because of a real or perceived conflict of interest.

Notably, the sections that I recommend for terms of reference in Box 3.8 do not include a commitment to keep minutes. In the 20 years I have worked in research, I have never heard a colleague ask for, or act on, detailed minutes from a previous meeting. On some rare occasions, research governance bodies are legally required to keep minutes – for example, a board of directors for a research institute that is incorporated is legally required to keep minutes. However, in most cases, research projects are better served by preparing an agenda marked up with decisions and action items because it takes less time

BOX 3.8. SECTIONS FOR A TERMS-OF-REFERENCE DOCUMENT

1 Background of project and purpose of committee
2 Information about committee composition, that is, defined committee roles such as chair (and possibly vice-chair), the number of members, required or desired diversity (e.g., in terms of gender), sometimes including the process through which members have been or will be selected
3 Scope and responsibilities, for example, project oversight, advice on risks and opportunities, the committee's role (if any) in financial decisions and strategic decisions that affect scope, schedule, or budget
4 Authority (e.g., whether the committee is advisory and, if not, what decisions can they make or not make)
5 Quorum (how many members need to participate for a meeting or decision to have validity)
6 Decision-making process
   a Try for consensus by majority vote, if necessary, or try for consensus and escalate if necessary
   b Which decisions can be made by the chair or a named subset of members
7 Commitment to keep a record of decisions and action items
8 Work commitment and meeting frequency (e.g., number of meetings and total hours per year and whether meetings will be in person or virtual)
9 Term (e.g., full length of project, if that is the expectation)
10 Appendix with names of chair (and vice-chair when applicable) and other members (updated when members join or leave).

to prepare and is more easily processed by research project team members and stakeholders (see Box 5.2, "Example Marked-Up Meeting Agenda with Notes and Action Items," in Section 5.1, "Running Effective Meetings").

Like the WBS and other project management tools, once a terms-of-reference document is established for one committee, it can often be reused, adapted, and applied to other committees and projects. In addition, any steering or advisory committees that you establish might also steer or advise other projects that are related in some way. The process of using a single governance committee for multiple projects can be more efficient and lead to the identification of strategic opportunities across projects that you might not identify if each project has a separate governance body (see Section 5.2, "Applying Project Management Tools and Processes to Research Programs, Operations, and Portfolios").

Box 3.9 presents a simple example governance and management plan for a multiyear project that brings all of the tools in this section together. In brief, it starts with defining roles and committees, including identifying someone who will serve as project manager (or equivalent), and specifies how tools such as status reports and meetings will be used during project implementation. Notably, the example governance and management plan specifies more meetings of governance bodies in the first year of the project, because that is usually the time when the more important strategic project decisions will be made, and because it is also when the team is most likely to identify and implement changes to the project plan. It also has more meetings with governance bodies in the final year to ensure opportunities for their expert advice to influence knowledge translation and planning for the next project or projects.

The example governance and management plan also prompts reviews of risks at multiple points and by management and governance bodies. You want to make sure your governance and management plan has these touch points to take a hard look at the project and pause to think about risks that might be bubbling up, and how you can address them.

BOX 3.9. EXAMPLE RESEARCH PROJECT GOVERNANCE AND MANAGEMENT PLAN

First Year
- Hiring or identification of the research project manager (or equivalent) to assist the principal investigator in developing planning documents that ensure a common understanding of scope, schedule, budget, and decision-making processes

- Identification of a single lead for each workstream and deliverable (add a RACI, if beneficial, to define who contributes via roles other than lead if that adds value for your project)
- Kick-off meeting that brings together the core team or teams (the subset of people who lead or conduct the research) and members of the broader research project team (e.g., knowledge users, intended beneficiaries, and other stakeholders)
- Establishment of management and governance body or bodies – for example, research executive committee, sponsor, steering committee, advisory committee or committees, scientific advisory committee – with terms of reference for each body
- Core team meetings (and, when applicable, research executive committee meetings) held every 2 weeks to monthly and focused on discussing topics and decisions that are strengthened by synchronous dialogue and input from multiple team members
- Determination of the format and frequency of status reports (usually every 4–6 months), and initiation of their issuance
- Establishment of a schedule for broader research project team meetings (or other forms of communication), including, at a minimum, at least one meeting of the broader research project team per year
- Once every 3–4 months, special core team meetings (and, when applicable, research executive committee meetings) focused on reviewing risks and progress in the context of the triple constraint
- Once every 3–4 months, direction and advice from governance body or bodies focused on review of progress and accomplishments and committee recommendations regarding strategic project decisions, negative risks, and potential opportunities.

Middle Years

- Core team meetings (and, when applicable, research executive committee meetings) held every 2 weeks to monthly, complemented and informed by status reports
- Meetings of the broader research project team at least once per year, complemented by small-group or one-on-one meetings and other communications with knowledge users, intended beneficiaries, or other stakeholders
- Twice per year, special core team meetings (and, when applicable, research executive committee meetings) focused on reviewing risks and progress in the context of the triple constraint

- Once or twice per year, updates and advice from governance body or bodies focused on review of progress and accomplishments and committee recommendations regarding strategic project decisions, negative risks, and potential opportunities.

Final Year
- Core team meetings (and, when applicable, research executive committee meetings) held every 2 weeks to monthly, complemented and informed by status reports
- Two to three sessions with governance body or bodies focused on completing the project knowledge mobilization and translation to ensure impact and next steps (e.g., for the next project).

3.5 USING PROJECT MANAGEMENT TO STRENGTHEN GRANT APPLICATIONS

Almost all academic research projects happen because they were selected for funding by an impartial committee of external experts who have no conflicts of interest or direct connections to the proposed work. In practice, this means that academic researchers are free to propose all kinds of projects, but they are often constrained by how review panels understand and view their research grant application in comparison with competing applications.

As a former research funder, and someone who has served as a reviewer for numerous provincial, national, and international research funding competitions, I have reviewed hundreds of research grant applications in the past 20 years and learned a lot in the process. As an aside, as per Barbara Sherwood Lollar's recommendation, I think one of the best things an early career researcher can do to improve their own grant applications is volunteer to serve on grant application review committees.

From my years of experience reviewing grant applications, I have observed that, quite rightly, research funding decisions are made primarily on the basis of the strength and innovativeness of the research that is being proposed. Research funders publish evaluation criteria that emphasize methodological rigor; innovativeness; scientific merit;

contributions to capacity development; and potential for social, health, economic, or environmental benefits, and they choose the grant applications that score the highest on those criteria. Project management tools and processes will not change that, but project management can strengthen research grant applications in important ways by helping to address the following common weaknesses:

- Uncertainty about what will be different if the research project is funded
- Lack of clarity about who is leading or contributing to specific elements of the project, especially if the team is large
- Unrealistic budget or a budget that does not seem to be allocated to the main deliverables of the project
- Projects that read as being overly ambitious and infeasible
- Concern about whether and how the different parts of the project will come together
- Typographical and other small errors in the application document.

One of the most common weaknesses in grant applications is that it is hard to know what will be different if the research is funded and goes as planned. Some grant applications do a very good job of framing the problem or knowledge gap that will be addressed, and describing the research methodologies that will be used, without being clear about what the research project will produce. That does not mean that every research project has to result in some measurable change, but it should be possible for reviewers to understand whether the goal is the creation of new knowledge, better understanding of a problem, evidence for policy and planning, a new or improved product or service, or some other output.

The project management tool that can help with this weakness is the WBS (see Section 2.1, "Scope and the Work Breakdown Structure." Because the WBS is a visual presentation of 100 percent of the scope that the project will produce, grant selection committee members can look at a one-page WBS and immediately see, at a high level, everything that the project intends to produce, including interim and final deliverables.

Some research grant applications allow for the submission of figures that do not count toward the maximum page count. I have reviewed many applications that include schematics with pillars, platforms, and ellipses intended to show how different elements of the project will come together and fit in context with other work. My personal view is that those kinds of schematics can be helpful when someone is in the room explaining them, but they rarely help reviewers understand grant applications, particularly when reviewers are assessing multiple applications that use similar words in different ways (e.g., one grant's pillar is another grant's enabler). In contrast, a one-page WBS is almost universally understood and processed. So, it is my view that if there is an option to include a figure in your grant application, a WBS is the best choice.

In some grant applications, especially large ones, the list of team members can be very long, and it is hard to know how all the named individuals will contribute. Reviewers might be convinced that the team, as a whole, has all the necessary skills and knowledge to perform the research but be uncertain about the extent to which listed team members will actually contribute their knowledge and skills. Two project management tools can help with this. First, simply adding team members' initials to the WBS to show who is the lead for each workstream and deliverable can do a lot to increase reviewers' confidence that the multiple research project team members will be deeply involved. For example, if multiple senior researchers have complementary expertise, adding their initials to show which workstreams and deliverables they will each lead would make it clear that the senior people will be much more than occasional advisors. The WBS can also be used to demonstrate that early career researchers will be provided with leadership opportunities by including their initials as leads at the subdeliverable, deliverable, or the workstream level.

The WBS is an excellent way to convey information about deliverable and subdeliverable leads, but, of course, there are roles other than lead. Including a RACI in a grant application provides additional details by identifying who will be the R: Resource, who will be the A: Approver, and who will be C: Consulted or I: Informed (see Section 3.3.5, "The RACI as a Tool to Define Multiple Roles"). The RACI (or a subset of the letters and roles) can be presented in tabular form in the grant application or incorporated into blocks of text to describe the roles and contributions that different team members will make to the project.

Table 3.3. Unrealistic High-Level Budget for a Fictional Large Research Project

Funder Budget Category or Subcategory	Cost/Year, $		
	1	2	3
Students	335,000	335,000	285,000
Postdoctoral fellows	200,000	200,000	200,000
Staff	175,000	175,000	175,000
Other personnel costs	150,000	150,000	150,000
Equipment	25,000	25,000	25,000
Supplies and services	85,000	85,000	85,000
Travel	30,000	30,000	80,000
Total	1,000,000	1,000,000	1,000,000

Another common weakness with grant applications is budgets that are not realistic or obviously connected to the work of the project. If your immediate reaction to the two high-level budgets in Tables 3.3 and 3.4 is that Table 3.3 looks unrealistic, you are not alone. Among other issues, the numbers in Table 3.3 add up to exactly $1 million every year, which is unlikely to occur because regular percentage increases in staff and trainee compensation mean that personnel costs rarely stay the same for multiple years, and most projects require fewer resources in their first year of implementation. Overall, Table 3.3 gives the impression that the applicants are either (a) asking for as much money as they can get without a real plan for how to allocate the funds they receive or (b) in need of more funding than the competition can provide so they are asking for the maximum. Either way, the budget in Table 3.3 does not work to the applicants' advantage.

In contrast, the budget in Table 3.4 gives the impression that the applicants have a plan behind their budget. It is also fictional, but it reads as being more realistic because it includes modest cost-of-living increases so the defined personnel costs increase a little each year, and it is based on actual compensation ranges for students, postdoctoral fellows, and staff as opposed to rounded numbers. Research funders require budgets to be submitted using the categories that they provide, but if there is space, providing a high-level description of the funded workstreams and the deliverables

Table 3.4. Realistic High-Level Budget for a Fictional Large Research Project

Funder Budget Category or Subcategory	Cost/Year, $		
	1	2	3
Students	308,813	419,985	428,385
Postdoctoral fellows	225,483	229,992	175,944
Staff	130,845	133,462	136,131
Other personnel costs	40,000	40,000	40,000
Equipment	10,000	85,000	10,000
Supplies and services	35,000	50,000	35,000
Travel	30,000	30,000	80,000
Total	780,141	988,439	905,460

would provide reviewers with more confidence that the applicants have the capacity to develop a real budget that is aligned with their proposed scope and schedule (see Section 2.3, "Deliverable-Based Budget").

In research funding competitions designed to attract highly innovative grant applications, proposals are sometimes so innovative and ambitious that reviewers question their feasibility. Risk management is a process that can help address that perceived weakness. Instead of leaving reviewers to wonder whether the applicants understand the risky nature of their proposal, including a risk management plan demonstrates that the research project team has thought about negative risks, in terms of likelihood and impact, and developed plans to mitigate the most important negative risks (see Section 3.2, "Processes to Identify and Manage Risks").

On a related note, it is sometimes not clear in grant applications how large interdisciplinary teams will work together or be able to make decisions if the realization of negative risks means that the project scope or plan needs to change. As noted earlier, it does not inspire a reviewer's confidence to read that a team of 20, 30, or 40 people will make every decision by consensus, particularly when the team includes people in different geographical locations. The tools and processes outlined in Section 3.4, "Decision Making, Governance, and Oversight," can help increase reviewers' confidence in the research project team's ability to work together on large and complex projects by identifying defined governance and management bodies and specifying how they will function in terms-of-reference documents that include details about how and by whom decisions will be made.

The last contribution that project management can make to strengthen a grant application is more about the development process than the application's content. It has certainly not been the case for the majority of applications that I have reviewed, but I have, on occasion, been presented with grant applications that show all the signs of being rushed. Sometimes they include typos or incomplete sentences. I have even seen applications that look as though they were prepared by cutting and pasting text from applications that had been submitted to other competitions (e.g., because they included the name or priorities of other funders). There have also been cases in which researchers have called me shortly before the deadline for an application because last-minute technical problems have complicated their submission. None of these inspires confidence in reviewers or funders.

The project management practice that can help with this weakness is building buffer into the schedule for grant application development (see Section 2.2.3, "Steps for Developing a Deliverable-Based Gantt Chart for a Research Project"). If you plan so that you are ready to submit your grant application days before the deadline, you can mitigate risks such as internet or power failures and ensure that there is time for someone other than the person who wrote the application to do a thorough proofreading of it.

Few things are more important to researchers than securing funding for their work. Regardless of whether you submit project management tools such as the WBS and RACI as part of your grant application, using them as the foundation for your schedule and budget will help ensure that you have a comprehensive plan

LEADERSHIP ADVICE CROSSWALK

3.9. RESEARCH LEADERS SECURE FUNDING

Colleen Flood, Jutta Treviranus, and Rich Zemel all spoke about the role of the research leader in securing funding, and Barbara Sherwood Lollar provided three concrete points of guidance on the topic for early career researchers.

that should be implementable if you are successful in competing for funding.

The project management community has come up with excellent ways of presenting project elements, such as scope, schedule, budget, risks, roles, and responsibilities. Applying adapted versions of these project management tools and processes can help to ensure a systematic and comprehensive grant application that fulfills the triple constraint by aligning scope, time, and cost, which can, in turn, increase its chances of success. Project management tools and processes will not turn an application that is deemed by reviewers to be non-fundable into one that is fundable, but it can help increase reviewers' understanding of, and confidence in, the research grant application, which can, in turn, help it earn higher scores from grant review committees.

Implementing and Closing Research Projects

4.1 PROJECT KICKOFF

Whatever work you and your team put toward developing your research grant application, it is small compared with the amount of work required to produce your deliverables during the project implementation phase (Figure 4.1). For that reason, upon receiving funding, it is important to check in with the team to take stock of the current situation before you move into implementing your plan. Because most research project proposals require a committee funding decision before they have the budget and human resources to start implementation, many things can change between the time that a proposal for funding is submitted and the date that the project starts (Box 4.1). These may be things that the team already identified as risks and determined risk responses for or as risks that need to be monitored because they may be realized again.

One of the single biggest positive things you can do for your project is to hold a kick-off meeting. In just a few hours, the kick-off meeting helps you to

- formally start the project,
- introduce the workstream or deliverable leads and other team members to each other,
- establish a common understanding of scope in terms of deliverables,

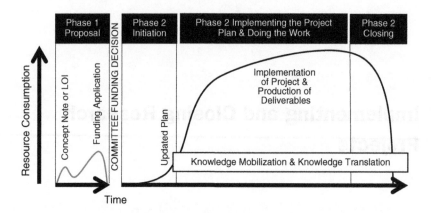

Figure 4.1. Project Phases and Resource Consumption
Note: LOI = Letter of Intent.

BOX 4.1. POSSIBLE RESPONSES TO THINGS THAT MAY CHANGE BETWEEN GRANT APPLICATION SUBMISSION AND THE START OF A RESEARCH PROJECT

- Funder drops out or decreases support → Find another funder (affects schedule) or decrease scope.
- Key team member leaves the team, and you no longer have the required expertise to perform the work → Find a replacement (affects schedule), take out the work they would have done (decrease scope), or hire a consultant to do the work (obtain budget for consultant by reducing other scope).
- While you were waiting to hear the results of a research funding competition, you find funds to start the work before the grant was awarded → Shorten schedule or add more scope.
- The team wants to undertake some work that was not in the grant application → Increase scope with corresponding budget and schedule increases, seek additional funder, or extend schedule or reduce other planned scope to make schedule and budget room for the new work.
- New regulations or requirements have been introduced that change scope, budget, or schedule → Revise the plan.

- communicate major things that have changed since the grant application was submitted,
- ensure that everyone knows about important dates and constraints,
- present the project's governance and decision-making processes,
- distinguish between the changes deliverable leads can make on their own and those that require additional approvals,
- make people aware of key opportunities for the project and high-level risks (but do not get into the weeds of negative risks because you want the kick-off meeting to be energizing), and
- begin to build relationships within the team.

> **LEADERSHIP ADVICE CROSSWALK**
>
> **4.1. START LARGE PROJECTS WITH A MEETING**
>
> Steve Farber, Zaïna Soré, and Stefaan Verhulst spoke about starting large research initiatives with meetings that bring people together and the importance of team members getting to know each other and build relationships.

If your kick-off meeting is virtual, you will probably want to limit it to 2 hours to ensure that it is an energizing experience for team members. A sample agenda for a 2-hour kick-off meeting is presented in Table 4.1. If the meeting is in person, the agenda could be expanded to include breakout groups and subteam discussions about specific deliverables and topics. If people travel to attend the kick-off meeting, it is probably worth adding more items and time together, such as a facilitated session on risk management.

Regardless of how long the kick-off meeting is and whether it is virtual or in person, early on in the agenda you will want to provide an opportunity for people to introduce themselves. How you approach this depends on the culture and needs of the team. Many readers have probably experienced meetings in which this part of the agenda drags on and decreases the energy of the meeting, sometimes because one person shares a lot of details about their background, prompting others to do the same. Two ways to mitigate the risk that introductions will take up too much of the agenda are as follows:

- As shown in Table 4.1, Agenda Item 3, instead of having people introduce themselves in detail, have them submit a biography

Table 4.1. Example Kick-Off Meeting Agenda

Item	Lead and Time Needed

1. Welcome and review of main meeting objectives:
  a. Share the vision for the project and its intended impact.
  b. Review the objectives for the grant and summarize what has changed since the grant application was submitted.
  c. Introduce workstream and deliverable leads and their plans.
  d. Do a high-level review of risks, key dates, and milestones.
  e. Provide an opportunity for team members begin to get to know each other.
	Principal investigator; ~5 minutes

2. Project vision and intended impact	Principal investigator and ≥1 knowledge user or intended beneficiary; ~15 minutes
3. Roundtable of what people hope the project will produce or accomplish (see also written biographies)	All; ~20 minutes
4. Review of objectives for the grant and summary of what has changed since the grant application was submitted	Principal investigator; ~15 minutes
5. Break	10 minutes
6. High-level approach for each workstream and major deliverable	Workstream and deliverable leads; ~30 minutes
7. High-level review of risks, key dates, and milestones	Project manager or principal investigator; ~15 minutes
8. Other business	All
9. Summary of action items and next steps	Project manager or principal investigator; ~5 minutes
10. Information items (generally not discussed unless there are questions)	

with a photo in advance of the meeting and at the meeting ask them to speak briefly about one thing they hope the project will change or accomplish. This can be a good way to energize the meeting and to learn about what different team members value most about the project. The written biography also has the advantage of providing some information about people who are unable to attend the meeting, and those people can also submit information about what they personally hope the project will change or accomplish in advance to be read during the meeting.

- Another option is to have people form pairs (or groups of three, if the number of participants is uneven) and learn another person's name, role, and, sometimes, their hope or fun fact. Then, instead of having each person introduce themselves, the person they just met introduces them. This approach has the advantage of giving people the opportunity to begin to get to know another person on the research project team, and, unlike self-introductions, introductions made by small group members rarely go over time because people will not have a lot to say about someone they just met.

Neither of these approaches, nor the sample agenda, are meant to rush the process of people getting to know each other. Some research project teams may require entire meetings, or more than one meeting, to get to the point at which trust is established, and people feel safe and comfortable making their contributions. As with all the guidance in this handbook, research project teams should approach the kick-off meeting in a way that meets the unique needs of their projects and team members. Done right, project kick-off meetings serve a technical purpose in terms of information sharing, can be the start for new or deeper interpersonal relationships, and reenergize the team after the wait to hear whether the project was selected for funding.

4.2 TRACKING AND DRIVING RESEARCH PROJECT PROGRESS

Readers who are thinking that they need something more than a single-page work breakdown structure (WBS) and schedule to manage a project during the implementation phase are correct. During the implementation phase, you will need more details than can be captured in those two documents to understand when things are progressing well and when individuals or teams might need help. For example, if you are planning a town hall to engage with members of the public, at least 1 month before that event you will need to know whether invitations have been sent, speakers have been arranged, the venue has been booked, and so forth. The trick to light-touch project management is not to have those details distributed over separate documents and emails or held in individuals' minds. You need some kind of a project management information system (PMIS).

It may be that your organization already has something that can serve as the foundation for a PMIS, such as a financial accounting system or workflow management system. If you do have something that already collects some information on project progress, it is worth exploring whether it can be used in a way that it helps you understand progress, negative risks, and potential opportunities at the deliverable and project level. One thing to watch out for with workflow management programs is their tendency to distribute work by assigning many detailed tasks to individuals. In general, people who are drawn to work in research are creative and prefer some autonomy and room to bring their ideas into their work. They are not usually people who get satisfaction from checking off 10 (or 20) small assigned tasks each day. So research leaders can experiment with using workflow management programs to understand project progress, but if the team pushes back, they will probably want to consider other approaches.

If you do not have anything in place, or if what you have is not suitable for monitoring progress, the tracking sheet (Table 4.2) is a very simple tool that can be adapted to add value in almost any environment. Templates and examples of the tracking sheet can be downloaded from https://researchpm.com/tools-resources/. The tracking sheet is created and populated in Microsoft Excel or your preferred spreadsheet program. It is a detailed working document that drives progress in the context of the WBS and deliverable-based Gantt chart.

Every 1 to 3 months, a new worksheet tab is populated in the tracking sheet file to provide a snapshot of project progress and near-term tasks and milestones. Each tab in the tracking sheet includes rows with deliverables and columns that present the lead, the last accomplishment, a status color (green, yellow, red), and upcoming tasks or milestones. The tracking sheet's simultaneous tracking of multiple upcoming tasks and milestones is important because if the next planned task or milestone is delayed for some reason, other tasks and milestones related to the deliverable are on the radar.

The tracking sheet is designed to help research project teams visualize project progress and issues because it uses variations in font and color to identify changes relative to the last project update (Figure 4.2).

Table 4.2. Blank Tracking Sheet Template for Research Projects

Deliverable or Subdeliverable Name	Lead Initials	Last Accomplishment or Completed Task or Milestone	Status[a]	Upcoming Tasks or Milestones and Target Completion Dates[b]				
				1	2	3	4	5

[a] Green = progressing well and within schedule and budget constraints and issues (if any) are minor and likely to be resolved without affecting other deliverables; yellow = low-impact risks have been realized or medium- or high-impact risks have the potential to be realized in the near future that could necessitate changes for deliverable or planning; red = progress halted, and significant decisions or activities are required to bring stream of work back on track.

[b] Changes relative to last version highlighted with bold italic font.

This means that the tracking sheet can be used to see, at a glance, which deliverables are progressing and which are not. Even though the tracking sheet presents a lot of information, the reader's eye is drawn to the color and fonts showing what has changed since the last update. The tracking sheet is not a smart tool that will automatically tell you when a change will have a negative impact on the project, but it does draw attention to all changes so the research project team can assess what, if any, response is warranted.

You can start using the tracking sheet at any time, not just at the start of a new project. Simply enter everything you know about the deliverables in regular font and put the date on the tab for the worksheet. Some teams that I have worked with have deliverable leads enter their own updates directly into an online version of the tracking

Tracking sheet (annotated): "Deliverables from WBS", "New accomplishments", "Target date changed for task", "Date of progress update"

Deliverable/ Subdeliverable Name	Lead Initials	Last Accomplishment or Completed Task/Milestone	Status[a]	Upcoming Tasks or Milestones and Target Completion Dates[b]				
				1	2	3	4	5
A2: Quarterly Steering Committee meetings	ED	*Fall Steering Committee meetings scheduled June 2022*	Green	*Steering Committee meeting Sep 19, 2022*	Final Steering Committee meeting Jan 2023			
A3: Evaluation plan	AG	Evaluation plan finalized and disseminated to team Jul 2022	Completed	not applicable				
A4: Updates to funders & stakeholders	AGD	*Status report prepared Sep 15, 2022*	Green	Interim preliminary findings shared Nov2022	Draft report shared Dec 2022	Final status update Jan 2023	Final report issued Jan 2023	
B1: Document review	MSP	Completed Jun 2022	Completed	Not applicable				
B2: Clinic & RHA data	KH	*Data collection completed Aug 2022*	*Completed*	Not applicable				
B3: Administrative data	SCM	*Access to data provided Oct 2022*	Green	Data collection complete Oct 2022	Data collection complete Oct 2022			
B4: Surveys	SEB	*Data collection started Sep 11, 2022*	Green	Data collection starts Jul 2022	Data collection complete Oct 2022			
B5: Interviews	SEB	*Data collection started Sep 11, 2022*	Green	Data collection starts Sep 2022	Data collection complete Sep 2022			
C1: Quantitative clinic & RHA data	AGD	*Analyses started Aug 2022*	Not started	Analyses start Aug 2022	Analyses completed Sep 2022			
C2: Quantitative administrative data	SCM		*Yellow*	Analyses start Oct 2022	Analyses completed Nov 2022			
C3: Qualitative	SEB		Not started	Analyses start Sep 2022	Analyses completed Nov 2022			
D1: Interim preliminary findings	AGD		Not started	Target Oct 2022 to share preliminary results				
D2: Final report	AGD		Not started	Work on draft report starts Dec 2022	Draft report shared for comment and review Dec 2022	Close review of draft report – first week of Jan 2023	Final report issued Jan 2023	

Date of progress update: 15 Jun 22   15 Sep 22

[a] Green = progressing well and within schedule and budget constraints and issues (if any) are minor and likely to be resolved without affecting other deliverables; yellow = low- impact risks have been realized or medium- or high-impact risks have potential to be realized in the near future that could necessitate changes for deliverable or planning; red = progress halted, significant decisions or are activities required to bring stream of work back of work back on track.
[b] Changes relative to last version highlighted in bold italic font.

Figure 4.2. Using the Tracking Sheet to Monitor Progress and Highlight Accomplishments and Changes

Note: RHA = regional health authority

sheet (e.g., in Microsoft OneDrive, Google Drive, or Dropbox). Others identify a coordinator to gather information and make regular updates to the document.

The research project team does not need to figure out exactly how they will use the tracking sheet as a tool from the moment they begin using it. Regardless of how the tracking sheet is updated, it may take a few iterations to get the level of detail in it right for your team. The team should feel free to adapt the tracking sheet and refine the level of detail in it over time. Overall, it helps to encourage people to provide the level of detail that they would want to see for a deliverable that they are not leading and to emphasize that it should not take a deliverable lead more than 10 minutes to update a row in the tracking sheet.

When it comes time to issue an update on the project's progress using the tracking sheet, simply copy the worksheet for the last update, put the new date on the tab, and make edits in the formula bar using color or font effects to identify the changes (Figure 4.2). The beauty of the tracking sheet is that you can see – and keep track of – all the deliverables on a single page. It also allows you to process which deliverables are proceeding well and which deliverables may need help. For example, even without reading the details of a row in the tracking sheet, if you see that new text has been added under the "Last Accomplishment or Completed Task or Milestone" column, that is usually a good sign. Alternatively, if you see a task or milestone that has not changed except for its target date, that can be sign that the deliverable is at risk or needs attention.

The tracking sheet helps to bring potential risks to the team's attention so that they can be investigated. It also prompts the team to think about the status of each deliverable. As with all of the tools in this handbook, the definitions for green, yellow, and red status can be modified on the basis of the team's preferences, but as a starting point, you may want to consider the following:

- Green: progressing well and within schedule and budget constraints, and issues (if any) are minor and likely to be resolved without affecting other deliverables
- Yellow: low-impact risks have been realized or medium- or high-impact risks have potential to be realized in the near future that could necessitate changes for the deliverable or planning

- Red: progress halted; significant decisions or activities are required to bring a workstream or deliverable back on track.

The advantage of this status labeling scheme is that it reserves red status for serious situations. Without that distinction, you may find that so many deliverables shift into red that the red status label ceases to have meaning. It is also important that people do not feel like red status is associated with stigma. If you want the tracking sheet to help the team identify and respond to risks early on, it has to be deployed in a way that encourages honesty. This means that deliverables with red status will need support, and it requires an agreed-upon decision-making process (see Section 3.4.2, "Decision-Making Processes") if resources are going to be transferred from one deliverable to support another.

The tracking sheet has many benefits. It displays groups of upcoming tasks and milestones for each deliverable so that they are all in the line of sight. It simplifies project communications and eliminates the need for many other documents, such as detailed minutes, lists of action items, or individual emails with project information. In this way, it minimizes the time required for project management and administration to a few hours for each tracking sheet update. In addition, the work required to update the tracking sheet can be distributed by having deliverable leads update their own rows, as long as one person takes overall responsibility for it. In practice, this might involve having the project manager, project coordinator, program administrator, or even a graduate student who wants to add project management to their résumé have a short conversation with the deliverable leads every month or two. Importantly, the tracking sheet decreases risk by providing details about what is happening between the start and end dates for each deliverable. It is also very easy to modify. For example, one organization that I worked for chose to add a column that identified the major risks for each deliverable.

A secondary benefit of the tracking sheet is that it provides a record of what actually happened during project implementation, as opposed to what the team thought would happen. If you adopt the practice of analyzing the data in your tracking sheet before developing a new deliverable-based Gantt chart, it will improve your project planning. The tracking sheet can also be a good source of information for other project documents, such as reports (see Section 4.3.2, "Status Reports") and meeting agendas (see Section 5.1, "Running Effective Meetings").

Depending on the nature of your project, and particularly if you are working in a regulated industry or sector, making a change to a deliverable may involve more than updating the tracking sheet. For example, if you are doing research on human subjects and want to change the protocol in any way, the amendment or revision would first have to be approved by a research ethics board. Similarly, if your research requires specific permits that include information about what you are planning to do, and those plans change, permits may need to be updated or reissued. So, although the tracking sheet can add value to most if not all research projects, it may not be sufficient for change tracking and change management, depending on the nature of the project you are working on and the sector you work in.

4.3 COMMUNICATIONS AND STAKEHOLDER INVOLVEMENT DURING IMPLEMENTATION

4.3.1 Communications Planning

The tracking sheet is just one example of a communications tool your research project team can use. It covers a lot in terms of raw information that the team will need, but the existence of information in a tracking sheet does not guarantee that team members or stakeholders will read or process it. Generally, you will also need synchronous communications, such as meetings and webinars, and simplified written materials for people who will not be interested in all the details captured in the tracking sheet.

You may find that the establishment of management and governance bodies together with stakeholder involvement drives a lot of your communications. For example, if you are going to have a steering committee, you can take it as a given that there will be an agenda and materials for its meetings.

Some research project teams find value in establishing a communications plan that formally presents the main mechanisms that will be

LEADERSHIP ADVICE CROSSWALK

4.2. GOOD COMMUNICATIONS SKILLS ARE ESSENTIAL

Many of the research leaders who were interviewed emphasized communications skills. They noted that you must be a good communicator if you are going to inspire and mobilize people (e.g., see Molly Shoichet, David Wolfe) and stressed that communications is much more than the circulation of written documents. Communications is a human activity that is mostly about speaking with and listening to others (e.g., see Steini Brown, Beth Coleman, and Aled Edwards). It is not enough to do good work; researchers need to be perceived by others as doing good work, and research results need to be visible (see Elspeth Brown, Barbara Sherwood Lollar, and Mohamad Tavakoli-Targhi).

used to communicate with various audiences. If you go that route, Table 4.3 presents some elements that you might want to include in a research project communications plan, and Appendix F includes a second example communications plan for a fictional research project.

A few things are worth noting about the example communications plan in Table 4.3. First, it includes meetings as a communications mechanism. Real-time discussions at meetings are essential for many people to process project information. Team meetings are also much better than email or other written communications if you want to have a generative discussion in which team members share and strengthen ideas (see Section 5.1, "Running Effective Meetings"), but that does not mean that team meetings are the only meetings you should have. It is not realistic to think that research project stakeholders will be inspired solely by words in print or that senior stakeholders will read everything that they are sent, so written materials need to be complemented by oral communications and meetings, in person when possible.

Second, the communications plan includes a website but notes that the website will be very simple. Over the years, I have seen several teams invest many thousands of dollars in research project websites that end up having few visitors outside of team members. In the worst-case scenario, the website content becomes dated (e.g., the most recent update may be months or years old). Out-of-date websites can give stakeholders and team members a negative impression and work against the interests of the research project team. For that reason, teams who develop project

Table 4.3. Example Research Project Communications Plan for a Generic Research Project

Format and Mechanism	Audience	Frequency
Tracking sheet posted online	Core team, research project team (others on request)	Monthly
Core team meetings and related materials	Members of core team (agendas and action or decision items shared with others as needed)	Every 2 weeks
Research project team meetings and related materials	Members of the core team, plus knowledge user partners, selected members of the intended beneficiary groups, and people who contribute to the project at specific points in time (e.g., legal counsel)	Kick-off meeting, then quarterly
Steering committee meetings and related materials	Steering committee (agendas and action or decision items shared with others as needed)	Quarterly, except 2 meetings in the 1st quarter of the 1st year and in the last quarter of the final year
Status reports	Steering committee, funders, knowledge user partners	Quarterly (timed with steering committee meetings)
Simple website (repository of downloadable documents and webinar video)	Core team, knowledge users, and intended beneficiaries; note that the aim is not to have a slick public-facing website but do include registration for people who want to receive information about findings by email	Updated no less than every 6 months
Stakeholder meetings[a]	Knowledge users and intended beneficiaries (beyond those who are members of the research project team)	Small-group or one-on-one meetings at least once per year and more frequently in the 1st and final years of the project
Webinars[a]	Knowledge users, intended beneficiaries, research team members who join midway through the project, and members of the general public who have an interest in the topic	One in the 1st year, at least 3 in the final year
Practice or policy briefs[a]		Timed to be available at the same time as webinars
Annual reports for funders in funders' specified format	Funders; can be shared with others on request, but status reports, briefs, and other formats are more likely to be well received	Annually
Final project report (1:3:25 format[b]), 100 print copies plus and ecopy to post on website and send via email	Funders, knowledge users, intended beneficiaries, and researchers on the team	1 month before the end of the funded period

[a] Reviewed and refined with knowledge users and intended beneficiaries who are on the research project team before being shared with stakeholders outside the research project team.
[b] See text for explanation.

websites are usually best off starting very simple. Most projects
will benefit from a repository where research project team members, and, in some cases, stakeholders, can access the final versions of project documents, publications, videos of webinars,
status reports, and the like. With readily available technology,
such as Microsoft OneDrive, Google Drive, and Dropbox, simple
repository websites can be established with minimal effort and
funds. Teams can build more sophisticated websites with more
features and functions if the simple repository website does not
meet the communications and information-sharing needs of the
team and stakeholders.

The 1:3:25 format for the annual report in Table 4.3 is a communications approach originally developed by the former Canadian Health
Services Research Foundation (n.d.; now the Canadian Foundation
for Healthcare Excellence). The numbers 1, 3, and 25 refer to the ap-
proximate length of three sections of the report:

- 1: Up to 1 page for the main messages of the report. The main messages can be thought of as how you would explain the significance
  of your research in plain language in 1 to 2 minutes, or how one
  decision maker might explain the work to another decision maker.
  This section is not a subset of the points presented in the executive
  summary.
- 3: Up to 3 pages for an executive summary that presents work and
  findings from the project as evidence to back up the statements
  made in the main messages.
- 25: Up to 25 pages of details about the background (including
  references), research questions, methods, limitations, findings, conclusions, and potential next steps.

Although the exact number of pages needed to communicate
information to stakeholders will vary depending on factors including the complexity of the topic and the amount of work completed since the last update, the 1:3:25 way of thinking should
always be considered. Research project communications materials should always begin with succinct summary information
with optional, more detailed information for stakeholders who
want it.

Figure 4.3. Quarter-Page Status Report for a Generic Research Project
Notes: Draft protocol circulated for comment with team and stakeholders March 1; target dates are mid-April for protocol submission and late May for approval of protocol.

4.3.2 Status Reports

Table 4.3, "Example Research Project Communications Plan for a Generic Research Project," includes status reports as one of the communications mechanisms. Almost all projects will require some kind of status update to help people quickly understand project progress, upcoming strategic decisions, and emerging risks. As with most things in research project management, a status report should start as a short and easy-to-process document, with more details added only when they are needed. Figure 4.3 presents a very simple status report that could work for a project with a straightforward plan and small team. Based on a template developed by the Knowledge Translation Program of the Li Ka Shing Knowledge Institute at Unity Health Toronto, it quickly conveys what is happening in the project at a given point in time.

If the project is more complex or if you have a governance body that wants to see more details in order to provide strategic advice, the two-page status report example shown in Figure 4.4 may be helpful. It begins with key accomplishments since the last update (information that can be taken from the tracking sheet) and key upcoming deliverables and milestones (which can also be taken from the tracking sheet). To keep the first page of this two-page status report short, you would not list everything that has happened or will happen before the next update, noting that you can always provide more detail to people who want it, including the entire tracking sheet on request. The last two sections of Page 1 of the two-page status report are key risks and a description of how the project is doing with respect to the triple constraint.

Page 2 of the two-page status report is a version of the deliverable-based Gantt chart, with a thick vertical line added on the date the status report was issued. As noted in the footnote below the schedule in Figure 4.4, everything to the left of the thick vertical line represents

Seniors' Health Clinics Evaluation Project Status Update, September 15, 2022

Key Milestones and Accomplishments Since Last Steering Committee Update

- Clinic and regional health authority data collection has been completed; analyses of these data started in August.
- All approvals to access administrative data have been obtained; access to data expected in October.

Upcoming Key Milestones, Tasks, and Deliverables

- Preliminary results will be shared with the steering committee in October 2022.
- All analyses are on track to be completed by November 2022.
- Draft report will be provided to steering committee in advance of third (and final) committee meeting in January 2023.

Key Risks and Planned or Implemented Responses

- Access to administrative data is expected to be provided approximately 1 month later than planned in the project schedule; we are accelerating our analyses of clinic and regional health authority data to free up resources for administrative data analyses once data become available.

Changes to Scope, Schedule, or Budget Since Last Update

- None – the delay in accessing administrative data does not affect the scope, schedule, or budget

Figure 4.4. Two-Page Status Report for a Fictional Seniors' Health Clinics Evaluation Project, Page 1 of 2

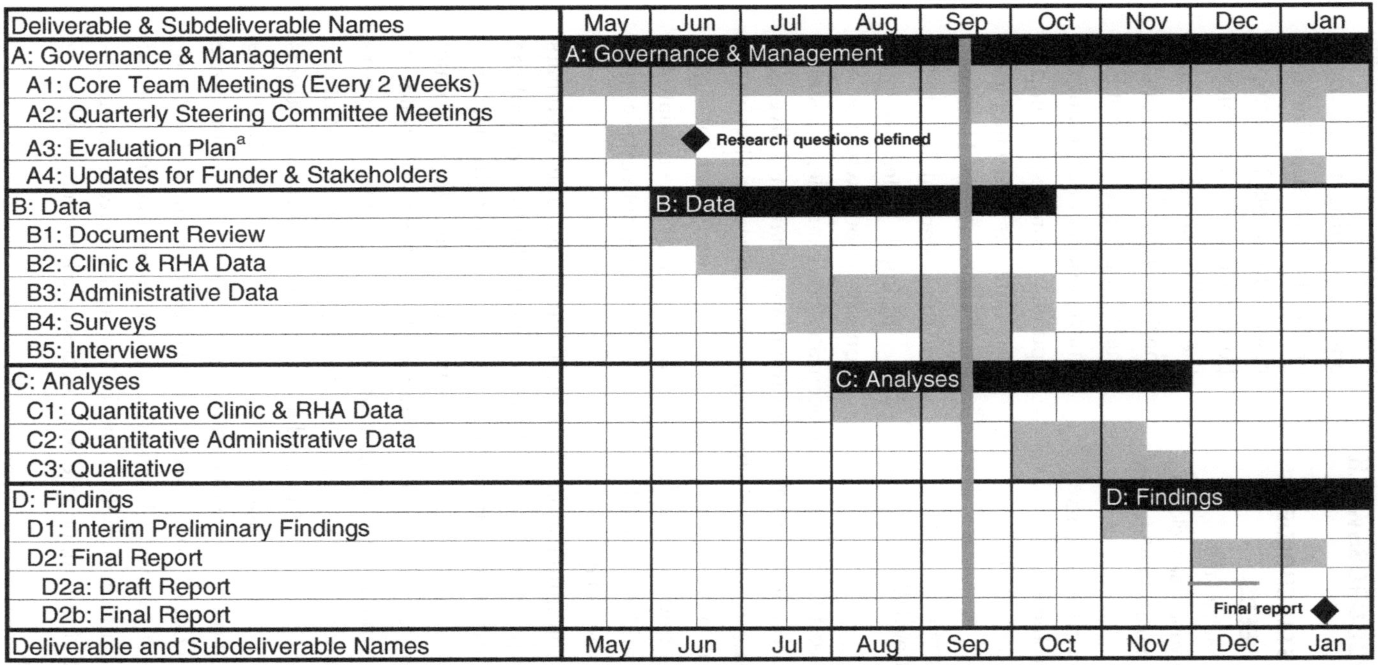

Deliverable & Subdeliverable Names	May	Jun	Jul	Aug	Sep	Oct	Nov	Dec	Jan
A: Governance & Management									
A1: Core Team Meetings (Every 2 Weeks)									
A2: Quarterly Steering Committee Meetings									
A3: Evaluation Plan[a]		Research questions defined							
A4: Updates for Funder & Stakeholders									
B: Data									
B1: Document Review									
B2: Clinic & RHA Data									
B3: Administrative Data									
B4: Surveys									
B5: Interviews									
C: Analyses				C: Analyses					
C1: Quantitative Clinic & RHA Data									
C2: Quantitative Administrative Data									
C3: Qualitative									
D: Findings							D: Findings		
D1: Interim Preliminary Findings									
D2: Final Report									
D2a: Draft Report									
D2b: Final Report								Final report	
Deliverable and Subdeliverable Names	May	Jun	Jul	Aug	Sep	Oct	Nov	Dec	Jan

[a] The evaluation plan includes A3a: Logic Model, A3b: Research Questions, A3c: Inventory of Data Sources, A3d: Description of Methods, A3e: Survey Questionnaire, and A3f: Interview Guide & Schedule.

Notes: The thick vertical line indicates the date of the status update. Shading to the left of the line indicates work that has been completed. Shading to the right of the line presents forecast completion dates for work that is in progress or not yet started.

Figure 4.4. Two-Page Status Report for a Fictional Seniors' Health Clinics Evaluation, Page 2 of 2 (*continued*)

LEADERSHIP ADVICE CROSSWALK

4.3. UNDERSTAND STAKEHOLDERS' COMMUNICATIONS NEEDS

Research leaders emphasized the importance of knowing your stakeholders' culture in order to communicate effectively with them (Aled Edwards, Zaïna Soré, and Sharon Straus) and provided examples of stories and other tailored ways to communicate with specific external stakeholder groups (e.g., see Lorna MacDonald, Jutta Treviranus, Zaïna Soré, Stefaan Verhulst, and David Wolfe).

work that has happened, and everything to the right of the thick vertical line represents forecasts for completion of future deliverables. If the deliverable-based Gantt chart is created in a spreadsheet program, it will not be a smart tool that automatically updates forecast completion dates as you enter project information. However, the thick vertical line helps to prompt reflection and honesty about whether the schedule will need to change to be accurate. For example, if a status report is issued on September 15 and the plan to have a deliverable completed in August was not achieved, the person responsible for the status report will have to manually modify the schedule on the right-hand side of the thick vertical line to show a new realistic end date for the deliverable and also adjust the schedule for other deliverables that are affected by the delay.

Finally, the communications plan in Table 4.3 includes webinars combined with practice or policy briefs – one in the first year of the project and multiple ones in the final year. This reflects the fact that it is often a good idea to create a quality communications product early in the project that can be shared with multiple stakeholders. Such products can end up saving a lot of time if new team members or stakeholders join or if stakeholders have general questions about the project. The communications plan also includes several products aimed at external stakeholders in the last year when the team has findings that are ready to be disseminated. In the table, webinars are paired with practice or policy briefs. This is because different individuals have different ways of learning, so using more than one format to present the same information can be a way to increase the likelihood that most, if not all, people will process the information you are communicating.

4.3.3 Stakeholder Engagement

The communications plan in Table 4.3 includes several references to communications products aimed at, and roles for, knowledge users and members of the intended beneficiary groups. For example, the row for research project team meetings notes that meetings will be held with knowledge user partners and members of the intended beneficiary groups.

Given the importance of good communications with external stakeholders, some teams may want to create a stakeholder engagement plan in addition to, or instead of, a communications plan. As noted in Section 2.4, "Involving Stakeholders in Project Planning," the term "project stakeholders" usually refers to external stakeholders, such as knowledge users, funders, and intended beneficiaries (e.g., members of the public, clients, and patients). The stakeholder engagement plan in Table 4.4 presents some examples of how to involve and communicate with stakeholders that overlap with some of the information in the communications plan but is organized on the basis of stakeholder needs. The format of Table 4.4 prompts the team to think about different external stakeholder needs and interests (which should be confirmed with members of the stakeholder groups) and how to address them.

There is no right or wrong when it comes to whether to establish a formal communications plan, a stakeholder engagement plan, both, or neither. However, it is a good idea to make sure that (one way or another) your project has the following:

1 A simple and concise way to communicate why the project is being performed and how it is progressing in two formats:

   a. A detailed update for research project team members and other researchers who work in the field
   b. A plain-language version for other stakeholders.

2 Deeper and different involvement of external stakeholders who are critical to the project's success (e.g., small-group meetings or inclusion of representatives on the research project team).

Table 4.4. Example Research Stakeholder Engagement Plan for a Generic Research Project

Stakeholder	Need or Interest	Engagement Plan (Must Align with Communications Plan Subdeliverables)
Intended beneficiaries (e.g., patients, clients, members of the public)	• To understand the opportunities and potential impact of the research • To have practical and accessible ways to influence the project and be involved in it • Some remuneration (e.g., honorarium) and expense reimbursement for members of the intended beneficiary groups who spend time in project meetings	• Include ≥2 people on the research project team who bring in the perspective of intended beneficiaries • Involve ≥20 people in the study design process who bring in the perspective of intended beneficiaries • Plain-language printed materials • Workshops before the implementation phase with ≥20 people who bring in the perspective of intended beneficiaries
Knowledge users (e.g., policymakers, planners, practitioners)	• Research findings that have the potential to change policy or practice • Easy ways to contribute to project planning and implementation	• Include ≥2 knowledge users on the research project team • Generate a list of interested knowledge user organizations and pay basic costs for representatives from these groups to come together (e.g., room rental, teleconference lines) • Create a webinar and pamphlet with basic information about the project in Year 1 • Establish project email address that people can contact for more information
Funder	• To be able to demonstrate that research funding has made a difference • To have confidence that funds are not being misused	• Annual report in funder's required format • Announcements that emphasize the importance of funder's contribution • Offer to meet and provide personal briefings according to the funder's format and frequency preferences
All of the above, plus core team and steering committee	• To be kept informed of progress, risks, and opportunities	• Quarterly email updates • Simple website that serves as a repository for resources referred to in quarterly email updates (e.g., presentations, reports)

Notes: Additional rows can be added for key stakeholders such as regulators, organization's research administrators, and so forth.

It is important that you get your communications with stakeholders right. To ensure that you do, consider asking someone who has a level of knowledge similar to that of your intended audience to review materials before you share them with stakeholders. Footnote a in Table 4.3 states that before materials for meetings with stakeholders are finalized, they will be reviewed and refined by knowledge users and members of the intended beneficiary groups who are members of the broader research project team.

Having external stakeholders review materials is a good way to formally bring in the expertise of team members who are not researchers or trainees. It is also good practice because, no matter how hard researchers might try, their deep and academic-oriented knowledge of the topics they research makes it unlikely that they will perceive materials the same way as their external stakeholders do. When you involve external stakeholders as reviewers, do not ask them, "Is this good?" If they know and like you, they will probably respond "yes." Instead, ask them, "What are your main takeaways from this document?" If they are not getting the messages you are trying to convey, you will know that more work is required for your communication to have its intended effect.

Also, before you send any materials to stakeholders, it is a good idea to have someone who has not been involved in producing the material review it with fresh eyes. Typos and grammatical errors can decrease stakeholders' confidence in written material and, by extension, their confidence and trust in the research project team.

An additional piece of advice about stakeholder communications comes from my years of working in government policy departments. As the director responsible for research, I would often be involved when research project teams presented their findings to government policymakers. From participating in those meetings, I learned that presentations to knowledge users and stakeholders should be very different from presentations to academic audiences. As part of the peer-review function, one of the roles of scholars is to pose probing questions about the methodology and validity of research. As a result, academic presentations often devote a significant amount of time to discussing the limitations of the research. However, when it comes to presentations to policymakers and other non-academic audiences, this focus on limitations can be distracting. When I worked for the Ontario Ministry of Health as the director responsible for research, there were occasions when, after a researcher's presentation, policymaker colleagues would ask me, "Why did they come in to present findings if they are so uncertain about everything?"

For this reason, my advice to researchers presenting to non-academic audiences is to not hide limitations but also to not overemphasize them. If you feel that your work presents some of the best evidence available on a topic, it is okay to let external stakeholders know that. Although they may not ask detailed questions about the method and limitations, many external stakeholders are experienced in using research evidence to inform policy and practice and will understand the caveats and limitations that apply when bringing research evidence into their environments. They will also pose questions for which you have provided detailed responses if they are unsure about the generalizability of your work to their context.

4.4 PREVENTING AND ADDRESSING COMMON PROBLEMS

Because of the uncertain nature of academic research, projects rarely, and perhaps should not, go exactly as planned. I am fond of saying that research project teams should plan on changing their plan, but of course that is easier said than done. If a research project team works hard to establish scope, schedule, and budget across multiple people and deliverables, and it turns out that their plan cannot be implemented, it can create conflict and problems for the project and the team.

There is nothing magic about project management, but there are ways that it can help prevent or address problems. For example, the project management tools and processes presented in Sections 2 to 5 can decrease the likelihood of the following problems common to academic research projects and help address them when they do occur:

- Research project teams that use a WBS and the triple constraint as the basis for planning are more likely to identify and correct misalignment problems before they start implementation (e.g., the triple constraint would prompt a team with an overly ambitious scope to decrease scope, increase budget, or increase the amount of time allocated; see Section 2.5, "Triple Constraint of Scope, Time, and Cost").

- Using the triple constraint to reformulate plans during implementation can help ensure that the research project team does not have a knee-jerk reaction to an issue and replace one problem with another (e.g., it would create a problem if a research project team made significant decreases to the budget for a deliverable during implementation without decreasing its scope).
- If a project is time constrained, fast tracking or crashing the deliverables in the first months or years of the schedule can help the research project team take calculated risks that allow them to complete the project on time (see Section 2.2.4, "Schedule Compression").
- Building buffer into the schedule decreases the likelihood that the quality of the final outputs of the research project will be poor (see Section 2.2.3, "Steps for Developing a Deliverable-Based Gantt Chart for a Research Project").
- A WBS that includes initials for leads, a RACI, or both can help research project teams understand who is carrying most of the workload for the project and help them to redistribute work if a team member is overwhelmed or cannot make their intended contributions for personal reasons (see Section 3.3, "Roles and Responsibilities").
- Negative risk response planning can decrease the likelihood that the research project team will be surprised and affected by negative risks (see Section 3.2.2, "Identifying, Prioritizing, and Responding to Negative Risks for Research").
- Defined, hierarchical, governance, and decision-making processes are helpful if a tough decision must be made, such as moving budget from one deliverable to another (see Section 3.4, "Decision Making, Governance, and Oversight").
- A communications plan, stakeholder engagement plan, or both decreases the likelihood that a person or group will inadvertently miss receiving updates on the project (see Section 4.3, "Communications and Stakeholder Involvement during Implementation").

- Establishing and using a RACI to clarify roles can help avoid the hurt feelings that may occur if a person or group is left out of decisions related to deliverables that they care about (see Section 3.3.5, "The RACI as a Tool to Define Multiple Roles").

The inclusion of an emotional and personal reaction in the last bullet point was deliberate. I cannot overstate that solving problems for academic research projects involves much more than having good documents, tools, and processes. Project management can help take the heat or emotion out of challenging situations, but the best way to prevent problems is to build human connections and trust between people.

The principal investigator and project manager (or equivalent) both have big roles to play on that front. The principal investigator is usually the one who sets the tone for the research project team and how people work together to solve problems. A key point is that although the principal investigator may have overall accountability for resolving problems, that does not mean that they should try to come up with solutions on their own. One of the first steps in addressing problems should be to mobilize the people on the research project team who have skills, experience, and ideas about how to resolve it.

Projects are most likely to go well if the personal styles of research project team members align, but that may not always be possible (e.g., if a new graduate student joins a team with a style very different from that of the rest of the team). In those cases, it is important that the principal investigator and project manager have interpersonal skills and compassion to help the team and the person work as effectively as they can despite personal differences. If the principal investigator and project

LEADERSHIP ADVICE CROSSWALK

4.4. LEADERS DO NOT HAVE ALL THE ANSWERS

Elspeth Brown, Molly Shoichet, Michael Schull, and Arjumand Siddiqi spoke about the fact that research leaders do not have all the answers. Demonstrating vulnerability and acknowledging their own weaknesses helps research leaders create an environment in which others take chances and do not feel that they have to be perfect to contribute.

manager get to know their team members on a personal level, they are most likely to benefit from what everyone can contribute. On a related point, if a principal investigator has the interpersonal skills to identify what motivates team members and inspire others, that will contribute much more to the project's success than any documentation related to those people's roles.

The principal investigator's and project manager's interpersonal skills are also very important for preventing and addressing problems with stakeholders. For example, whenever there is interaction with knowledge users and the intended beneficiaries of a research project, it is very important that the research project team members be attentive and responsive to negative feedback, including non-verbal cues expressing concern. In my experience, research project teams can get in trouble with project management if they become so attached to their plan that they miss or ignore stakeholder reactions to what they are doing. Furthermore, principal investigators and project managers should certainly not assume that stakeholders have read and agree with everything in a plan simply because it was sent to them.

Although a lot of the project manager's work during project implementation involves preparing and distributing documents, nobody should believe that is sufficient to prevent or solve problems, no matter how thorough the documents are. For example, identifying someone as the lead for a deliverable on the WBS is better than having someone be uncertain about whether they are responsible for a deliverable, but it does not guarantee that the person has the time, skills, or personal motivation to lead the work. If, during project implementation, the person who is identified as the lead is not able to produce a deliverable, it is extremely unlikely that an email from the

LEADERSHIP ADVICE CROSSWALK

4.5. MAKE HUMAN CONNECTIONS

The language in many research leaders' interviews presented research as a "people person" profession that relies on human connections (e.g., see Steini Brown, Beth Coleman, Aled Edwards, Colleen Flood, Lorna MacDonald, Barbara Sherwood Lollar, Michael Schull, Sharon Straus, Zaïna Soré, and Mohamad Tavakoli-Targhi). Research leaders used words such as "passion," "inspire," "humility," "nurture," "motivate," and "joy" and talked about dialogue and the importance of how research leaders make others feel.

project manager or an update showing that their deliverable status is "red" will resolve the problem. What would be more likely to help is a conversation with the person to identify ways to address the problem, which could potentially include more time, people to help with the work, or shifting the lead role to someone else who has the time and skills to take it on.

Principal investigators and research project managers also need to be aware that, because of the natural power imbalances within research project teams, even simple things such as asking for a status update might create stress for some team members. The routine pushing out of documents or requests for updates that is common for project managers in non-research environments is often perceived negatively by research project teams that tend to favor conversations and personal interactions over documents.

In summary, when it comes to preventing and addressing problems in academic research projects, project management tools and processes can help, but only if they are coupled with interpersonal skills. Research is done by people, and human connections matter more than documents, tools, or processes.

4.5 CLOSING THE PROJECT AND CAPTURING THE LESSONS LEARNED

All projects have beginnings and ends, which means they do not go on forever. For a research project, however, the end of a project may not be obvious because new research questions are constantly being generated, so projects may blend into each other rather than stop when grant funding ends. For non-research projects, the importance of proper project closure is widely acknowledged and typically includes confirming that the intended scope was achieved and deliverables have been accepted by the client, performing an audit or assessment of how the project schedule and budget compared with the plan, releasing the team or reassigning them to other projects, documenting the lessons learned, and capturing all the information in a project management information system. For research projects, because it is more acceptable, and sometimes desirable, for research projects to deviate from their plans, there is usually less emphasis on technical completeness and analysis of variation in project implementation versus the plan, but there is still value in having formal project closure.

Unfortunately, forces and factors outside of the research project team's control can work against good research project closure. For example, there may not be a natural or obvious end to the project, funding for a new research project may prompt people to leave the project abruptly, or a project may end because a key person leaves, funding is withdrawn, or because the team determines that it is not possible to study or generate what they had hoped. Even for research projects that are completed as planned, team members might be eager to move on to the next project and resist investing time in project closure that is seen as administrative work. However, a small number of research project closure activities are worth considering because they can add a lot of value (Box 4.2).

BOX 4.2. RESEARCH PROJECT CLOSURE ACTIVITIES

1 Locate final copies of all key project documents and move them to a dedicated folder separate from the rest of the project files.
2 Identify any outstanding requirements related to closure (e.g., final report for funder), and assign specific people to complete each of them.
3 Hold a lessons-learned session.
4 Have a celebration; it can be small and no cost, but it is good to recognize people's contributions and project accomplishments even if the project did not go as planned.
5 Set reminders to follow up with knowledge users and intended beneficiaries.

The value of the first project closure activity – creating a dedicated folder for final materials – is probably self-evident for anyone who has ever had to resort to searching email for the definitive final version of project documents. Just a little bit of work to organize files at the end of the project can save a lot of time down the

LEADERSHIP ADVICE CROSSWALK

4.6. GOOD PROJECT CLOSURE

Several research leaders spoke about the importance of activities related to project closure. For example, Zaïna Soré talked about preparing final products in formats that non-academic knowledge users can use, and Steini Brown, Molly Shoichet, and Jutta Treviranus spoke about making the most of opportunities to learn from mistakes and failures. Research leaders also spoke about the fact that research does not have to have an obvious impact to be successful; sometimes the impact is in preventing something from happening, sometimes it would not be appropriate for any change to be made solely in response to the research, and sometimes the impact is a lesson that has been learned about what does not or cannot work (see Colleen Flood and Arjumand Siddiqi).

road and mitigate the risk that you share or use the wrong version of a project document in the future. The second activity – assigning responsible individuals to complete outstanding tasks – is important because those requirements can sometimes extend months after the research stops, so assigning specific people to them releases the time and energy of other team members while ensuring that all binding requirements are fulfilled.

For those unfamiliar with lessons-learned activities, they can be thought of as focused and intentional efforts to capture what was learned during project implementation so that it can inform future work. There are many lessons-learned templates available online; however, most of them are meant for non-research projects and focus on technical completeness. The templates do, as a rule, encourage people to think about think about what worked well and what the team would do differently in the future, and these two categories of information are also important for research projects. Research project lessons learned can be as short as one to two pages, and they often include

- risks (negative and positive) that were realized during project implementation,
- approaches that worked well and might be adapted and reused in future projects,

- things that did not work well and should be avoided in future projects, and
- a list of the individuals who participated in creating the lessons-learned document and their roles on the project.

The emphasis is on documenting, at a high level, the risks that were realized, things that worked, and things that could have been improved. There should also be a section to record who participated in creating the lessons-learned document because, just like the risk management plan, the content will vary depending on who is involved in the process of capturing the lessons learned. On a related point, interpersonal skills are as important as project management skills if you want to identify and capture the main lessons learned from a research project. It may be that your project achieved all of its objectives but in a risky or time- or resource-consuming way, and the only people who know the full extent of the room for improvement are not senior members of the research project team. You also want honest dialogue about what the lessons were. For that reason, it is often a good idea to have a 30-minute to 1.5-hour synchronous meeting for lessons learned (in person or virtual) that makes use of facilitation techniques (see Section 5.1.4, "Facilitation Techniques and Processes") and live anonymous polling to draw out the lessons from the project.

The final recommended closure activity enumerated in Box 4.2 – setting reminders to follow up with stakeholders – is an easy thing to do that can make a big difference for project impact. Because of their innovative nature, research projects' impact is usually not realized until months or years after they end. Therefore, it is a good idea to follow up with knowledge users and intended beneficiaries months or years after a project has been completed. In the case of basic research, this may mean checking in after 1 or 2 years to see who is referencing and building on the scholarship. For applied research, it is a good idea to check in with knowledge users and ask questions, such as "Were you able to apply the knowledge or findings generated by the research project in practice?," "Do you need additional support with knowledge translation?," or "Now that one knowledge gap is filled, is there another that research can help with?" Commonly used software makes it very easy to set up reminders so you can focus on other work. For example, "snoozing" an email so that it will reappear 6 months in the future or entering 0-minute meetings in your calendar (so that they do not interfere with scheduling other meetings) can automatically remind you to check in without requiring you to consult some other document that is not part of your daily work routine. If the reminders appear at an inconvenient time, you can simply snooze them, as long as you do not dismiss a reminder until you have acted on it or until you decide that you are not going to act because the window of opportunity has passed.

You do not need to wait until the end of a project to perform research project closure activities or document the lessons learned. Sometimes it makes sense to capture learnings after a phase or key milestone, such as grant application submission or a summit event with stakeholders. If you have different research project team compositions for different phases of a project, it is a good idea to close off and perform a lessons-learned exercise at the end of each phase. Additionally, if you find yourself in a situation in which team members are expressing relief after having completed a challenging deliverable or milestone, that is usually an indication that there is a lesson to be learned and shared. Good project closure is about performing small amounts of work that can be done at the end of the project or project phase to benefit future research, so you want to do project closure activities while research materials are accessible and before people's memories fade.

Cross-Cutting Topics

5.1 RUNNING EFFECTIVE MEETINGS

5.1.1 Value of Meetings

For something that is often low to no cost (except for the funded time of meeting participants and travel, when applicable), meetings can make a big difference for research. In research, it is rare for things to go exactly as planned, and meetings are one of the main mechanisms through which team members bring together their collective expertise, experience, and judgment to decide how to respond to changes. They are also one of the main ways in which people on the team get to know each other and build trust. For those reasons, meetings can literally make or break million-dollar projects and initiatives. With the increasing size and complexity of research, the need for productive meetings has never been greater.

The two most important things that you can do to have a successful meeting are to (a) identify a meeting chair and (b) establish a good agenda to ensure that live synchronous time is used for discussion and decisions.

5.1.2 Role and Responsibilities of the Meeting Chair

Every research team meeting should have a chair because there are specific responsibilities that may not be fulfilled if no chair is identified.

Often the chair will be the lead for a committee, the principal investigator, or the project manager (or equivalent), but the chair's responsibilities can also be delegated to others, including to team members who are earlier in their careers to give them some experience with chairing a meeting.

The primary role of the chair is to confirm the meeting objectives at the start of the meeting and manage the meeting time to achieve the objective to the extent possible. During the meeting, the chair has a role in making sure that there is clarity about what decision is being made because for research projects it is not uncommon for the scope of a decision to change as discussions progress or for a single decision to be split into multiple decision points.

Some research teams include people who process information rapidly and are quick and frequent speakers. If that is the case, the chair has a role in making sure those people do not dominate the discussion and that others have an opportunity to contribute. If a meeting consists mostly of one person speaking about a topic, you are not really getting the benefits of live synchronous and generative discussion.

The chair also has a role in keeping the discussion flowing, helping to identify when all key inputs have been obtained and when people are ready to move to the next agenda item. Finally, before the meeting adjourns, the chair has a role in confirming that all meeting participants have a common understanding about what was decided and who is responsible for the next planned steps. In the absence of this step, participants may exit the meeting with a vague sense that there was agreement but uncertainty about the specific decisions that have been made and who is responsible for acting on them. Additional tips that may be helpful for research meeting chairs are presented in Box 5.1.

BOX 5.1. TIPS FOR CHAIRING RESEARCH MEETINGS

- Confirm the meeting objectives and obtain buy-in for them before the meeting starts.
- Immediately before a decision is made, clearly state the decision point (e.g., "We are choosing to do X" or "We are selecting Y over Z").

- If certain people in the meeting have a tendency to dominate the discussion, create time and space for less vocal participants to contribute.
- Keep the discussion flowing in a productive way, for example, by introducing and managing the convention whereby a participant raises both hands (not just one hand) if they want to make a point that is directly related to a point somebody else has just introduced.
- Gauge how close the group is to consensus, for example, by using the five-finger method whereby participants display fingers to display their support for the proposed decision (a fist = zero fingers = cannot or will not support, an open hand = five fingers = 100% support).
- Manage the agenda time allocations, to the extent possible, and identify which agenda items to defer or compress in cases in which the entire agenda cannot be completed.
- Limit the amount of group meeting time used for topics that concern only a few of the participants; if a subset of meeting participants only requires 2 to 3 minutes to complete their discussion, it is often a good idea (and more productive overall) to let them do so during the large group meetings, but anything longer should be moved outside the meeting time.
- At the end of the meeting, summarize what was decided at the meeting and who will do what after the meeting.

5.1.3 Research Meeting Agendas

Most meetings of the core team, research project team, and (when it exists) the research executive committee will be between 1 and 2 hours long. Often, for those kinds of meetings, a good agenda will set out objectives and allocate time for two or three discussion or decision items (Table 5.1). Because many meetings focus on addressing negative risks and issues, a nice and positive practice can be to include a brief review of accomplishments and things that have gone right near the start of the agenda, so meetings do not take on a negative tone. However, the ability to keep those brief positive updates early in the agenda depends on the team and the meeting chair. Some teams cannot resist the temptation to talk at length about accomplishments or question the details behind them. If that happens, there may not be enough time for group discussion and consensus decision making, in which case you should move the accomplishments to the final part of the agenda under information items.

Occasionally, you may want to use meeting time for a presentation to make sure that the whole group hears and processes new information at the same time and has the opportunity to ask questions together. More typically, you will want most of your meeting time to be allocated to group discussions using a predetermined decision-making process (Box 3.7) that aims for consensus and defines what will happen if consensus is not achieved. If your meeting has more than seven participants, each discussion or decision item will usually require at least 20 minutes (i.e., at least 2–3 minutes for each participant to contribute) and more if the topic or decision is complex. It is good practice to schedule the discussion and decision items that are most important or that will benefit the most from live synchronous discussion at the beginning of the agenda.

The rationale for the last three sections of the sample agenda in Table 5.1 are as follows:

- **Other business** – This agenda item is included in case there is extra time available, and a team member wants to bring an item to the attention of the entire group.
- **Summary of action items and next steps** – This agenda item provides a prompt for the meeting chair or project manager to briefly review the list of what was agreed regarding decisions and who will do what after the meeting and an opportunity for other meeting participants to ask clarifying questions or add to the list if the meeting chair or project manager missed something.
- **Information items** – The bullet points under this agenda item can have a surprisingly beneficial impact because they are more likely to be complete and easily processed than oral top-of-mind roundtable updates. Also, because they are provided before the meeting (as opposed to in meeting minutes afterward), written information items provide other participants with the opportunity to ask clarifying questions.

The agenda in Table 5.1 is not meant to imply that all meetings must have structured and formal agendas. In some cases, you may want to have a meeting that has the sole objective of helping team members get

Table 5.1. Example Research Meeting Agenda with Decision Items

Item	Lead and Time Allotted
1. Welcome and review of main meeting objectives: (a) Objective 1 (b) Objective 2 (c) Objective 3 (having two main objectives is preferable)	Chair (can be committee chair, principal investigator, or their delegate); ~5 minutes
2. Optional: Brief review of selected key accomplishments or milestones since last meeting: (a) Accomplishment or Milestone 1 (b) Accomplishment or Milestone 2 (c) Accomplishment or Milestone 3 (d) Accomplishment or Milestone 4 (e) Accomplishment or Milestone 5	Chair or project manager; ~5 minutes
3. Discussion or Decision Item 1 (circulated agenda includes key points related to the item, for example, why it is being presented and the anticipated outcome, e.g., is it the first preliminary discussion of a potential opportunity or risk, or a decision that needs to be made. If there are major risks or issues that require whole-team input to resolve or decide on, this is where you would want them on the agenda). (a) Point 1 (b) Point 2 (c) Point 3	Lead for deliverable or decision
4. Discussion or Decision Item 2	Lead for deliverable or decision
5. Other business	All
6. Summary of action items and next steps, orally summarized, typically by the project manager, who keeps a list during the meeting (a) Restatement of all decisions that have been made (b) Other items (e.g., action items identified as a result of the discussion)	Chair or project manager; ~5 minutes
7. Information items (detailed statements are included in the circulated agenda, one per bullet, e.g., • Item X, which was left open until we heard from AGD, has been resolved by consensus; everyone agreed.... • Detailed Statement 1 [e.g., the travel budget for the June stakeholder meeting is set at $75,000] • Detailed Statement 2 [e.g., could state plan to address risk identified on project tracking sheet that does not require group discussion: "Activity x is behind schedule; Y and Z will convene a meeting and bring the proposed resolution to next team meeting"] • AGD will be away July 24–August 12)	Individual who is the lead for the content of a bullet point can speak to the point if questions arise

to know each other. That is not just okay, it can be beneficial for many research projects, particularly near their start. It often takes more than one meeting to have people begin to know, trust, and appreciate each other's contributions. Even in the case of a "get to know each other" meeting, however, you will still want an agenda so that people are on the same page regarding what the meeting will accomplish. For example, you do not want a situation in which half of the attendees think the main purpose of a meeting is for the team members to get to know each other, whereas the other half are hoping to have group discussion and make an important decision.

When the meeting ends, instead of issuing minutes, you may want to consider the less time-consuming practice of preparing a marked-up agenda that summarizes key decisions points and action items (Box 5.2). In a few circumstances, minutes are a legal requirement. For example, the boards of directors of incorporated organizations must have accurate minutes. However, for most research projects, minutes are not required, and, more important, they are not particularly useful compared with the time it takes to prepare them. In contrast, a marked-up agenda leverages agenda content that is already in writing and can be prepared quickly. In one organization where I worked, the team's very efficient coordinator would make edits in real time on a large screen that all meeting attendees could see, which focused the team's attention on what was being decided and who needed to do what as next steps.

5.1.4 Facilitation Techniques and Processes

Depending on the nature of a meeting discussion or decision item, you may want to use a facilitated process to bring participants' expertise together. Facilitated processes can be an excellent way to draw out the expertise and judgment of diverse research team members and convert it into tangible and actionable next steps. Typically, facilitated processes involve an opening stage (e.g., brainstorming, sometimes accompanied by tools such mind mapping to ensure a thorough consideration of all the relevant topics), a discussion stage (e.g., reviewing the ideas that were generated to ensure everyone understands them in the same way, sometimes grouping them by theme), and a prioritization or closing stage (e.g., consensus discussion or voting to pick priority topics for the team to focus future work on).

BOX 5.2. EXAMPLE MARKED-UP MEETING AGENDA WITH NOTES AND ACTION ITEMS

AGENDA – XXXX Research Project Team Meeting, [Time and Date]

Notes and Action Items added by KJH on [date]

Item

1 Review of meeting objectives, i.e., to
   (a) Consider input from consulted groups; finalize XXXX.
   (b) Discuss response to risk that the lower value of the Canadian dollar will affect required purchases and leave insufficient funds for other project work.

2 Summary of accomplishments since last meeting:
   (a) Research ethics board submission on [date].
   (b) Good advice and positive feedback from stakeholders on study design.

3 Decision or Discussion Item 1 – The advice from multiple stakeholders has been integrated into the attached draft stakeholder engagement plan; as noted in the comments, there are a small number of outstanding decisions to be made:
   (a) number, content, and timing of webinars – *There was agreement to have three webinars – one midday, two in early evening – in the last year of the project; the planned content foci (which may change as study findings are produced) were XXXX, XXXX, and XXXX.*
   (b) language – *Decision to have the webinars presented in English with live simultaneous French-to-English interpretation and French and English text side by side on all slides.*
   ACTION: KJM to arrange for interpreters after receiving a minimum of three quotes.

4 Discussion Item 2 – Given the recent decrease in the value of the Canadian dollar, there is concern that procurement of XXXX will be over budget, decreasing the amount of funding for other project work. We would like to have a team discussion about options for responding to this risk.
   ACTION: KJM and PAP to develop a plan to bring to the next meeting, taking into account the main suggestions during the meeting.

• Confirm that we need the full functionality for the purchase of XXXX (models with less functionality may be cheaper).

- Talk to at least three other academic colleagues who have purchased XXXX in the past for their advice on preferred venders and essential versus nice-to-have functionality.
- Approach the vendor about a possible discount.
- Identify deliverables that could be decreased to ensure sufficient budget for XXXX.

5 Other business – ***none noted***

6 Summary of action items and next steps ***(see above)***

7 Information items (generally not discussed unless there are questions)
   a. Have completed document requesting access to data; will be submitted as soon as research ethics board approval is obtained.
   b. Next meeting we will discuss planned publication and authorship.
   c. EPD is away for the month of [month]; JD will cover for her for the duration.

Participants: AAAA, BBBB, CCCC (regrets), DDDD (regrets, sent EEEE as delegate), FFFF, GGGG, HHHH

Section 3.2, "Processes to Identify and Manage Risks," and Section 4.5, "Closing the Project and Capturing the Lessons Learned," both outline the use of facilitated processes. Many other facilitation techniques, and free internet resources for them, may be helpful for research teams, including minimum specification requirements facilitation (Lipmanowicz & McCandless, n.d.) and multivoting (American Society for Quality, n.d.-a). In addition, there are free versions of technologies that make it possible to capture participants' ideas in their own words, help people build off each others' ideas and suggestions in real time, and allow participants to vote ideas up or down and suggest their own ideas to add to the voting (e.g., Poll Everywhere [https://www.polleverywhere.com/], Mentimeter [https://www.mentimeter.com/], and Miro [https://miro.com/]).

If you are going to conduct a facilitated process, it is important that you identify one person, ideally someone who is not part of the research team, to manage it. In the absence of having one person responsible for overseeing the facilitated process, you may find that it is hard to move past the opening and discussion stages of the facilitated process and perform the closing phase, which determines the next steps after the session. If you have a facilitator who is also a member of the research team, there is a tendency for any input they provide to be interpreted as the last word on a topic because of the perceived authority of their role as facilitator. If that happens, it is very hard for others to contribute on an equal footing.

Facilitated processes can provide many benefits to research teams, particularly if the teams are large and diverse. Most significantly, they make it possible for multiple ideas to be generated and presented in parallel as opposed to one at a time. However, facilitated processes are not silver bullets that work in all circumstances. It is critical that you choose the right facilitated process to achieve your objective. For example, if you know that knowledge and experience related to a topic are unevenly distributed among team members, you do not want to pick a process that gives everyone an equal vote in deciding what to do about it. Additionally, although anonymous polling techniques can be good for identifying issues when there are power differences among team members, it may not be possible to resolve an issue unless someone feels secure enough to identify themselves and present the details of the issue. Therefore, before committing to a specific facilitated process with the team, it is a good idea to think through potential unintended consequences of that process, which may lead you to choose a different facilitation process out of the many that are available.

In closing, the time that research project teams spend in meetings is extremely valuable. The last thing you want to use your meeting time for is having someone read text on slides that participants could read on their own time or to have two people discuss a topic that nobody else needs to know about. The whole point, and value, of meetings is that people come together to discuss and do something synchronously that they could not do alone, so meeting time should focus on supporting live discussion and good decisions.

5.2 APPLYING PROJECT MANAGEMENT TOOLS AND PROCESSES TO RESEARCH PROGRAMS, OPERATIONS, AND PORTFOLIOS

Projects are a form of work that has a beginning and an end and produces something unique. By its nature, most research is performed as projects that focus on one or more unique unanswered questions, create knowledge that has not been produced by prior research, or both. However, there are other ways of thinking about and organizing the work of research. More specifically, groups of research projects can be managed together, and some research work is better understood as operations. Unfortunately, similar to governance, this is another topic for which variation in how people use terminology means that there are no universally understood definitions to draw on. What one person, or organization, might think of as a large project with subprojects, another might call a program. For the purposes of understanding how to adapt this handbook's project management guidance to other forms of work, I use the following working definitions:

- *Research program:* A group of related research projects with program-level management, governance, or deliverables (e.g., program-level supervision or a program-level advisory board)
- *Research operations:* Ongoing research and research support work that has no specific end date and is often repetitive or regular (e.g., responding to requests for library services, maintaining a data platform, running a research institute)
- *Research portfolio:* research projects, programs, and operations that are brought together with overarching management and governance (e.g., a principal investigator's lab or a research institute that has a mix of projects, programs, and operations that are managed collectively as a portfolio).

In general, the management and leadership of programs, portfolios, and operations are more complex than the management of individual projects. At a minimum, taking management and governance beyond the project level requires some coordination or integration of work that is being performed by different teams with different objectives. The differences between project management and program, portfolio, and operations management are significant. Guidance on the effective leadership and management of organizations often includes, but goes far beyond, project management, and both the Project Management Institute (the organization responsible for the *PMBOK® Guide*; Project Management Institute, n.d.) and Axelos (the organization responsible for *Managing Successful Projects with PRINCE2®*; Axelos, n.d.) offer distinct certifications for program and portfolio management. There-

> **LEADERSHIP ADVICE CROSSWALK**
>
> **5.1. LEADING AN ORGANIZATION IS DIFFERENT THAN LEADING A RESEARCH PROJECT OR PROGRAM**
>
> Michael Schull spoke about the many ways in which leading an independent research institute is different than leading your own research program – for example, governance in the form of a board of directors with legal accountability for the corporation, the fact that hundreds of people depend on the organization for their employment, the critical importance of relationships with funders and partners, and the reality that running an organization requires a team with business skills that a principal investigator probably does not have.

fore, the guidance presented here on these topics is meant to illustrate how the project management tools and processes can be applied beyond projects rather than to provide comprehensive guidance on the management and leadership of research programs, portfolios, or operations.

The core piece of advice is that the mindset of "define, then deliver" can be applied beyond the project level and that project management tools and processes can help any team doing research-related work to establish a common understanding of the scope of what they are trying to accomplish. Figures 5.1 to 5.3 present the work breakdown structures (WBSs) for a fictional research program, operations for a fictional virtual research center or network, and a research portfolio for a fictional new investigator, respectively. In each case, the WBS presents the complete scope in tangible terms but at a higher level than was done for project WBSs. For example, Figure 5.1 includes a single box for each of the three different projects it includes.

As was the case with project-level WBSs, circulating a draft program, operations, or portfolio WBS to team members and stakeholders is an effective way to identify any differences in opinion regarding what the research program, operations, or portfolio will entail.

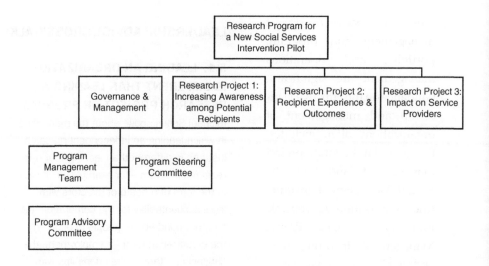

Figure 5.1. Work Breakdown Structure for a Fictional Program of Research for a Social Services Intervention Pilot

In the same way that WBSs for different research projects can have similar deliverables, the WBSs in Figures 5.1 to 5.3 have some things in common, even though the fictional new investigator's research portfolio would be much smaller in scope than the program of research and the operations of a virtual network or center. Notably, each of the three non-project WBSs includes one or more management and governance bodies that oversees multiple projects and activities. This is one of the main advantages of coordinated program, operations, or portfolio management. Instead of having separate siloed governance and management bodies, you can identify synergies and strategic opportunities across projects and decrease the total number of people and total amount of work required for effective governance and management. The guidance presented in Section 3.4, "Decision Making, Governance, and Oversight," can be adapted to apply to more than one project (e.g., see Box 3.7, "Two Common Options for Consensus-Based Decision Making for Research," and Box 3.8, "Sections for a Terms-of-Reference Document").

The amount of additional planning and management control that is needed for subelements of programs, operations, and portfolios will depend on the needs of the team or organization. Usually, there will be benefit in establishing, at a minimum, a one- to two-page program-,

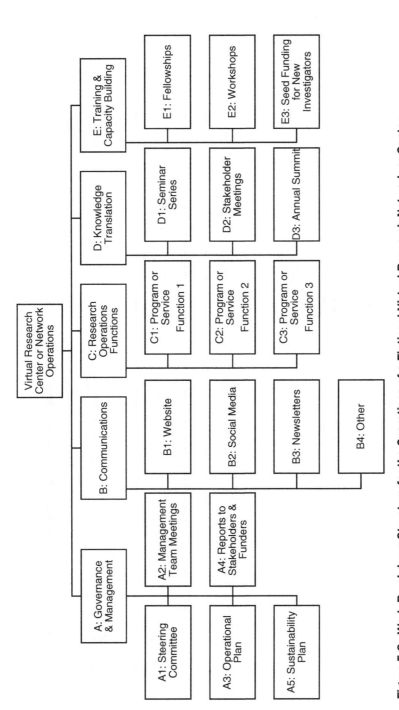

Figure 5.2. Work Breakdown Structure for the Operations of a Fictional Virtual Research Network or Center

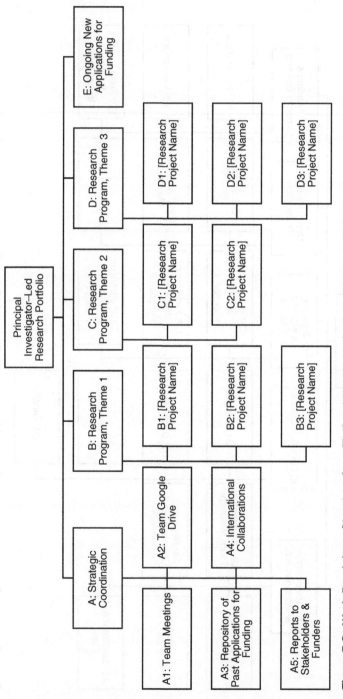

Figure 5.3. Work Breakdown Structure for a Fictional New Investigator's Research Portfolio

operations-, or portfolio-level schedule and budget by adapting the guidance in Section 2.2, "Deliverable-Based Schedule," and Section 2.3, "Deliverable-Based Budget," to apply at a higher level. Most of the time, a modified version of the tracking sheet, which has one row for each box on the WBS, will also add value (see Table 5.2 and Section 4.2, "Tracking and Driving Research Project Progress"). Because the program, operations, or portfolio tracking sheet is one level higher than that for a research project, each row tracks the major project deliverables and milestones (instead of tasks and milestones for deliverables).

For some elements of academic research programs, operations, and portfolios, high-level planning and monitoring (e.g., with the tracking sheet) may be all that is needed. For other elements, the team may need to break down a project or other elements of the program, operations, or portfolio by creating a separate WBS for it. For example, Figure 5.4 presents a detailed breakdown of the ongoing applications for research funding element of the fictional principal investigator's research portfolio presented in Figure 5.3.[3] Even though applying for research funding is an ongoing activity that never has an end, there can be value in establishing a WBS and setting up leads for work-streams under it to ensure a comprehensive approach to grant applications that leverages the content of and experience from previous competitions.

The guidance in this section on adapting the WBS, deliverable-based schedule, deliverable-based budget, tracking sheet, and governance to programs, operations, or portfolios just scratches the surface. Other guidance in the handbook, including that related to risk management, team development, communications, and stakeholder engagement, can also be adapted and applied to research programs, operations, and portfolios. The main point of this section is to illustrate that tools and processes that were developed for project management can have applicability beyond the project level but need to be adapted to work for programs, operations, and portfolios.

---

3 There is no agreed-upon formatting convention, but if you routinely use rectangles for program, operations, and portfolio WBSs and circles for project WBSs, it can help people distinguish between the different kinds of WBSs.

Table 5.2. Tracking Sheet Template for Research Programs, Operations, or Portfolios

Project or WBS Element Name	Lead Initials	Last Accomplishment or Completed Deliverable or Milestone	Status[a]	Upcoming Deliverables or Milestones and Target Completion Dates[b]				
				1	2	3	4	5

[a] Green = progressing well and within schedule and budget constraints and issues (if any) are minor and likely to be resolved without affecting other projects or WBS elements; yellow = low-impact risks have been realized or medium- or high-impact risks have the potential to be realized in the near future that could necessitate changes; red = progress halted, and significant decisions or activities are required to bring work back on track.
[b] Changes relative to last version highlighted with bold italic font.

5.3 AGILE APPROACHES AND RESEARCH PROJECT MANAGEMENT

Agile approaches are a hot topic in project management right now, and some readers may be wondering how the guidance presented in this handbook relates to them. In brief, agile approaches do not have the overarching plan that is at the heart of traditional project management methods (sometimes called "predictive" or "waterfall" methods because the Gantt chart flows from the upper left-hand corner to the lower right-hand corner). Instead, agile approaches involve frequent meetings that focus on work in the upcoming days and weeks for a phase of the project and flexible approaches that rapidly respond to stakeholder needs.

Agile approaches have their origins in software development and the "Manifesto for Agile Software Development" published decades ago (Beck et al., 2001) and kept current by the Agile Alliance (n.d.). In the context of software development, the manifesto authors note that they favor "individuals and interactions over process and tools" and "responding to change over following a plan" (Agile Alliance, n.d., para. 1). Methods that follow the "agile philosophy" include Scrum (https://www.scrum.org/resources/what-is-scrum) and eXtreme Programming (http://www.extremeprogramming.org/). In addition, both the Project Management Institute and Axelos have published guidance and offer certification in agile project management.

Agile approaches are very popular for software development and other projects in which the members of a project team have a clear and shared understanding of what the team is working toward (e.g., a new website) but need or want to be open to many changes in the details of what they are producing. When these project teams encounter issues or opportunities, it does not make sense for them to wait days or weeks before they can meet together or meet with their client, and they do not want to be bound by a detailed master plan that was developed before anybody knew about the issue or opportunity.

Given the flexibility of agile approaches, it is natural to ask whether they might be good fit for uncertain and innovative research projects. In brief, my view is that agile approaches can work well for some research project deliverables and in cases in which the team has a very clear and shared understanding of what the project's outputs will be (e.g., the development of a new mobile device app), but, overall, a high-level traditional approach is likely to produce better results for academic research than agile approaches for several reasons.

The first and most significant is that many academic research projects do not have narrowly defined outputs, so, in the absence of an overarching high-level plan, there is a risk that diverse research team members will slip into different interpretations of what the project is meant to produce. This risk is heightened when research team members are spread across multiple locations,

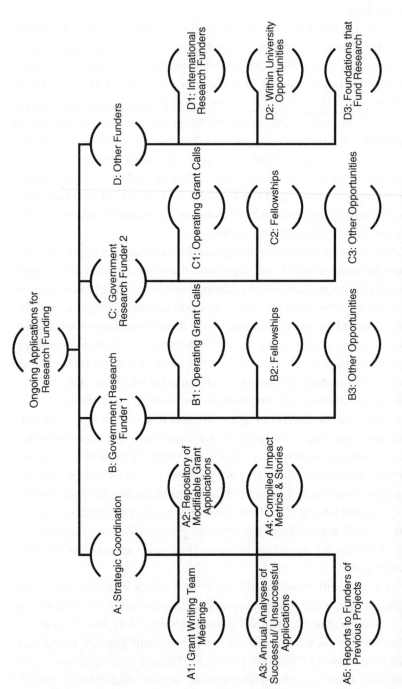

Figure 5.4. Work Breakdown Structure for Fictional Ongoing Applications for Research Funding

organizations, and disciplines, as is often the case with large academic research projects. Second, for many academic research projects, the cadence of progress and availability of team members does not align well with the agile approach of having frequent scheduled meetings. Because research project team members often have responsibilities that go beyond a single project (e.g., other research projects, teaching, or attending graduate student courses), it is unlikely that there will be meaningful content to present every day or even every week. Also, on a practical level, it may not be possible to find a regular meeting time slot that works for all research project team members because of their other commitments.

For these reasons, I recommend a high-level and strategic application of traditional project management tools and processes to academic research projects that can provide some of the benefits of an agile approach – that is, allowing deliverable leads and teams the flexibility to innovate and being open to large-scale changes in scope – without losing the benefit of an overarching plan. Nothing prevents research project teams from bringing in agile approaches that are appropriate for certain deliverables, but I encourage academic research project teams to focus on light-touch versions of traditional high-level project management approaches over agile approaches.

5.4 ADAPTING RESEARCH PROJECT MANAGEMENT AND LEADERSHIP SKILLS ON THE BASIS OF CONTEXT

5.4.1 Modifying Academic Research Project Management Skills for Other Sectors That Perform Research and Development

It is no secret that there are more graduate students than there are academic positions for them to move into and that many PhD and master's degree graduates end up working in careers outside of academic settings (CHSPRA, 2015). In addition to emphasizing their research and subject matter skills, job applicants can draw attention to their research project management skills when applying for jobs with business, governmental, and not-for-profit organizations; however, they will often need to modify their project management practices to work in non-academic settings.

If you use a federated search engine to look for project manager job postings in any urban area, you will find thousands of active searches for project manager candidates, including many postings with the keywords "research project management." Most of these job postings include qualifications related to budget management and communications skills combined with some experience working in research or research and development (R&D), either as a project manager or as a researcher. Many of the job postings emphasize stakeholder engagement, organizational skills, and general management and leadership skills. Sometimes, but not usually, research project manager job postings reference or state a preference for experience with specific project management software (e.g., Microsoft Project [https://www.microsoft.com/en-ca/microsoft-365/project/project-management-software]) or project management certification.

Even though the job descriptions for research project manager positions might read as being similar across sectors, in practice project managers will often be asked to take on different roles and responsibilities in the private (i.e., business), government, or not-for-profit sectors than in the academic sector. Some of the variation in what research project managers are asked to do arises because of differences in project certainty (see Figure 1.1).

In general, but with some exceptions, investigator-driven academic research will have less certainty than R&D projects in other sectors, and this will translate into different levels of detail and control in both project planning and implementation (see Table 5.3). By extension, people applying or interviewing for jobs outside of an academic setting might want to highlight knowledge and skills corresponding to the right-hand column of Table 5.3.

To secure a job outside of the academic sector, it is also important to demonstrate that you understand the context and ways of working for the organization you are applying to. Some common differences between business R&D projects and academic research projects are as follows:

- Business R&D projects are more likely to be experimental development or applied research than are academic research projects (see Box 1.2).

Table 5.3. Differences in Research Project Management Practices Depending on the Certainty of the Project

Most-Certain R&D Projects (e.g., Experimental Development at a Private-Sector Organization to Refine a Commercial Product)	Least-Certain R&D Projects (e.g., Principal Investigator–Driven Basic Research at an Academic Institution)
Long and detailed project planning and management documents	Short and high-level project planning and management documents
Tighter monitoring and control of changes during the implementation phase (e.g., 1- to 2-page change request template for every change)	High-level monitoring and control (e.g., the tracking sheet) plus, where applicable, documents required by regulation or policy (e.g., research ethics applications, study protocol amendments, permit changes)
Many standardized processes (e.g., formal review and acceptance of project outputs, including assessment compared with predefined specifications)	Few formal processes – only those that are perceived by the team as adding value
Detailed roles and responsibilities with formal and regular performance evaluations	High-level definition of roles and responsibilities and less formal (or absence of) performance evaluations
Formal quality standards and clear articulation of what is considered successful on the basis of the standards	Definition of success that can change during project

Note: R&D = research and development.

- Business R&D projects are usually selected for funding by people or committees within the organization who will benefit if the project is successful.
- The main criterion for selecting business R&D projects is their ability to generate a return on investment and directly or indirectly contribute to the business's profit and the company's value.
- Most business R&D projects have plans and steps that are very similar to those of projects the business has conducted previously (e.g., businesses will have a set way of performing clinical trials, market research, information technology software or hardware development). As a result, over time, company R&D staff can become highly qualified specialists in terms of both their content knowledge and their process expertise.

- Because there are commonalities in the ways in which regulated companies perform R&D, if a business needs to bring in additional capacity to accelerate progress on an R&D project, contract research services and personnel are often an option.
- If a business R&D project needs additional funds to move forward quickly, mechanisms exist to redistribute funds across the business's portfolio of projects to ensure that the highest-priority projects proceed at the fastest possible rate.
- Low-performing or low-priority business R&D projects may be terminated on the basis of opportunity cost considerations – that is, because the business determines that it is better to put the resources toward another R&D project that is more likely to produce a greater return on investment.

On the basis of these characteristics of the business R&D environment, business employers often value project managers who know the tools and processes of the *PMBOK® Guide,* the method outlined in *Managing Successful Projects with PRINCE2®,* or both, very well and are skilled at applying them to detailed projects. Businesses often rely on project managers to be able to manage the details of complex projects, programs, and portfolios and to understand and act on interdependencies within and between projects. The R&D project manager in a business environment is an expert planner or implementer of a detailed project plan. They must have good content and sector knowledge, understand client and regulatory requirements and company research and sales priorities, and have good knowledge of risks and mitigation strategies in the company context. In regulated R&D-intensive industries, such as the pharmaceutical sector, businesses also value people who have the communications skills and composure to interact directly with regulators.

Public-sector research is performed by government agencies, and sometimes by governments themselves (e.g., policy research). It depends on the specifics of the environment, but, overall, the context for public-sector research project management has some similarities to that of academic research and business R&D. For example, like business R&D projects, public-sector research projects are usually directed toward generating knowledge that can be applied in some practical way, but like academic projects, governments and government agencies will also fund projects solely for the knowledge they generate as opposed to expecting a specific return. Like businesses, government agencies and governments often have a dedicated, permanent full-time staff who perform research, which means that decisions about research funding are, for the most part, decisions about which projects to allocate staff resources to. Like academic projects, the scope of public-sector research projects can change in major ways during project implementation on the basis of political factors and the results of government consultations with stakeholders. For example, a government agency's research team focused on developing a diabetes strategy could change from a focus on telemedicine and self-management to one on medication in response to a political party's agenda or stakeholder feedback. Even if the scope changes in major ways, the government agency's project might still have the same name, team, and high-level purpose (i.e., in the earlier example, to decrease the negative effect of diabetes on society).

Because of their focus on research that serves the public and aligns with political priorities and realities, government agencies and governments value research project managers who have some political acuity and an ability to "read the tea leaves." When public-sector research staff work directly with external stakeholders, they need excellent communication skills (including the ability to communicate research and science to non-expert audiences), and interpersonal skills (e.g., the ability to notice and respond if a stakeholder is having a negative reaction to a proposed deliverable or course of action). Because the scope of a public-sector research project can change in major ways during the implementation phase, government agencies and governments also value research project managers who have an excellent ability to estimate and quickly develop high-level plans that illustrate the options as to what can be achieved in what time with what resources.

There is a lot of variation in the approaches and skills that work best for not-for-profit research project management because research in not-for-profit organizations varies depending on the source of funding and the objectives of the not-for-profit organization. One of the main differences relative to other research-performing organizations is that not-for-profits often have little (or no) core funding to cover basic costs such as rent, electricity, office supplies, and staff salaries, so they rely very heavily on having their proposals selected for funding in competitions. In those cases, not-for-profits require research project managers who have many of the skills required for other sectors – that is, people who can write persuasive proposals and produce results that align with the needs and interests of other organizations.

If not-for-profit organizations do large-scale research, it is often done in partnership with groups in the academic or business sectors, which tend to be larger and have more funds for research. Some not-for-profits focus on providing research grants and overseeing research portfolios rather than performing research themselves. In those cases, they might seek individuals who have portfolio management skills – that is, the ability to monitor and provide oversight of a large number of projects – as opposed to leading or supporting individual research projects.

In summary, there is no single right way to apply project management to R&D. There are some fundamental differences among academic research, business R&D, public sector research, and not-for-profits' research that should be reflected in the ways in which project management skills, tools, and processes are used. Depending on the characteristics of the project and the environment in which it is being conducted, research project managers will need to take different approaches and use different skills to successfully compete for jobs and succeed in non-academic roles.

5.4.2 Applying the Guidance in This Handbook in Your Environment

There are many different ways in which a project can be successfully managed, as illustrated by the different approaches described by the research leaders interviewed for this handbook. This variation in project management practice can be beneficial and appropriate when it is done to meet the needs of research teams, projects, and environments.

Depending on the environment in which research teams work, there may be existing project management systems, frameworks, and required documentation. Different organizations may use different terminology and labels for their project management tools and processes such as "workplan," "charter," "project plan," "project dashboards," and so forth. In general, if the tools and processes in the organization where you work are helpful and add value, they should be leveraged as opposed to discarded in favor of the tools and processes presented in this handbook. However, if there is no preexisting project management method or framework, or if the existing approach is not working, the tools and processes presented in this handbook can constitute a complete light-touch method when combined with other documentation that includes project-specific details required by regulators or stakeholders (e.g., study protocols, ethics submissions, permit applications).

Although the names of the tools, templates, and processes can vary, it is important that the mindset of "define, then deliver" (Box 2.1) is being followed before moving into project implementation. If it is not, then no template, project management information management system, or leadership style can ensure that a project is starting off in the right direction. Regardless of the details or labels applied to an organization's project management tools and processes, there is likely flexibility to incorporate the mindset of "define, then deliver" somehow or in some way by

- defining the main deliverables of the project,
- identifying who is responsible for leading each deliverable,
- establishing a high-level schedule to guide when and how the deliverables will come together, and
- establishing and populating a tool to monitor project progress during implementation and drive the near-term activities that are required to produce the deliverables and achieve the project's objectives.

If you are tasked with developing a complete research proposal in an unstructured format, the collection of tools and processes presented in this handbook can be the foundation for a complete project or program plan that will typically be 15 pages or fewer before the details of the methodology are added (see Appendix F, "Example Full Project Plan for a Fictional Natural Sciences Research Project That Is Part of a Multidisciplinary Program"). The good news is that most of the information for the complete project plan or program plan probably already exists within your organization, in which case only a small amount of work would be required to modify the existing content and bring it together into a formal plan or proposal (see Table 5.4).

In closing, this handbook was created to provide guidance that provides individuals and research project teams with some concrete

Table 5.4. Existing versus Recommended Content for a Research Project Plan or Program Plan

Existing Content (and Source)	Content of Full Research Project Plan or Program Plan[a]
Objectives and purpose (grant application or proposal)	Objectives and purpose
Scope (grant application or proposal)	Scope – *WBS with leads*
Assumptions and constraints (grant agreements or institutional policies)	Assumptions and constraints (bring key ones forward from grant agreements and institutional policies)
Roles and responsibilities (grant application or proposal)	Roles and responsibilities *defined for workstreams and deliverables*
[Governance] (grant application or proposal may or may not mention)	Governance *deliverables defined*
Schedule (grant application or proposal)	*Deliverable-based* Gantt chart
Budget (grant application or proposal)	*Deliverable-based* budget
[Stakeholder engagement] (grant application or proposal may or may not mention)	Stakeholder engagement, *communications plan, or both*
[Risks – negative] (grant application or proposal may or may not mention)	Risks – negative *and positive*

Note: WBS = work breakdown structure.
[a] Items that may be new are in italics.

examples of research project management and leadership in practice. Rather than constraining principal investigators, project managers, and other research project team members, it is intended to increase awareness of approaches that might be beneficial.

All research is performed with the goal of making a difference in some way. I hope that the contents of this handbook will help individuals and teams to articulate and share their vision so that they can develop and implement plans to produce deliverables that are steps on the path to a positive impact.

Interviews with Research Leaders

I am indebted to the 19 research leaders who shared their knowledge and advice, which makes up approximately one-third of this handbook. Many of them are people with whom I have worked as a research team member or when I was a research funder at the Ontario Ministry of Health. In other cases, I have provided coaching or project management services to them or their teams. As a result, there are a disproportionate number of Canadian research leaders, even though I approached only a small subset of the many people who have inspired me with their research leadership over the years. In addition, research leaders who focus on applied research in the areas in which I work (health sciences, data-intensive research, data governance, and public engagement) are overrepresented relative to the percentage of researchers who work on those topics.

Of course, the 19 people who agreed to share their research leadership advice in this handbook do not constitute a representative sample of research leaders. No group of 19 (or 50 or 100) people would be representative of all disciplines, all perspectives, and the diverse backgrounds of people who lead research. However, most of the advice they provide is not discipline specific, and the situations they describe can occur in different research fields.

These research leaders were not asked to focus on any particular topic or provided with each other's interview write-ups as background. As a result, and on the basis of my personal relationships with research leaders, my advice is to not read anything into the absence of content on a particular topic in any one research leader's interview. Put another way, if I had specifically asked each research leader about involving stakeholders, developing and supporting students and junior staff, equity, and accountability, I am sure that the interviews would have been longer and have more content on those topics. However, it is remarkable that so many research leaders independently provided advice that followed similar themes (see the 10 themes in Section 1.5). The individual research leader interview write-ups are provided here to add details and context that help explain how and why those themes are important to them.

6.1 ELSPETH BROWN: STARTING A NEW LEADERSHIP ROLE WITH A LISTENING TOUR

Research Leader: Elspeth Brown, associate vice president research and director of the Critical Digital Humanities Initiative, University of Toronto Mississauga

What does research leadership mean to you?

In my role as associate vice president [VP] research, research leadership means understanding and identifying the kinds of research that faculty members are doing and learning what they need in order to meet their research goals. Sometimes it is about having a conversation with faculty to help them understand what the opportunities are and where they can go with their research. Part of the role is helping people to be ambitious and reach for a goal that maybe they had thought they weren't ready for.

What leadership situation will you share with readers?

I'm going to speak about the listening tour I started when I began my role as associate VP research in 2020, what we did based on what we heard, and some reflections on the whole process.

What did you think and do in that situation?

As background, I'm very motivated by questions of social equity. My commitments to equity, diversity, and inclusion [EDI] determine how I organize my time and energy in relationship to the limited resources that are available. That is not to say that I'm not happy to support others. I try to make people feel included and use the resources that are available to benefit everybody, but I also have to make decisions. I chose to start my listening tour with associate professors who were marginalized in one way or another, for example, because they were BIPOC [Black, Indigenous, or people of color] or because they were LGBTQ [lesbian, gay, bisexual, transgender, or queer]. I wanted to underscore how we could support those researchers in some way.

The listening tour identified some concrete activities to help meet faculty needs. One example is a funding program available for BIPOC researchers working in any field and for other faculty working on BIPOC questions. We also started a first-book manuscript workshop as a new initiative to support faculty members who have recently received their PhD and started their academic work. We organize a workshop and an external reader who convenes a seminar of colleagues to provide feedback to strengthen the manuscript before it is submitted for publication. The first faculty member selected for the workshop had an exceptionally strong proposal and also happens to be an Indigenous person. We have convened a group of other Indigenous scholars who are helping to strengthen their manuscript. So, everyone wins in terms of moving forward, the overall program, as well as the EDI goals.

What did you learn?

It's important to note that everything I'm talking about is in the context of me being the first associate VP research at University of Toronto Mississauga, and the first who is in social sciences and the humanities. I've also seen other Canadian universities hiring associate VPs research who are women, and/or working in humanities or social sciences, and who are often BIPOC or LGBTQ. So, we now have more people from groups that have been underrepresented in leadership positions, and we are learning more about what faculty from under-represented groups need.

One of the things I've learned is that people just need to be asked or prompted to think about EDI because discourse about it is not necessarily front and center. My role has been to find ways to bring EDI into the conversation around program design and budgeting. For example, if there is a desire to create a training program for undergraduate students over the summer, I might suggest that there be a bursary to support marginalized students so that they can participate. There has never been any opposition to these suggestions, and people are happy to implement them; they just may not have thought of them depending on the backgrounds and disciplines of the people involved.

Similarly, I've found that it helps some faculty members to be prompted about new opportunities. For example, people who have received a partnership development grant may need somebody to tap them on the shoulder and say, "Great job" and ask, "How about this other opportunity?" "Have you considered it?" "How can we help you move your research to a new level?" That kind of work can have a lot of value, so you need to have structure in terms of scheduled meetings that create opportunities for conversations. You need to talk to faculty to understand their needs and do work that is relevant and actually supports them.

In my listening tour, we heard that faculty were concerned that their research was not visible on the campus. I share that concern and agree that doing a better job at amplifying faculty research is really important. It's important because we want people to know about our faculty members' research, but it's also important for the faculty members themselves. If you're doing research and nobody seems to care or notice, that's not great for morale. Faculty need to feel like they are part of their workplace and part of a shared enterprise. Based on what we heard, we were able to bring in an additional part-time communications officer to the VP research office. This is a position we've never had before. We probably need to do more, but it's a start.

After a couple of years on the job, my final learning is that you must guard against getting into your own leadership bubble with other senior administrators or faculty administrators. It's really important to keep connecting with constituencies and faculty members. I'm continuing to use the term "listening tour" because I'm continuing to meet and have conversations with faculty members about their research.

Do you have any additional leadership advice based on your own experiences or advice that you've received from someone else?

There are two things I find myself advising faculty members who are either senior assistant professors or just tenured. Often, they have very ambitious research plans that involve a lot of partners, and they've got their own individual research agendas alongside their partnership, collaborative research agenda. The first piece of advice is to recognize that the work of doing research is a form of labor, so they need to acknowledge that and delegate. Some of the work – like setting up meetings and work-study contracts – is not the best use of a faculty member's time. It's much better to create a project manager position within the research team. But it's more than that. When the research leader takes the back seat, it gives others the opportunity to share and use their skills. One of the very specific things that I do is to have a different person lead each weekly meeting. It could be a senior colleague or a work-study student. It's not just about the leadership or facilitation that they provide; it's about having somebody else's voice be the leading one in the meeting. And I have found that amazing things have happened because of this. For example, a research manager on my team who has a theater background starts meetings in very creative ways. Last week she put up six images on Zoom and asked us each to say which image resonated on that particular day, and why. Things that are real and important in people's lives emerged. It only took 10 minutes of our meeting time, but activities like that are absolutely critical to building trust within the team.

The other piece of advice I have for new leaders is about learning how to be human and vulnerable and recognizing that you don't have all the answers. The situation for new research leaders can be similar to how people feel when they first start teaching. There can be a stiffness and anxiety about not being able to answer questions, sometimes an imposter syndrome. When people become more experienced, they also become more relaxed. If they get a question they can't answer, they are honest about it. There's a kind of openness that emerges. And it seems to me that it's important to figure out how to create that kind of openness and collaborative research leadership moments, where there's that kind of capacity to communicate with honesty and vulnerableness.

The role of the leader is to mentor and support people, and help them prepare, so everyone can benefit from different approaches. And there is an equity issue, too, in terms of who are the ones to contribute. I think it is an art to create a collaborative, functioning, and productive environment for research teams in which everyone feels included. I'm fascinated by the topic and always happy to learn more about it.

6.2 STEINI BROWN: RESEARCH LEADERSHIP SHOULD FOCUS ON THE TEAM, NOT THE LEADER

Research Leader: Adalsteinn (Steini) Brown, dean, Dalla Lana School of Public Health, University of Toronto

What does research leadership mean to you?

Research leadership can mean two things to me. The first is that some research leaders are the people that find new ways and approaches to define what is going on in a field, or even redefine what a field means. The other kind of research leadership is all about the fundamental skills of being able to support really highly trained and highly qualified personnel to do innovative, rigorous work. It's different than research management because it's not about managing a process, it's about finding ways for teams to be engaged and inspired to achieve more.

What leadership situation will you share with readers?

I'm going to speak about a project that I led that started with an inspiring but focused scope that ultimately became the hospital report card series involving more than two dozen researchers from four universities.

What did you think and do in that situation?

When I started in the project in a leadership role, I saw myself mostly as a person who was managing a process. That was partly because we hadn't staffed up to the right level so that someone else could provide management support, and partly because I'd come from the private sector where I saw myself as a manager-leader. To start, the project was scoped to produce a single report that analyzed hospital performance by region with the Ontario Hospital Association and the University of Toronto as the main partners, but once that report was issued, interest and scope grew. Building on that success, we were able to expand and bring in additional funders, three more universities and a lot more researchers, and the Canadian Institute for Health Information (CIHI) and ICES as well as the Ontario government as a funder. The scope grew from one report with regional analyses to a series of reports that analyzed the performance of individual hospitals' acute care, emergency department care, complex continuing care, rehabilitation, women's health, and mental health. The increased scope meant new teams with new partners, including many more hospital-based researchers, some of whom I hadn't worked with before.

What did you learn?

It was really important that I realized that the scope had grown to the point that I could not, and should not, try to manage everything. I also realized that my job wasn't to vet or validate the research of others – there was no way that I could or should do that. Instead, I learned that it was my job to make sure that things came together, which was a very different focus than I had when the project started. It meant that I had to spend more time up front trying to make sure that people were set up for success. I also gained a much deeper understanding of my colleagues' strengths, which led to a different way of working that was much more helpful to my colleagues than my initial approach.

The real lesson for me personally was realizing how to get out of the way and focus on supporting other individuals in doing the work. In the first year of the project, I felt that I had a responsibility to be the person out in front of it all. But as I reflected and learned, I was able to shift to being a leader who was more of an enabler, for example, by working with my colleagues to set goals, or just making sure that peo-ple were working well with each other and feeling supported. When the scope expanded from a single report with regional-level analyses to multiple reports with hospital-level analyses, at first, I was con-sumed by the project. But when I learned to stand back and support others, both the team and I were able to increase the scope of what we could take on and accomplish more.

The other thing I want to say is that, on reflection, my approach at the beginning of the project was pretty clumsy. The changes in my leadership style, and shift of my focus, were probably the result of tolerant colleagues providing a lot of advice back to me about how to think about things differently.

Do you have any additional leadership advice based on your own experiences or advice that you've received from someone else?

One of the defining research moments for me was the very first piece of high-profile research that I published on cost-effectiveness, but it wasn't because of my leadership, it was because of the leadership of my mentor. He was asked to do some work for the Blue Cross Blue Shield Association of America, which, for him, was the kind of thing he could have done in his sleep. But he knew that the work was high profile and set things up for me to lead the work as a postdoctoral fellow. Because of his reputation, and the way that he had engaged with folks in the past, he was able to organize things effectively and keep the rest of the team moving along and contributing to the work, even though all of them were more senior than me. I really appreciate the sacrifice he made. It was a gift to me.

In terms of advice that I pass on to others, three things come to mind. First, you don't have to be the smartest person in the room. If you try to be that person, you may do the best work and be the most knowledgeable, but you won't be demonstrating the skills you need to be a research leader, and you and your teammates will find your leadership frustrating. The second thing, as one of my mentors constantly reminds me, is that you want to do a lot more listening than talking. And when you are talking as a research leader, it will mostly be because you are feeding back what you've heard from others as you find ways to work across the whole team and help the team move forward. The third piece of advice is that you really need to focus on incentives for researchers. You cannot pay researchers or scholars enough to do something that they aren't interested in. So, you have to pay attention to things like why a researcher would be intrigued by a project and the quality of the environment they are working in.

Researchers are incredibly rational when it comes to the big picture and intrinsic-value incentives, and when you get them right, it's actually one of the most inspiring things about being a research leader.

The last thing I'd like to share is that research leaders learn a lot more from their first set of failures than they do from successes later in their careers. That means that we need to give less-experienced researchers the opportunity to try things that they may not succeed at, and the people around them need to be willing to tolerate failure. It also means that mentorship is critical. We're trying to expand the range of skills we teach future researchers to be stronger leaders. I believe it's going to lead to more satisfying careers for them and a stronger and more sustainable health system.

6.3 BETH COLEMAN: STARTING UP THE UNIVERSITY OF TORONTO BLACK RESEARCH NETWORK

Research Leader: Beth Coleman, director, University of Toronto Black Research Network, and associate professor, data and cities, Institute of Communication, Culture, Information and Technology, University of Toronto Mississauga/Faculty of Information, University of Toronto

What does research leadership mean to you?

For the kinds of wicked problems that we work on, research leadership is a combination of internal work to put together dynamic, strong interdisciplinary teams and external work on knowledge mobilization so that our research has a societal impact.

What leadership situation will you share with readers?

I will talk about the work I've been leading to start up the Black Research Network at the University of Toronto (U of T). The Black Research Network is one of a small number of institute strategic initiatives that are funded by the university to accelerate innovative research across sectors. But, unlike some of the other institute strategic initiatives, the Black Research Network has a very broad mandate.

Our ambition is to help support and amplify Black research excellence across the three U of T campuses and across all disciplines.

What did you think and do in that situation?

One of our objectives is to make Black researchers across the U of T tri-campus visible to each other and to the broader research community. To do this, early on we launched a campaign using the Black Research Network website as a portal for people to find rich content about the researchers in the network. As people began using the website to find out about Black-led research and to look for people to join interdisciplinary teams, we started to build momentum. The website is helping us to be seen as a trusted network that is the foundation for powerful research collaborations.

Part of good leadership is having the right team, and right does not always mean big. It is about understanding what roles need to be filled and bringing in people who are well positioned to do the work and continuously learn from each other. The first staff person I brought in to help with the launch of the Black Research Network was a program lead with project management experience. Now we are expanding to include a program administrator and a communications person. We have also identified the need to have team members who manage third-party resources, e.g., to create videos about researchers. We're small, but we're working well and learning together, and will continue to evolve.

What did you learn?

It's important to have a big vision, but equally important to take that big vision and organize it into discrete chunks. You need small and actionable goals that allow you to build capacity in the team over time and provide opportunities to reflect on what is working and what should be done differently.

On that point, having the right culture is as important as having the right team members. Inevitably something will go wrong, or not go as planned. When that happens, you need a culture where people trust each other so that you can use the experience of the whole team to resolve issues.

For the wicked and complex problems that we look at – like vital factors in health outcomes or the complexity of underrepresentation of Black, Indigenous, and People of Color in science, technology, engineering, and mathematics practices – multifactorial and interdisciplinary teams are needed. Leaders need to recognize that when they create these teams, they also must commit to the difficult but necessary work of figuring out a common language and way for people to work together.

I have also learned that research leaders need to do some curation around who is at the tables they convene. For me, it is an important aspect of leadership practice to have a vision about whom you are bringing together to address a complex problem. But it is equally important to be flexible and adapt your approach. You may find that not everyone you invite to the table stays. They may recommend a colleague who is a better fit for the expertise you are seeking or may not have the time to participate in the ways that you had imagined. Research leaders need to be fluid in terms of learning in the moment and gaining from whatever advice or expertise people have to contribute.

Do you have any additional leadership advice based on your own experiences or advice that you've received from someone else?

From my own experience, I'd emphasize how important it is to listen to your team members and to make sure that they listen to each other. Team members are often the first to see emerging issues and opportunities. In research, you get what you give, and it is very important to keep a spirit of generous engagement.

I've also learned from one of my mentors who would lead by engaging in dialogue. The act of asking people what they need and where their skill levels are, then supporting them and amplifying their strengths has been really gratifying, and fun. It is a lot of work, but it is worth the effort.

In closing, it has been delightful for me to support other people in learning how to do some things better. To see how team members' organizational skills, synthesis skills, and communications skills have grown, and the ways that their strengths have taken our network in different directions. Being able to rely on the people around us to help produce the best outcomes or learn better together is extremely rewarding.

6.4 ALED EDWARDS: LEARNING YOUR PARTNERS' CULTURE THROUGH IMMERSION

Research Leader: Aled Edwards, founder and chief executive, Structural Genomics Consortium, and professor of medical genetics and medical biophysics, University of Toronto

What does research leadership mean to you?

My dad is a very accomplished choir conductor, and his job is to get 80 people to sing in balance. Not everybody is the best singer on planet Earth, but working together they can make a great choir. I think of research leadership that way. It's about inspiring people to reach a common goal and leading the work in a way that everyone has a part in it.

What the leadership situation will you share with readers?

Twenty-five years ago, I took a year off from my university work to start a biotech company to better understand the biotech sector, and then 10 years ago, I spent 4 months at the global research and development headquarters of a large pharmaceutical company to better understand that sector.

What did you think and do in that situation?

It wasn't about learning the mechanics of project management methods or operations of the organization; it was about culture, people, and decision making. To start, I focused on understanding the culture, but then I focused on how to use the patterns I saw as means to influence culture and decisions within an organization.

What did you learn?

I found that in large corporations, champions are the ones who get things done. Research leaders who want to partner with external organizations need to find and develop those internal champions. A nuance of partnering is understanding how best to support your champions within their organizations. Also, you need to develop a range of champions at partnering organizations, because what you quickly learn in the modern industrial sector is that people move jobs. You need to be prepared, mentally and practically, for your champions to leave the organization.

Do you have any additional leadership advice based on your own experiences or advice that you've received from someone else?

It's not what's taught, but I build organizations around people, not functions. I think it's healthy to embrace different leadership styles, and it's a mistake to try to make square pegs fit in round holes. Indeed, I think the lack of diversity of thought in organizations, including universities, is that we recruit one personality type for our leaders. We associate words like "bold," "innovative," and "ambitious" with leadership. And while that describes some people, other leaders use different styles and are just as effective.

This also applies when you build teams. There are people who are the happiest when they put the period at the end of a sentence, and others who are happiest never to finish that sentence. A research leader needs to recognize the range of different personality types – there aren't that many – and be flexible enough to accommodate different people's ways of being successful. The tension in research project management is that some of the people you need on your team are the ones that don't follow rules. That is actually what enriches the science, especially when you pair the dreamers with practical people. A leader has to balance providing air cover for the creative folks who never finish the job, who are never on time, who bring up the same issues over and over, and supporting the folks who like everything on time, who plan weeks in advance, and who are so critical to actually accomplishing anything. I've never met a project management person who is not frustrated by these types of scientists. In general, I think it's one of the hardest parts of building an organization – appreciating that people "not like you" are exactly what will make it successful.

One of the differences between leading a small group and a large project is that, as the leader of a large research project, you have to pay attention not just to the best performers and high flyers, but to everyone. A reality of the academic system is that a professor running a research laboratory can do quite fine if a couple of the people in the lab produce high-impact papers and some folks publish nothing. But in a large research project usually the goals are collective, and the research leader must ensure that everyone gets due attention. This is important not only for the project and the person, but also because the morale of the organization will suffer if there are unhappy people. In contrast, the team performance will go up if everyone knows they matter.

Another interesting situation is how to balance keeping people happy with maintaining the highest scientific standards and really challenging the team. You have to be scientifically rigorous with students and postdocs, but also find the Goldilocks middle in terms of criticism. You need to prepare people and help them understand how to defend their science in front of the world, which can be harsh, while making it clear that your criticisms are designed to make them better scientists. This can be hard for graduate students, many of whom are high achievers and may never have received such criticism before. It can also be hard and awkward for young professors to find that balance, because they might be close to the same age as their postdocs and students, and they are both peers and mentors.

After seeing hundreds of mentors and leaders over my career, in several universities and dozens of companies, I think the best ones set clear scientific expectations but have optimistic and encouraging styles. Leadership, certainly in the university research setting, isn't about being dogmatic about the way it "must" be done or rules that "must" be followed. It's about being open to differences – embracing students and researchers who are not like you – and being empathetic.

6.5 STEVE FARBER: LEADERSHIP TO ADVANCE A CONCEPT INTO A CODEVELOPED RESEARCH AGENDA

Research Leader: Steve Farber, associate professor, geography and planning, University of Toronto Scarborough

What does research leadership mean to you?

For me, the meaning of research leadership is twofold. The first part is about creating opportunities for others. Sometimes this refers to the people I advise – my postdocs and grad students – but I'm also trying to give back to other scholars. I love the idea that I'm creating new space for people to do work and new resources for people to use.

The second part is about pushing and pulling the disparate parts of a research project together toward a central set of goals. The research leader is not the only person to do that, but they are one of the few people on the research team that really knows how everything fits together. In this sense, research leadership is about helping other researchers drive their individual projects into alignment with our overall research mission.

What leadership situation will you share with readers?

I'm going to talk about how I led an interdisciplinary group of people from the concept of "mobilizing justice" to an operating network with non-academic partners and a full research agenda.

What did you think and do in that situation?

I first wrote down the idea of mobilizing justice as part of an application for University of Toronto interdisciplinary seed funding to support new collaborations between engineers and social scientists like myself. The original nucleus of the mobilizing justice idea was to look at the changes that are taking place in the transportation sector because of technological innovations and revisit metrics for studying transportation performance in light of those changes. We were especially interested in metrics that look at performance on social dimensions, not whether buses are running on time or other typical measures of network performance. We wanted to understand performance in terms of people's experiences and how transportation works in their lives. We started off with some collaborative research data analysis and review activities, but along the way, we decided we would share the results and create a community of researchers and practitioners who are trying to do similar things in Canada.

In 2019, we held a 2-day in-person workshop of about 40 people, mostly Canadian and American and some additional international people. The idea was to create a space for academics and practitioners – like government policymakers and transportation planners, and some representatives from the technology firms who are pushing new technologies into the transportation sector – to think about the social and equity implications of transportation technological changes. The objective of the workshop was to develop some common goals and a shared vision for the future of equity in the transportation system. The second half of the workshop focused on identifying the research needed in order to support that movement. We organized all sorts of activities to co-create research ideas and developed these into a research agenda. The outputs of the workshop ultimately were funded by a Social Sciences and Humanities Research Council Partnership Grant.

What did you learn?

It was super important that people from municipalities across the country were part of the workshop. We asked them all to make presentations, and without any prompting, they had very similar stories in terms of what they were trying to accomplish when it comes to equity in transportation planning and what their pinch points were. With academics and people from multiple cities in the same room, we came to the realization that we're all in this together and we're all struggling to do better. We started to talk about transportation equity like a community of practice. We all felt like we were creating something much bigger than ourselves, and that there was a lot of excitement and enthusiasm and a clear connection that mobilizing justice was needed and that it would be really, really useful for our non-academic partners.

The researchers were able to hear the specifics of what the practitioners were struggling with and generate a research plan that was grounded, very concretely and undeniably, in what our partners needed. This was possible because of the concentrated effort to galvanize support from the non-academic partners and the fact that we made sure the academics were responsive to things that the non-academic partners were asking for.

Another important outcome of the workshop came from the debates that we held. In the United States, there are equity requirements for transportation that stem from the Civil Rights Act in the 1960s. Essentially, those require that any federal spending must be subjected to an equity analysis to make sure that money is being used across racial groups in an equitable way, e.g., combating systemic lack of investment in Black communities. Canada has no such legislation. During the debate, the Americans told us that their guidelines and rules have had a negative impact because they set the bar too low. On the other hand, we heard Canadians saying that guidelines and thresholds were needed to get decision makers to agree to support equity goals with money. It was through this debate that we all agreed that we needed to find the sweet spot, i.e., set guidelines and thresholds in meaningful ways within a Canadian context, that could perhaps, be spread to the world afterward. This all came out of the in-person workshop and wouldn't have happened otherwise.

Do you have any additional leadership advice based on your own experiences or advice that you've received from someone else?

People did advise me to make sure that the partnership grant was what I wanted, and I do think that is an important question for people to ask themselves. For someone like me, who loves doing my own research, data analysis, report writing, and paper writing, I just don't get to do that as much as I used to. This dispersed portfolio project is a full-time job for multiple people, two staff and about half of my own time. It is a massive undertaking, and you need to have the resources there to do it, too.

Also, a partnership grant isn't a way to grow your own lab. My own team is resourced to do their work under the grant, but 90 percent of what comes in for the project goes out to others across the country. My leadership of the grant won't necessarily show up in conventional ways, like my Google Scholar page. So, you have to realize that you're making a trade-off to support other people and to have influence and benefit a common goal.

6.6 COLLEEN FLOOD: FORWARD THINKING AND SCENARIO PLANNING FOR POLICIES RELATED TO VACCINATION

Research Leader: Colleen M. Flood, University Research Chair and director, Centre for Health Law, Policy & Ethics, University of Ottawa

What does research leadership mean to you?

Research leadership means bringing people together and bringing disciplines together to solve difficult problems, and doing our very best to get our findings and recommendations out in a variety of ways.

What leadership situation will you share with readers?

I'm going to talk about a recent collaboration focused on vaccine passports and mandatory vaccination. It was co-led with my colleague Kumanan Wilson with funding from the Canadian COVID-19 Immunity Task Force.

What did you think and do in that situation?

Kumanan and I have been friends and collaborators for many years. He's an internal medicine specialist and holds the University of Ottawa Faculty of Medicine Clinical Research Chair in Digital Health Innovation. Early on in the pandemic, we both came to the realization that the topic of vaccine mandates was going to be important. Other people doubted that it would come to pass, but based on our reading, Kumanan's expertise in epidemiology, and my work on law and public health, we thought that vaccine passports and mandatory vaccination would likely be needed.

We wanted to get out there early with some forward thinking and scenario planning and write about the topic in a way that would get people thinking. The goal was to avoid a scramble or panic if policy had to be made. If it turned out that we really did need to roll out vaccine mandates and vaccine passports, then at least we would have planned for it.

Some among the health law community, which is my community, were a bit shocked that we were coming out and talking about the topic, and some criticized us for doing so. But we had done some earlier related work on the issue of vaccination and kids, and I'd been teaching a course called the law of modern-day plagues, so we had precursors that meant we had more expertise than many others to write on the topic. Also, Kumanan and I are both okay with ruffling feathers when needed. We're both at a fairly senior level and asked the question, "If we can't say what we think needs to happen, then who can?" For me it's a duty. I'm publicly funded for my work, and I have to try to improve the lives of Canadians as best as I can, with the resources that I've got.

We were really fortunate to have Bryan Thomas on the team as a senior research associate. Bryan is an outstanding writer and an expert in law and religion and has a background in philosophy as well, and he helped us bring in all these different disciplines to the table to make the research richer.

We set up Zoom meetings every 1 to 2 weeks so that we could actually see each other. Sometimes we would talk about the details of our work, other times we would just chew the fat about what is going on in the hospital world and in the legal scholarship world as a team with our graduate students. We all learned from each other through the very simple mechanism of having regular Zoom meetings.

What did you learn?

Working across disciplines was essential, and also joyful. I love to hear how other researchers from other disciplines think about questions and how they approach them. I always learn something. Sometimes you realize that there are different ways to think about things but also, interestingly, you often find that different disciplines approach topics in very similar ways. It makes you ask the questions "What can we say together?" and "How can we pool our expertise together to say something important?" I think working across disciplines really improves the research product at the end of the day.

But it's not always easy to find people from other disciplines that you connect with. It's a little bit like dating; if it doesn't work, well, then go try another. Eventually you'll find the right ones to click with. And it's worth it. Collaborations, like the ones I've had with Kumanan, have been the most powerful kind of experiences for me. You don't always have to be the best of friends with your collaborators, but you do need to trust each other and have a sense of each other's capacities. The best collaborations are where everybody lifts their weight without prompting. So, what I've learned is that you need to have really good connections within the team. If you don't have relationships, you have to build them in different ways. Sometimes it is about having dinner together, or having a coffee, or actually spending a little bit of time with them so that you see each other as people and not just folks that you send emails to.

Over the past year, people have come to realize that we were prescient in understanding that vaccine passports and vaccine mandates would need to be thought through. To balance thinking about the cost of precautions, we brought in thinking about the rights of people to health care and the right to not be infected. But even as people understood the value of our work, we were very careful to add caveats and emphasize that that our recommendations were based on the science of the moment and that they could be proven wrong in this fast-moving pandemic because things change quickly.

Years ago, I gave up thinking that my work would have an immediate impact, but I'm optimistic that the more high-quality research we put out there in different ways, the more we support good decision making. When there is an opportunity for a decision maker to make a difference, they will have the support of strong research evidence to do it. As researchers, we don't really know all the different constraints of the world that policymakers have to work within. So, if we can provide them with a buffet of evidence about important issues, over time we can make a difference.

Do you have any additional leadership advice based on your own experiences or advice that you've received from someone else?

I had a wonderful supervisor at the University of Toronto, Michael Trebilcock. His advice was that you have to be able to explain your thesis over a pint of beer. By the time the beer is finished – or pint of orange juice, if you prefer – you need to able to cogently explain to the person on the other side of the table what it is that you're doing, how you're doing it, and why you're doing it, i.e., how you think it could make a difference. I feel that he taught me that it is an art to make complex things simple. Going for clarity is a good test for whether there are gaps or problems in your own thinking. So that's my advice for graduate students – go to the pub.

Another piece of advice from another brilliant friend and colleague of mine is to avoid what she called "word salad." That refers to putting a lot of words together in a way that sounds superficially smart but doesn't actually mean anything. I've seen students do this, and researchers do it in grants, and it doesn't get you anywhere. It's like papier-mâché. Peer reviewers will sense it, and their views of the project will be diminished because you haven't used every word in the grant application with purpose.

From my personal experience, I have four additional pieces of advice:

- Sometimes making a difference as a researcher means stopping bad things from happening. In my case, trying to defend the public health care system against privatization. So, it may be that nothing much has changed based on your work, but in a way, that is a victory. Interpretation of the outcomes of research may need a little bit of nuance and thought.
- Do not take it personally if you apply for funding and don't get it. Our first application for the project I described above was not successful, so we tried again and were successful with the COVID-19 Immunity Task Force. For any competition, only a few people get funded. The most successful people dust themselves off and get back in there and reapply.
- Researchers need to know how to say no politely. This can be very difficult when you get excited about a lot of different things, and you see possibilities and prospects. But you have to be able to figure out when to say no in order to be able to enjoy your life and avoid working on something that really isn't what you love.
- If you can find one thing that you are really good at, then that is to be celebrated. Don't worry about the fact that you're not amazing at all the other parts of a researcher's role. Some people are great at knowledge translation, but others are much better at technical and analytical thinking, done alone by themselves. That is fine. People can work with others in the system as opposed to necessarily doing everything themselves. For me that is an insight not just for deans and for heads of departments, but for everyone to apply to themselves. As a researcher, you don't need to be all things to all people.

6.7 LORNA MACDONALD: CREATING AND LEADING TWO PRODUCTIONS OF A HISTORICALLY-BASED OPERA

Research Leader: Lorna MacDonald, Professor of Voice and Lois Marshall Chair in Voice Studies, Faculty of Music, University of Toronto

What does research leadership mean to you?

For me, research leadership is like other types of leadership; it is about accountability and responsibility. It means always being willing to take full responsibility for the successes and the failures of the work, and sometimes making tough decisions. Being a research leader requires you to be open to the fact that the process you have in mind will change and that you may even have to pivot from what you planned. As a research leader, you need to identify the best people to associate yourself with, the ones who can help with the work.

What leadership situation will you share with readers?

I led a Social Sciences and Humanities Research Council grant to write and produce *The Bells of Baddeck*, a large-scale historical music drama based on the lives of Mabel and Alexander Graham Bell. I'll talk about how I approached the first production, which premiered at Parks Canada's Alexander Graham Bell National Historic Site on July 3, 2015; what we learned; how that has changed; and how I'm leading work for an expanded and enhanced production scheduled for August 2, 2022, the centennial of Bell's death.

What did you think and do in that situation?

Back in 2013 when I got the grant, I knew that I had to build teams to do the work. I'm not sure I was aware of the importance of the choices I made at the time, but in retrospect, the teams were very clear and had specific functions. The first one was the Parks Canada team, which related to the community. That team focused on all the things that had to be in place when working with a federal agency. It was a huge learning curve.

Then there was the creative team, which was much easier for me. I went with people whose work I was familiar with and who I knew would value the story that I was telling. It took a long time to find people who would honor the story and feel passion for it, but when I found them, I knew they were the right ones.

Finally, there was the performance team. I wanted to create the best performance experience and opportunity for them that I could. As a performer myself, I know what it feels like to be treated well, and it was really important to me that we provide work for young artists at a high level. The teacher in me understood that *The Bells of Baddeck* was giving artists the opportunity to create new roles. These were roles about historical people who had lived, and their descendants would be attending the show. Our production was the first time that the Bell family had given permission for character representations of Alec and Mabel. So, we had to make sure that the performance team was being faithful to the family without taking away from the creative values. It was important to me to earn the family's trust and then, in turn, to have my cast earn their trust.

Another thing that I learned was to bring in outside expertise. For example, at first I wasn't aware that the University of Toronto would provide a financial officer to help, but when I learned about that resource, it made a huge difference. Similarly, my initial plan didn't include equity contracts for the lead performers (under the Canadian Actor's Equity Association), but I realized there was value in paying for the contractual expertise of others. Prior to *The Bells of Baddeck*, I had only signed contracts – never written them.

What did you learn?

I remember feeling alone when I got the grant, and wondering "Where do I start?" What I relied on was my performance background and a very clear vision of the outcome that I wanted. That allowed me to work back from the outcome and determine the procedural steps. The three very deliberate teams worked well. It took a lot of time to find the right people, but it was time well spent, and I'm doing that again for the second production.

The main learning, and difference for the second production, was not to focus only on bringing in people who understood what needed to be done, but to focus on finding people who can actually do the work. For the first production, I would take on anything because I felt it was all my responsibility. I even did the costume laundry when I couldn't find someone do it. For the second production, I'm finding people that can lead elements of the work and delegating to them. For the first production, I didn't know that there is a system in place at the university that can help me; now I know about it, and I'm taking advantage of that.

Another big lesson was the realization that there has to be something for everybody in the research. From the start, I knew the outcome I wanted, but over time I learned more about what the work meant for other people, not just what I envisioned. Just for example, we had to understand how the community perceived the production. It was when I got to know the leaders in the community, I realized that some people were reading a lot into the fact that it involved the federal government and Toronto. The singers were opera singers, so that didn't help with the perception that it was "sophisticated" and maybe not for local people. But coming from Cape Breton, I know that Cape Bretoners love singing and that they would come to the show once the word got out that it was really good. So, we organized events to give people exposure to the music and spread the information that "Yes, you can make out all the words," "Yes, it's in English," "No, you don't have to get dressed up." That was all a part of the process that I never anticipated.

Do you have any additional leadership advice based on your own experiences or advice that you've received from someone else?

People should know that there is tension as you go from leading something independently and owning it completely to expanding the work by involving other people. When you are doing it alone it can be overwhelming, but it is also easier to keep the artistic values and human values front and center. It's hard to let go, especially when you've had success running things based on your approach. That is something that has been, and remains, a conflict for me.

You also have to know from the outset that, whatever your creativity is, there will be criticism. You want to please people, but not everybody will value what you do. My advice in those cases is to maintain your highest standards. Let the criticisms fall away as best you can because the highest outcome you first envisioned is likely where your best idea was.

Leadership in research is essentially teaching – your team, yourself, and your community. My background as both a performer and a teacher gave me a strong personal foundation for the research project.

6.8 KIM MCGRAIL: LAUNCHING A NEW PAN-CANADIAN NETWORK

Research leader: Kimberlyn McGrail, chief executive officer and scientific director, Health Data Research Network Canada; scientific director, Population Data BC; and director of research, University of British Columbia Health

What does research leadership mean to you?

Research leadership is about helping the whole be greater than the sum of the parts. It is about connecting and drawing out strengths and helping people see how working together could achieve a larger objective. It is facilitation ... and bushwhacking. I favor research leadership that makes space for others to take ownership and control of the areas that they can. It is a kind of shared leadership that relies on a lot of trust in the capabilities, capacities, and outcomes of other people.

What leadership situation will you share with readers?

In October 2018, I was principal investigator of the team awarded $39 million from the CIHR to create a data platform under Canada's Strategy for Patient-Oriented Research. Our team had worked together on a proposal for a pan-Canadian data platform for years, but the moment we heard that we had been awarded the grant marked the beginning of a new phase. I'm going to talk about the first steps we took to use that funding to create Health Data Research Network Canada (HDRN Canada).

What did you think and do in that situation?

The first reaction when we heard that we were funded was pure excitement, and that immediately led to a feeling of responsibility. The whole team recognized the importance of getting this opportunity right, because we knew that there would not be another similar opportunity for years. We felt like it was our chance to make a difference in the space of multiregional research and related topics, like Indigenous data sovereignty and public engagement. That quickly brought me and the team into an operational frame of mind.

On a practical level, one of the first things I realized was that I needed to have a staff person to help with the funding agreement and other administrative and start-up requirements. At that point, it was really important to have someone that I had worked with in the past, whom I could trust to understand what was being asked of them, and who would seek clarification when they had questions. We weren't in a position to hire the operations director at that time; that came a few months later. What I needed at the start was someone who would help lay the groundwork for what later became the operations director and other roles. The person had to have strong communications skills, oral and written, and be comfortable presenting this brand-new project out in the world.

Another thing that I did was establish regular meetings of what ultimately became our executive committee and formalized leads for elements of the work. The entire HDRN Canada team recognizes that the success of this particular network depends on everybody in the network, and everybody holding together in a certain way. So, I fundamentally felt that it was important to spread the leadership roles and capabilities across the team, with a collective and, as much as possible, consensus voice.

What did you learn?

It's not that everything has gone perfectly, but in terms of our fundamental approach, there isn't anything that I'd do differently in the future. I think this is because, from the start, we have all been willing to revisit, reconsider, rejig, redo, and adjust. It's not a matter of "change management" of our plan. I believe that we should be constantly evolving in the way we do things, and that change is a function of what we're doing. The context is changing, the opportunities are changing, and we have to adapt to that.

Also, I remember distinctly a conversation when members of our executive committee told me that it is good and fine to work with and toward consensus, but in the end, somebody has to be in charge in a network that is large and diverse like HDRN Canada. There have been times when I have been on the receiving end of an autocratic leadership style. I really didn't like it, and I don't think it works in the academic space, particularly when we're talking about a network of people who are leaders in their own right, in their own circumstances. So, I've learned it is important to constantly balance consensus-focused work with the fact that decisions do need to be made, and sometimes the research leader will be the final arbiter.

Another thing that I learned was how important it is to establish principles up front. Long before we were awarded funding, we completed the "forming" and "storming" stages of team development. For us, the outcome was a common view of what was needed and agreement on the contributions that different centers and individuals would make to HDRN Canada. We paid a lot of attention to the principle of equitable distribution of funds; in our proposal. This doesn't mean completely equal distribution of funds; it means a commitment to using grant funding to level up and build capacity, understanding the different needs and contexts of small versus large data-holding organizations and northern versus urban sites. Another principle was that we would take and include data-holding organizations as they came and not require them to adopt specific policies or practices in order to be part of HDRN Canada. These principles gave us a big head start when we were funded because they gave us the foundation and trust to work through challenges.

Do you have any additional leadership advice based on your own experiences or advice that you've received from someone else?

Early in my independent researcher career, I was speaking to Jerry Hurley about changes we were thinking of making to our research plan after we received funding. He told me, "Kim, if you use your CIHR grant to do exactly what you wrote in your proposal, then you have learned nothing along the way." This was very helpful advice. It gave me the permission and freedom to make changes that benefit research projects, and, as I mentioned above, I now see change as a function of research.

As a leader, you can get into situations where you're proposing new work that seems to be so closely tied to the organization you represent that it looks like a conflict of interest or self-promotion. In those cases, it helps to change the conversation to a discussion of *what* is needed rather than *who* will do the work. Once the function or outcome is agreed on, then you can come back to deciding which organizations and people have the skills and capacity to do the work.

You can do a lot of work virtually through web meetings, but something special and different happens during discussions that you have in person, or when you have a beer or a meal with someone. Leaders need to be aware of that.

A final point is that when you're working on something as large and complex as a pan-Canadian network, there will be days when it feels like the work is so complicated with so much going on that it's hard to imagine how you'll move the needle. That's why it's important to step back and take stock of what you have accomplished. For HDRN Canada, when we bring together summary information for CIHR or our board, it highlights just how much parallel work is going on, and it is all work that would not be happening in the absence of HDRN Canada. The HDRN Canada executive's and my talent is about holding all of those pieces together, making sure that we understand the intersections and connections among the pieces, so that individuals can do their focused specialist work without having to worry about the details of how it will fit into the bigger picture.

6.9 MICHAEL SCHULL: WHEN A CLINICIAN SCIENTIST IS THE CEO OF A RESEARCH INSTITUTE WITH MORE THAN 200 STAFF

Research Leader: Michael J. Schull, chief executive officer, ICES, and professor, Department of Medicine, University of Toronto

What does research leadership mean to you?

Leadership means responsibility and accountability for something, whether you are a soccer coach or the president of an organization. As a research leader, you might be responsible for a research project, a research program, a research team, or a research institute or some aspect of it. As the scale and scope of what research leaders are responsible for increases, they often have to let go of their personal research agendas and running individual research studies. Research leadership becomes about the leadership work in itself and a broader view of what constitutes success.

What leadership situation will you share with readers?

Beginning in fall 2013, I became chief executive officer (CEO) of ICES (formerly the Institute for Clinical Evaluative Sciences), an independent not-for-profit research institute with more than 200 staff and seven sites across the province of Ontario, Canada. ICES encompasses a community of research, data, and clinical experts and a secure and accessible array of Ontario's health-related data. ICES's mission is to translate data into trusted evidence that makes policy and health care better and people healthier.

What did you think and do in that situation?

One of the things that I reflected on early was how privileged I was to have the opportunity to be the leader of ICES. For any role worth having, there will always be stiff competition. Whether or not there is a fixed term, people don't typically stay in a single research leadership role for decades, so I also saw it as a time-limited privilege. That helps to focus the mind on what you want to achieve. I was inspired by an interview of Dr. David Naylor when he became president of the University of Toronto in 2005. I recall him saying that he wanted to focus his presidency on the undergraduate student experience. It struck me as a very strategic thing to single out and focus on one very important goal even though the job obviously included many other responsibilities.

At that time, ICES's work with Indigenous Communities and organizations was relatively new and relied a lot on personal relationships with individuals at ICES. I realized that we had to build upon and institutionalize those relationships to build trust with ICES as an organization more broadly. To be clear, that didn't mean that I was going to be at the center of the work. It was about assembling teams and empowering them while demonstrating CEO-level and organizational commitment to the partnerships with First Nations, Inuit, and

Métis organizations and developing ways of working with Indigenous Communities more broadly. Though I've singled out this topic,
in a lot of ways my early leadership of ICES was focused on building
teams for all of ICES's work and trying to give them what they needed
to succeed.

What did you learn?

I think research leaders often come into CEO jobs based on their successes leading large grants and research programs, but that's not the
same as leading an organization. Research accomplishments and scientific "street cred" are essential, but research leadership requires a
completely different mindset than what I think many researchers are
used to. Just, for example, as the leader of a research institute you
have to understand the ambition of the whole institute, the role of
the board of directors, and relationships with funders and other
key stakeholders. You need to learn how to manage teams and individuals, budget development and financial accountability, and the
distinction between a research grant to study a topic and a contract
that binds your organization to do specific things. As a research leader,
you have to pretty quickly identify what your gaps and weaknesses
are – everyone has them – and figure out how to account for those. In
some cases, you might seek additional training, but more typically,
and in my case, it was about assembling a team that fills those gaps
and understands the business of the research institute. You also want
to build excitement and opportunity across the organization to try to
make it a magnet for great people.

   To start, team development might focus on addressing operational
issues and getting the mechanics of the organization running well,
but the bigger question is what is the organization as a whole trying
to achieve? What's our strategy? What are our priorities? The whole
strategic planning cycle – including developing ICES's mission, vision, and values – which I think some people see as bureaucracy, was
actually an important process to go through. Research institutes need
a practical strategy that identifies key domains of work and achievable
objectives within those domains. If you develop the strategy in a way
that is inclusive, so that people shape and see themselves in the plan,
it can be a very effective tool. I'm proud of ICES's 2020/21–2022/23

strategic plan, in particular. It includes commitments to topics like public engagement and innovation in data science that show how ICES has evolved and grown over time. And to be clear, those were not just my ideas. As a CEO, I think you need to attract the smartest, best people you can, give them clear guidance on what you want to achieve, and largely stay out of their way as they come up with and implement ideas. That's how you are most likely to succeed. It's not going to be because you have all the answers.

Do you have any additional leadership advice based on your own experiences or advice that you've received from someone else?

As mentioned earlier, I recommend picking a small number of key big-picture things to move the dial on, in addition to fulfilling all the regular responsibilities of the leader's role. I think when you start as the leader of a research organization, you need to figure out whether it will be "steady as she goes" leadership or more transformative change. Maybe there's some fundamental risk or threat that you need to take on. I think we have had some of those in the past few years, and I needed to figure out how to clarify what transformation we wanted to achieve and bring together everyone that is needed (the team, partners, and stakeholders) to codevelop the vision of the transformation so that they buy in and embrace it. And then there is the work to operationalize that vision – getting from A to B in terms of where you are now and where you want or need your organization to be.

Some advice that I've shared with others, and benefited from myself, is the idea that if you really want to be loved by everybody all the time, a leadership role probably isn't for you. Sometimes leaders need to dive in and intervene when they see friction in relationships or an issue developing, no matter how hard or uncomfortable it feels. Sometimes you have to stick your neck out to address an issue.

And there is always going to be someone who thinks you're doing the wrong thing, or someone who is opposed to what you're doing, and will let you know. There are days when it's demoralizing, days when you question whether you are doing the right things. At those times, and really always, it's important that leaders reach out to trusted mentors and advisors, but also have faith in their own instincts. There have been times where I've learned things the hard way because I trusted someone else's instincts instead of my own and ended up making a mistake.

A few other pieces of advice that I hope are helpful are that a sense of humor is a huge asset in any leadership role; be willing to acknowledge your mistakes when they happen; you can never have too many mentors and advisors; and if you feel like you're overcommunicating something, it's probably just the right amount of communication. Research leaders need to be available and responsive. It takes courage and stamina to be a research leader, but research leadership matters.

6.10 BARBARA SHERWOOD LOLLAR: UNDERSTANDING THAT RESEARCH OPERATIONS ARE FUNDAMENTALLY ENTREPRENEURIAL

Research Leader: Barbara Sherwood Lollar, Canada Research Chair, Dr. Norman Keevil Chair in Ore Deposits Geology, and professor, Department of Earth Sciences, University of Toronto

What does research leadership mean to you?

In a single word, research leadership is community. Frankly, the most rewarding part of being a researcher comes from community interactions, volunteering, and getting involved on the leadership side of research. In the long term, research leadership is about what you leave behind. As I've spoken with other research leaders over the years, they always say the people are what they remember and value the most. Research leadership is not just about the big papers, grants, or even big discoveries. If you're getting into the research game, you are doing so because you are a people person.

What leadership situation will you share with readers?

I'm going to speak about how the foundational base of successful research in science and engineering is fundamentally entrepreneurial. And I don't mean entrepreneurial in terms of commercial contract work done by academic researchers, or patenting, or the creation of start-up companies, though those can all be part of how researchers are entrepreneurial. I'm talking about the role of a professor in acting like an entrepreneur to secure funds for their research vision. From that perspective, even pure academic research is entrepreneurial in its nature.

For example, as a proud researcher of the University of Toronto, I am grateful to receive my salary, physical space for my research team (including heat, electricity, etc.), and access to the library, computer power, and other university resources. But, beyond those basics, I am responsible for securing funding for everything else in my lab, from the half-a-million-dollar mass spectrometer to the paper clips. Similarly, I have to find funding for the 10 to 15 people that are in my lab at any given time, including postdoctoral fellows, technicians, research associates, and students. While scholarship funding does exist, the majority of the funds for the support and research these people do is not raised by the University of Toronto; I need to do that. So, as professors we need to write grants and proposals for funding agencies all over the world in order to lead the research that is a core element of our jobs.

I jokingly refer to this model using a Tim Horton's franchise analogy. My point is that, just like franchisees, research leaders need to run small businesses and bring in revenue. We have a role in job creation, with leaders in the sciences and engineering groups bringing in millions of dollars of revenue each year, most of which is used to pay salaries and student stipends. I think it is important to talk about the need for researchers to secure their own research funding because some young professors do not understand the very nature of the career they are choosing.

What do you recommend that early career researchers do?

New and early career faculty need to understand that they will arrive at their jobs with teaching obligations and an expectation that, within 3 years or so, they will be ready for their preliminary evaluation for tenure. So, the real name of the game for new faculty is to quickly secure research funding that will allow them to show some results. For Canadian sciences and engineering funding, I think we do support that quite well through programs like the National Sciences and Engineering Research Council (NSERC) Discovery grants. NSERC

Discovery is a gem of a program. The grant funding amounts are not large, but the grants are very effective because (a) they are completely blue sky and don't constrain research in any way, (b) they provide a stable level of base funding for 5 years, and (c) they focus on early career researchers. That's why I always say that NSERC Discovery grants are like intellectual venture capital.

As good as NSERC Discovery grants and their equivalents are, they were never intended to support researchers' entire research programs and long-term goals. Faculty need to diversify their funding and go after lots of grants. That does not mean scattershot applications. I always recommend that new faculty do the following three things, which may seem obvious, but in my experience are not done consistently:

1 Read every single part of the competition instructions and submit exactly what the guidelines tell you to submit. Understand what the competition is seeking and fulfill everything.
2 Get coaching and seek mentoring. Talk to as many people as you can who have written those kinds of grants before or who have served on review panels for them. Ask for advice, and also ask if anyone is willing to share a successful grant application that you can use as a model for what you submit. If or when you are asked to be part of a review panel, say yes (though this may not happen in the first few years) because it is an excellent way to learn how the systems works and how grants are scored and selected for funding.
3 Don't just go after the same pots of money that you see the people around you are applying for. Branch out, and work to secure a diverse portfolio of funding. Just like an investment portfolio, you want some proposals focused on funding for projects that you know you can deliver on, and others that are higher risk or have some high-risk elements.

What have you learned?

It is important to say yes if you are asked to be on a review panel, not just because it helps you understand what makes for a successful proposal, but because our entire research community runs on people who volunteer to review grant applications and manuscripts and serve as editors for journals. It is a massive infusion of people power into the system and the basis of peer review. But most importantly, for new faculty, actually being involved as a member of your community is a big part of your personal success strategy. A classic mistake that people make is believing they need to say no more. Instead, I advise students and early career researchers that they need to learn how to say yes to the right things.

I hear some people advising early career researchers that they need to focus on just one thing so that others in the research community have a clear sense of who they are. Personally, I don't think that's true. Of course, researchers shouldn't overextend themselves, but it is important to do different strategic things. There are peaks and troughs in research funding. If you have a diverse portfolio, you are more likely to be able to weather the changes and keep your team rich and productive even if funding becomes scarce in some areas. It is about making strategic decisions about the multiple research areas you will focus on.

Do you have any additional leadership advice based on your own experiences or advice that you've received from someone else?

Foremost, I think we need to spread the message that researchers are entrepreneurs to everyone, not just early career faculty. Canadian universities are mostly funded with public dollars, so the public should understand what university-based researchers do. In particular, I think it would help if more people understood the role of university professors in job creation.

I also think is important that early career researchers not only do great work, but that they are seen as doing great work. If you are the kind of person that works hard and assumes people will know you are working hard, that probably isn't going to be enough. I let young folks know that they should not wait until their third year to make a good impression on the people who are going to be evaluating them for tenure. Nobody wants to be the person who runs around blowing their own horn all the time, but everyone should be doing small and subtle things, like short hallway conversations about new papers, research findings, and promising new students. My advice isn't to hide things that aren't going well. But it's not a good idea to wait until you have a problem to resolve to talk to the people that will be evaluating you. You want a trickle of good news too.

That's true for everyone, but it is even more important if you are one or more degrees different from the perceived norm or stereotype of what a university researcher is. There are many papers and studies about the "Matilda Effect," which is a bias against acknowledging the achievements of women scientists whose work is instead attributed to their male colleagues. I think that if you differ from the norm not only in gender but in other intersectional ways, the risk is even greater due to ongoing issues of implicit bias, and some people won't perceive you as the driver of research excellence, particularly if you are part of a team. So, it's not enough to hope or assume your great work will be recognized. It's a really proactive and defensive strategy to make sure that the good work that you are doing is seen, and that people understand that you are the driving force and vision behind it.

Overall, academic researchers have to be incredibly entrepreneurial because what you end up doing is very much driven by what you can securing funding for. It's exciting because it means that we really are, to a large degree, our own intellectual bosses. But it is tough, too, because it means we spend an extraordinary amount of time writing grant proposals or nurturing partnerships with other professors, other institutions, or industry or not-for-profits, all to secure funds for our research visions.

6.11 MOLLY SHOICHET: SUPPORTING STUDENTS IN LEARNING THEIR OWN LESSONS

Research Leader: Molly S. Shoichet, University Professor, Michael E. Charles Professor in Chemical Engineering, and associate chair, Graduate Studies, Chemical Engineering and Applied Chemistry, University of Toronto

What does research leadership mean to you?

Whether someone is a corporate leader or research leader, leadership is about inspiring others to achieve excellence and to achieve their goals. A research leader isn't like a king or queen that gives out instructions and expects people to follow them. Research leadership is about having people who will engage with your ideas, and work with you to develop those ideas.

What leadership situation will you share with readers?

I'm going to speak about a situation where two of my brilliant graduate students wanted to try something that we had never done in the lab before.

What did you think and do in that situation?

The details of the research aren't important, but in brief, the students wanted to bring something called "environmental enrichment" into studies that we were performing as part of our stroke research. I knew that environmental enrichment was important, but I was concerned that our lab did not have the capacity to do it. So, I tried to convince the students not to try it. But they were persistent, and at the end of the day, I funded and supported the research that they wanted to do.

What did you learn?

Unfortunately, I was right, and the students weren't able to integrate environmental enrichment into our research. I wasn't happy that they failed, but just from a learning perspective, it was fantastic. They learned so much more by trying and failing than they ever would have learned by me convincing them not to do it. In research, we are constantly trying to advance knowledge, and I always tell people the reason why research takes so long is because we fail most of the time. So, what we mostly learn is how to pick ourselves up after we fail and keep going.

In the situation above, I was right, but there have been many other times when I've been wrong. For example, there was a situation where some students wanted to try making hydrogels with lipid nanoparticles in them, and, for the students' approach to work, the lipid nanoparticles would have had to exit the hydrogels. I thought their strategy was fundamentally flawed and that the particles would stay immobilized in our hydrogels. But again, I let the students try their idea, and in that case, they proved me completely wrong. As a research leader, there can be situations where you disprove your own hypotheses, and you need to have the confidence in yourself to be proven wrong.

There are so many reasons why research can fail. For example, it can be because you don't have the right tools or knowledge, in which case you try to address those deficits by bringing in tools or collaborating with others. It may be that you don't have the capacity to do the work, or that the tools you need don't exist yet, or maybe you started with a flawed idea. In those cases, you can't repeatedly beat your head against a wall; you need to take what you have learned and move on and try something different. And whether your original hypothesis was right or wrong, you advance knowledge, which is core to what we do as researchers.

Do you have any additional leadership advice based on your own experiences or advice that you've received from someone else?

When I was a graduate student, I had an advisor who played a lot of tennis and would say that research is all about "returning the serve." Thirty years later, I still think of the analogy of research being about staying in the game. I encourage my students to get a PhD because it opens up so many opportunities for them, and it's not easy to go back and get a PhD once you start working. Once they've got their degree, staying in the game means continuing to use the intellectual capacity that they have developed, whether it is in industry, government, or in academia.

My last piece of advice is about collaboration. For us, it is critical because we need brain power from other people in order to work on the really complex questions that we're trying to answer. We always collaborate with people who bring in complementary skills and ideas, and we look for people who are trying to answer the same, or similar, questions. We collaborate with lots of people – from biologists who do basic science to surgeons – in many different fields, including regenerative medicine, cancer, and small molecule drug design. Our collaborators are fantastic people, intellectually and in terms of being awesome people to work with. What's so wonderful in research is that you can be intellectually curious and, if you can convince others that you've got a good idea and you've got the capacity to execute that good idea, then you get to fulfill those dreams.

In closing, I think of research as inventing the future. To do that, we need to take risks and bring in the best minds in order to succeed and, when we fail, have the confidence to try again.

6.12 ARJUMAND SIDDIQI: CONTRIBUTING AS A RESEARCHER WHEN YOU'RE NOT CERTAIN THAT YOU'RE RIGHT

Research Leader: Arjumand Siddiqi, Canada Research Chair in Population Health Equity and associate professor, Dalla Lana School of Public Health, University of Toronto

What does research leadership mean to you?

I've always been a little cautious about thinking about myself as a leader, and it's not because of modesty. My dad is an academic, and from what I observed with him while growing up, I see science as a non-hierarchical scenario where the job of the people who are ostensibly in charge is to guide the people who are in the starting phases of their careers. So, I'm not sure "research leadership" is a meaningful term for me. But, if it is anything, I might say research leadership is the nurturing of people and ideas. It's about what you do in order to facilitate people becoming what they want to become. It's also about coming outside of your own skin and your own narrow area of expertise to think and talk about the field, the discipline, and the society in which we are embedded, to help people think about issues going forward.

What leadership situation will you share with readers?

I'm going to talk about two situations I'm involved in, where I'm not certain that my understanding of the situation is correct. The first has to do with the fact that it is very hard to get funding for equity-focused research even when you have a strong record of scholarly publications.

The second is about the practice of community engagement for research focused on race or race-based data.

What did you think and do in that situation?

In the case of the lack of funding for equity-focused research, I think that the issue might be a combination of a shortage of people with expertise who can be on review panels and the fact that the people who are reviewers are also everyday citizens and may not be intellectually or politically oriented to understand or endorse the importance of equity research. But I could be wrong about that. There could also be purposefulness about the neglect of equity research or the way that it's been handled in funding. And it matters what's happening, because if it is an accidental constellation of a number of factors, it could be fairly easy to initiate a conversation about change. On the other hand, if funders don't think there is a problem, or aren't open to change, nobody – including me – wants to spend their time screaming from the mountaintop to no effect. So, for now, I'm raising the issue in public forums and trying to get a conversation going.

On the second topic, there has been a lot of recent discourse about community engagement in order to use race and race-based data. Many of my very close friends and colleagues are very much in favor of this. Personally, I don't know that it's always the best way to go. I worry that we might be setting an expectation that academics partner with communities or other organizations for every single research project, even for projects where the data being used have already been collected through a consented process. I don't think that would be right because it privileges questions that seem to immediately translate into action for those communities and organizations (or at least questions for which communities and organizations perceive the research as readily translatable to action). My concern is that there are other big important questions that aren't politically expedient or that won't result in a program tomorrow. These include questions about large structural forces and major policy issues. And I think there is a risk that those kinds of fundamental questions can fall by the wayside because no community member or organization is going to sign up to do that kind of research. It will seem far too removed from everyday reality. And yet, these are often the most fundamental issues affecting the health of those communities. For example, what if you wanted to study white supremacy? Or income inequality? These studies hold little promise of changing these issues. Rather, they will interrogate them and establish what is happening and who is responsible. And if you, as an academic, can't change things, does that mean you shouldn't study them? That seems like an awfully misguided notion, and one that demonstrates very little understanding of how societies work. Structural forces of society are simply not moved by single academic studies. So, I struggle with that a bit, but I'm also not sure that I'm right, particularly in the Canadian context where I sense there is a commitment to community-partnered research for health. For this topic, I've had to reflect on how I might be wrong and, even if I am right, have a little humility and support my colleagues who clearly see community partnerships as being important.

What did you learn?

When you agree to get involved in an issue or a project, it's very important that you begin by making sure that you, yourself, understand what you think is happening. And I'm being very careful in saying "what you think" is happening because, just like in science, there can be alternative explanations and interpretations. I feel like I can often make good guesses, but that isn't the same as being certain.

This way of thinking doesn't just apply to the two situations described above. I'm often called on to talk to various audiences about equity. Sometimes that takes the shape of talking about race, ethnicity, and data collection. Sometimes it takes the shape of talking about the substantive research in these areas. And sometimes it's because people who focus on a particular method or topic area, such as artificial intelligence, need a lens of equity. In those cases, the first thing I've had to figure out is where it makes sense for me to be a part of a conversation. Showing up for the conversation is no small part of this, because you can't be a part of every single endeavor where someone needs an equity person. You need to make decisions about what to prioritize. And when I do get involved, a lot of thought has to go into figuring out what I can tell the audience before me that will help them understand the issues in ways that are actionable, or at least explains what I think is happening.

I don't want to be someone who just shows up and states what my opinion is. No organization should change what it is doing solely based on any one person's opinion. But for some of the groups that I work with, they may not be speaking to anyone else about equity. So, what I try to do, in the media and at events, is to be very clear and systematic about my analysis of the situation and distinguish between topics when I'm comfortable presenting my understanding of what's happening and topics where there is more uncertainty.

Do you have any additional leadership advice based on your own experiences or advice that you've received from someone else?

I've had a lot of fantastic mentors, which is probably common for people who find themselves in leadership roles. One that I'm thinking of, in particular, is Clyde Hertzman, who passed away, too soon, in 2012. He was a giant in population health work and an incredibly generous scholar in terms of nurturing people. He told me that he always works with people he likes because it makes the work better. That always stuck out for me, and I do try to prioritize spending time with people I enjoy, and it makes for better ideas and better work.

I also credit Clyde with the fact that my students have often told me that they feel like colleagues with me. It isn't just that they see me as a colleague, it's that they can tell that I also feel that way about them. Clyde believed that you can always learn something, and you have no idea whom you are going to learn it from. It could be the taxi driver. It could be the CEO. So, he would engage with the people he encountered and give them his full attention. It wasn't just that he wanted to make them feel good; he wanted to soak in everything they had to say. And that's stuck with me; I want to soak the whole world in and learn from everyone around me.

6.13 ZAÏNA SORÉ: WORKING WITH PARTNERS TO TAKE RESEARCH INTO PRACTICE

Research Leader: Sougrynoma Zaïnatou Soré, head, Capacity Development Office, International Institute for Tropical Agriculture, Ibadan, Nigeria

What does research leadership mean to you?

Research is about rigor and using the right methods to collect and analyze data. Research leadership is about stretching ourselves to be curious and doing things differently. It is about being open to different inputs, and even surprises.

What leadership situation will you share with readers?

I'm going to speak about a project that I led that included many partners and both research and program design elements.

What did you think and do in that situation?

The project started with a scoping study of value chains, a skills gaps assessment, and an analysis of youth employment and potential youth employment in the agricultural sector in the states of Ogun and Plateau in Nigeria. The research component was focused on mapping the value chains of rice, casava, yam, and maize and looking at private-sector organizations and potential for youth employment. Based on that research, with our partners, we designed training programs that would directly meet the needs of labor markets. It was a very interesting process because we had to work back from research findings and a research database and translate those into effective training programs that had a more practical and pragmatic focus.

The core team required a lot of expertise and was large. We had researchers and people who were experts in value chains, socioeconomics, economists in education, the technical team, people from the Nigerian National Board of Technical Education, and the donor (Deutsche Gesellschaft für Internationale Zusammenarbeit). So, the core team meetings had 12 to 13 people at them, and as many as 25 people at stakeholder validation meetings.

What did you learn?

It took some time before we got to a level where everyone on the core team could understand each other and actually work very smoothly.

The issue was that the consortium had formed before we joined the project as researchers, so we had to go back and forth many times to understand the expectations of different groups and what each party was bringing to the table. There were many moving pieces and information coming in bit by bit, even as we moved into the implementation of the project. A lot of frustrations came out of that. So, if I were to do such a program again with so many actors, I would start with a workshop just for the actors to get to know each other and state their expectations, so we could design the program together based on what everyone needed.

The other thing I learned was about how important it is to take research, and the outputs derived from research, and turn them into blueprints that people can copy and use in other development projects. We were trying to design something that could help the National Board of Technical Education to reform or raise the quality of technical education and from a data-driven, science-backed perspective. So, translating the outputs of the research and fieldwork into something that technicians could also understand was important. I think this – finding ways to write science in a way that people who are not scientific can use it and apply it – is important in science overall. Unfortunately, a lot of research outputs can sit on shelves because they aren't really understood by end users. For this project, it took a lot of work and several versions of the documents to get it right. We would create documents and share them and ask people, "How do you understand it?" or "What's the story you want to get out of this?" It was really important to have everybody involved, from the technicians to researchers. Researchers can be narrow and focused in our ways of thinking, and that can make it difficult for somebody that thinks outside of the box to feel like they are valued. We had to make room for everybody's opinions. There was a very interesting mix of people with different experiences, different backgrounds, and different perspectives. So, yes, we had to have academic rigor, but we also had to be open minded and respect non-academic views just as much as the research outcomes. We had to rework the document several times, but through that we got something that everyone was satisfied with.

I really enjoyed coordinating the project and learning from the different partners that were involved in it.

Do you have any additional leadership advice based on your own experiences or advice that you've received from someone else?

When I first took on this leadership position at the International Institute for Tropical Agriculture 3 years ago, my supervisor told me if somebody gives you advice, say "thank you." Whoever gave you the advice took their time to think about the challenge that you're facing and talk to you. So, even if you aren't going to apply their solution, or if it was something you knew already, or if you think is a bad idea, thank them for their suggestions. There may be a time in the future when you will need their advice, and if you don't express gratitude and appreciation, they may not offer it. I think this is important advice about human connections in research and humility in research leaders. Research leadership is more than just doing good research; you have to respect your collaborators and let them know that their opinions are valued.

The second piece of advice is that research leaders need to continue to build their skills, including soft skills. For example, the project management training that I obtained helped unlock some of the challenges I was facing with coordinating programs. Research leadership is a craft. Skills beyond core research are critical to being successful as a research leader.

6.14 SHARON STRAUS: USING RESEARCH SKILLS AND METHODS TO ACHIEVE CHANGE

Research Leader: Sharon Straus, Professor of Geriatric Medicine, University of Toronto; geriatrician, Tier 1 Canada Research Chair in Knowledge Translation and Quality of Care; and physician-in-chief, St. Michael's Hospital–Unity Health Toronto

What does research leadership mean to you?

Whether it is in health care, or research, or some other sector, I think leadership is about having a moral compass and sticking to your core values and principles. As a research leader, you cocreate a vision and work with others to achieve it. My vision is to improve outcomes for patients and impact the health care system. That vision determines how I pick projects, whom I work with, and what I decide not to work on.

Research leaders need to always stay true to their values and beliefs. As a research leader, you should feel good about what you're doing and believe in what you're doing. This has been a thread throughout my career. For me, it is what research leadership is about. Research leaders should be role models by demonstrating how we use our privilege and leveraging our skills to answer questions that are messy and are causing distress for people in society.

Research leadership is also about building capacity and supporting others in developing their own research pathways. Being an effective research leader means that you support and mentor other researchers and create opportunities for them, so that they can achieve their own research goals.

What leadership situation will you share with readers?

I'm going to speak about how I realized that I needed to do more to increase diversity and inclusivity at my research institute, and how I used my research skills to initiate change.

What did you think and do in that situation?

Years ago, after I presented to an audience of researchers and physicians about a national research initiative I was leading, a woman from the audience came up to tell me that I was the first woman clinician scientist that she had met at my institute. When she had been recruited as a physician early career researcher to our institute, she had been given a list of many people to meet with, but there had not been a single woman on the list. Apart from me, she said that she hadn't met any women who were both physicians and scientists since joining the institute.

It really made me sad to think about her experience, and how I might have normalized the situation because I was used to being one of a handful of women in meetings and was used to experiencing inequities in my own career path. And I was not looking beyond my own research program. My research team is large, often has more women than men, and is very diverse with respect to research discipline, career stage, ethnicity, and language. My team also works hard on being truly inclusive, making sure that people's voices are heard in research and that everyone is included in every step along the way.

But hearing the experience of the physician early career researcher made me think that I had become too insular. I hadn't really been noticing what was happening outside of my team within the research institute, and I hadn't been making the pathway easier for others outside of those in my professional networks by taking leadership on this issue and trying to effect change.

At the time, I didn't have a leadership role beyond my own research program. The experience of the woman who had approached me disturbed me and made me think about how I might have contributed to what she experienced or how I failed in my role as a researcher at the institute. I know that I'm very privileged as a white woman in academics and being a physician scientist. Her story helped me realize that I needed to use my privilege to address diversity and inclusivity issues outside my team and professional networks. Talking about inequity isn't sufficient; action (including using privilege and social capital) is needed to effect change.

I started by looking at the local data on our research institute because while people remember the stories, it is important to start with the data. With colleagues from my research team, we looked at data by gender, race, job descriptions, and financial support. We used a sequential mixed-methods approach, gathered and analyzed quantitative and qualitative data, and presented it to the research institute's leadership. We then presented it at research rounds within the institution.

Several changes were initiated, including formal search processes for all positions, including standardized, transparent guidelines. A research equity committee was developed within the research institute. A commitment was made by the research leadership to monitor recruitment and align with the Dimensions Canada requirements. Mentorship was also facilitated with implementation of mentorship workshops for scientists to build capacity. Recognizing the need to explore the intersection with the university, our team subsequently built on this work to conduct a similar initiative across the Department of Medicine, University of Toronto. This led to the creation of a new portfolio, vice chair, mentorship, equity and diversity, in which data were used to drive change within the department.

What did you learn?

I learned that we can use our research skills to achieve change. I don't believe that we would have got the traction that we achieved on diversity and inclusivity at our institute without the data and analyses we presented. Our methods, expertise, and scientific credibility helped convince the institute's leadership that we had a problem that needed to be addressed.

More generally, over the years, I have learned that if something bothers you as a research leader, you should try to use your research skills to do something about it. There have been individual patient and caregiver experiences that led me to take on new projects, and this also happened during the pandemic in response to the inequities experienced by groups and communities. I think that it is good for research leaders to take on projects based on feelings of anger, or anxiety, or moral distress. As research leaders, we are incredibly privileged in that we can use our skills to shed light on issues, or develop interventions, or tackle complex questions in ways that many other people in society cannot do because they don't have the infrastructure.

Do you have any additional leadership advice based on your own experiences or advice that you've received from someone else?

One of the things I learned from my mentor, David Sackett, is that people are loyal to other people, not institutions. I've always enjoyed the places where I have worked, not because of the buildings or facilities, but because of the people. That's why it is so important to build and nurture relationships with the people you work with. It keeps you energized and connected.

I've also been influenced by Dave's speaking and writing about "compulsory retirement for experts." The idea is that experts must step aside in order to make room for the next generation of researchers and their ideas to flourish. I've noticed that some people struggle with stepping aside, perhaps not realizing how well it reflects on them as mentors to have their mentees do great work independently. Regardless, I think we have an obligation to make way and create opportunities for others. If we don't, people stay in the same roles and things stagnate, and where's the fun in that? I think one of the most important things about being a good mentor is giving opportunities to others and knowing when to step aside.

It's also important that mentors do more than support individual researchers. They also need to advocate for mentorship within their research institutes and programs. This means advocating for mentorship and encouraging and rewarding mentors, for example, by having mentorship be part of promotion packages.

If you look at my CV, you'll see how many times I've shifted my focus to new research topics. This was partly about creating space for the next generation of researchers to take leadership roles, but also because I get interested in different things, and changing my research focus keeps me fresh. For each of those shifts in focus, it was important for me to be strategic about what I say yes and no to. It is always a struggle for researchers to say no to things, but they must do it, particularly when they are just starting their careers. Something else I learned from Dave is how to be strategic about the decisions that I make and to say no nicely when that is my decision. When you say no, and for any decision that a research leader makes, respect, integrity, kindness, and transparency in communications go a long way.

6.15 MOHAMAD TAVAKOLI-TARGHI: CREATING VIBRANT RESEARCH COMMUNITIES IN THE HUMANITIES

Research Leader: Mohamad Tavakoli-Targhi, Professor of Historical Studies, History, and Near and Middle Eastern Civilizations, University of Toronto Mississauga

What does research leadership mean to you?

Being a research leader means doing top-notch research yourself and creating intellectual communities and supportive environments for the success of your students and colleagues.

What leadership situation will you share with readers?

I will speak about 30 years of experience building research communities in the humanities and creating forums for researchers to present and publish their work.

What did you think and do in that situation?

I had my first experience creating a research community when I was a graduate student at the University of Chicago. I was part of a group of students who established a weekly seminar series that we called the Middle East History and Theory Workshop. As graduate students, we invited speakers, posed questions, and presented our own research alongside faculty. Later, I used a similar approach to mobilize lecturers and create a community of scholars at Illinois State University.

I have also been the editor of journals and compendia that mobilize and support research communities. Beginning in 2001, I served for 10 years as the editor-in-chief of *Comparative Studies of South Asia, Africa and the Middle East,* and currently I am leading work on two compendia, one for Iranian cinema and one for Iranian women poets.

What did you learn?

All of these research communities accomplished things could not be achieved by individual researchers in isolation. We helped and supported each other in many ways, including by promoting the research of community members to help them get external attention and recognition for their work.

Research communities can be created anywhere and give a sense of empowerment to their members. Interactions between students, new faculty, and senior faculty benefit all parties because they provide equal access to knowledge and produce exceptional research.

To create and lead communities, research leaders must do top-notch research themselves. Other researchers are much more likely to present at a conference or contribute to a publication if they are approached by someone who is doing outstanding scholarship. In that sense, the labor that research leaders put into their own research is an investment in their ability to mobilize communities that include world-class scholars.

Do you have any additional leadership advice based on your own experiences or advice that you've received from someone else?

I would encourage people who teach university courses to organize a student conference at the end of the academic term. Instead of having students simply submit their papers for grading, I ask them to compile a portfolio of the work that they have done for the course, do a self-evaluation, and present their paper. We invite many people outside of the course to attend, and encourage students to invite their parents and friends. I have found that the act of presenting a paper to an open community of scholars embeds a desire to excel in students. The course conference makes a big difference in terms of how family and friends see the students and how the students see themselves. Students have come back to me years after their coursework was completed to tell me how the end-of-term conference was vital in enabling them to become academics.

In terms of hiring and developing young faculty, I learned that it was important, but not sufficient, to increase the diversity of whom we hired. You may have world-class scholars coming into your university, but if they feel isolated, their potentials will not be realized. Research leaders need to demonstrate that they care about younger scholars by listening to them and spending time with them beyond administrative responsibilities. If you do that with students and early career faculty, they feel like they matter and are part of a vibrant community. That has been the key to my success. Investments in colleagues' success are an investment to ensure that whatever we establish can be sustained and self-perpetuating. Research leaders benefit when they invest in others.

6.16 JUTTA TREVIRANUS: SHIFTING THE CULTURE OF RESEARCH FUNDING TO MORE INCLUSIVE APPROACHES

Research Leader: Jutta Treviranus, director, Inclusive Design Research Centre, and professor, Faculty of Design, Ontario College of Art & Design University

What does research leadership mean to you?

Research leadership for me started in the late 1980s and has consisted of decades of making mistakes and learning from them. When I reflect on what research leadership means for me now, it is largely about leading from behind. A lot of what I'm trying to do is about increasing the human capacity within the community and encouraging voices that have not been heard in research, because those are the innovative voices.

What leadership situation will you share with readers?

As background, people need to know that our team is divergent from the average conception or conventional thoughts of what is research. We critically ask questions like "What is rigorous academic practice?" "What is scholarship?" "How do you go about inquiry?" and "Who are the researchers, who are the subjects?" So, the situation that I'll talk about is one where we were successful in pushing the boundaries in an application for funding focused on digital inclusion. Instead of taking the funding criteria to heart, we looked at them more fundamentally and made the point that, in order to meet the spirit of the competition, we were proposing a way of doing research that should be judged differently.

What did you think and do in that situation?

In this instance, one of the criteria was that the team include research leaders with high impact scores with many years of scholarship. We said that wasn't right for our proposal because we wanted to create a system whereby individuals who were currently digitally excluded could participate in the internet, the web, etc. For digital inclusion research, we need people who are not entrenched in a particular view, who are going to work across disciplinary boundaries, and who have new and fresh perspectives and are able to see and support emerging trends as opposed to protecting a particular established view.

And that was just one of the criteria we challenged. Where the competition asked for economic potential and marketable products, we said that we would make our work open source. Where the competition asked for scalability, we argued that formulaic replication wouldn't work, but we would scale by diversification and localization. The norm for the competition was for researchers to partner with providers of expensive high-end enterprise equipment and count the discount from the company as an in-kind contribution. Instead, we create code and apps that run on equipment that anyone can buy inexpensively, and we release our products with open licenses so that companies can integrate them without worrying about proprietary restrictions, which helps the code and apps we create propagate to more systems.

I also should note that this way of presenting our work to funders was grounded in years of learning how to adaptively frame inclusive design. Harnessing societal interest in artificial intelligence (AI), we found two ways of communicating that really sparked the imagination, not just of the general public and policymakers, but also of AI developers, statisticians, and mathematicians. The first is the "lawnmower of justice." It was aimed at AI researchers working on predictive models. The lawnmower of justice refers to chopping the top off a Gaussian curve so that there will be no more than a certain number of repeats of any element, removing the advantage of being like the majority, and ensuring the learning model attends to the full spectrum of data. We have lots of data that tell us that the people at the edges of the Gaussian curve are the ones to focus on when it comes to innovation, because they are innovators by necessity. Design, education, work, and even democratic decisions that are based on majority rules don't work for people who experience exclusion or marginalization. For those people life is, to some extent, a series of continuous attempts to be resourceful, to be innovative, to try to make things work that are not designed for them. So, when we are looking for innovation, to improve things, for new insights, the people at the edges of any population data distribution are the individuals who add the most valuable perspectives. AI that doesn't consider the entire spectrum not only amplifies, accelerates, and automates disparity and inequity but also misses the weak signals of threats to come.

The second illustrative anecdote was based on a true story about early programming for autonomous vehicles. Back in 2015, we tested a range of machine learning models that were designed to guide automated vehicles through intersections. When presented with the data of a friend of mine who (unlike the majority of people in wheelchairs) pushed her wheelchair backwards, many of these systems and models chose to proceed and run her over. And when more data were added to "improve" these systems and machine learning models, we found that they would run her over with greater confidence.

The lawnmower of justice and the story about autonomous vehicle systems and the backward-moving wheelchair prompted people to question the treatment of minorities and outliers in quantitative analytics and AI. The interesting thing is that we were able to use AI as the mechanism for communicating a whole other range of ideas and risks, because AI made a lot of the theoretical things that we've been talking about manifest. The issues illustrated by the lawnmower of justice and the autonomous vehicle and wheelchair anecdote are also present in fundamental and long-standing practices, like majority rules decision making (which rules against outliers or minorities), or statistical reasoning (which makes predictions that are true for the average, but wrong if you're at the tails). Because there was so much attention and so much hope put into AI, it gave us a lever to get our message out and caused reflection about underlying assumptions.

What did you learn?

The situation above was one where we were successful in our grant application, but there were many other times that we weren't. The way that our community thought about it was that even if we didn't get funded, at least we would have prompted people to think about these issues and start to question research funding criteria. But I also learned that we need to be so careful about the expectations of the community – letting them know that only a small percentage of grant applications are funded and preparing them for the possibility that our proposal may not be funded. This was hard for the communities that we work with to accept when the things that we were proposing were so obviously valuable and critical to their lives. It also means we have a lot of work to do with communities after a negative funding decision to take care that communities aren't hurt by the hope of possibility when the risks that we won't be funded are so high.

Another thing I've learned is to not pull back from the approach we want to take just to get funding. In one case we did that, but the funded research plan that we had to implement was so ill-fitting. That has taught me to not ever do that again. Don't agree to do something that really doesn't jibe with the values or the process or the nature of the team and the community you have.

We're also learning that the funders are changing. There are proposals that were completely refused at one point that are now integrated into the criteria for funding. Changing the culture of investors, of funders, of government grant programs, of the granting agencies and peer reviewers is a slow process. But it is like water dripping on a rock; eventually a groove forms for the water to flow in. In fact, of late, things have been shifting so fast that there have been times when we were almost caught unaware. We have become so used to being opposed that we started pushing even when we didn't need to push.

Do you have any additional leadership advice based on your own experiences or advice that you've received from someone else?

In my presentations, I use an image of white-water canoeing to describe the process for culture change. You never know what's coming around the next bend, so you have to react and be resourceful, see where there is give, and use the power of the water to take you there. It's also like some of the martial arts where you use the strength of whoever is opposing you to your advantage. When you are working on change, you want to find a way to capitalize on the energy of those you are trying to convince but retain your own values.

It's also important to delegate and foster a succession plan early on. You don't want to come to the end of your term without someone to fill your place. Part of that is a willingness to let go and support creativity that comes from other people. I'm so grateful for the people who stuck with me through times when it was really difficult. Because of them, we have now been able to start new things that I couldn't have imagined. They bring in constant renewal and fresh ideas and areas to explore. That's what keeps research alive – being open to dissonant, divergent, unanticipated areas and then supporting people to pursue them, and to make mistakes, and seeing those mistakes as valuable and encouraging them to try again. I really love the group of people that are taking the research that I started in different new directions.

6.17 DAVID WOLFE: DISTINCT LEADERSHIP REQUIREMENTS FOR LARGE RESEARCH GRANTS WITH BUSINESS PARTNERS

Research Leader: David A. Wolfe, Professor of Political Science, University of Toronto Mississauga, and codirector, Innovation Policy Lab, Munk School of Global Affairs & Public Policy, University of Toronto

What does research leadership mean to you?

Research leadership means defining a project, assembling a team, and obviously getting funding for the research. But then, once you've done that, it can be like the dog catching the car it is chasing – you need to figure out what you are going to do with it. For research, the critical step after getting the funding is working out a detailed project plan and determining where and how the team you have assembled is going to help you realize the objectives laid out in that plan.

What leadership situation will you share with readers?

I've led three different major interdisciplinary collaborative research projects, all funded by the Social Sciences and Humanities Research Council (SSHRC). The first two had central directive leadership. The third one was a partnership grant with business partners and more bottom-up leadership from multiple researchers. I'm going to talk about leading all three grants and the critical ways in which the partnership grant project was different from the first two projects.

What did you think and do in that situation?

All three projects were large and interdisciplinary. Each one had between 15 and 26 case studies and academic researchers with different ideas about how to approach the grant based on their respective disciplines. So, the first 6 months for each project had me leading by example to establish the project design, cajoling, pushing, strong-arming, whatever it took.

Once we had agreed on the overall project design and laid out the project plan, we had to implement the design and manage the process

in a way that we could understand if people were actually producing their deliverables. Two things made a big difference. I got some
advice early on from SSHRC to create agreements with each of the
researchers that I would be transferring funds to on a multiyear basis.
So, we had each researcher draw up a proposal for their deliverables
for each year of their grant – this many interviews, this amount of data
analysis, presentations at our annual conference, this many external
conference presentations, journal articles, etc. – and we turned those
proposals into memorandum of understanding agreements (MOUs).
During project implementation, the MOUs specified that we wouldn't
transfer the funds for the following year until the deliverables from
the current year had been completed. In this manner, we were able to
establish an internal accountability mechanism between myself as the
principal investigator and the various team members.

Also, back at the start of my first project, I was very fortunate to
hire a person with experience in managing projects within the university. She continued to work with me through the three SSHRC projects
and one Canada Foundation for Innovation grant until she retired in
2019. She had great strengths and a system to manage budgets with
built-in Gantt charts and timelines for each researcher, spelling out
how much funding each researcher got to conduct their piece of the
research, the general administration costs we covered, etc. Each grant
had annual meetings where the academics would come and present
their research findings and updates on their latest research. She was
also responsible for organizing our annual research network meeting
each year, which was held in a different city each time. Given that
we had between 60 and 80 people attending, including researchers,
postdocs, grad students, and partners, this was a major undertaking
to organize.

For each grant, about midway to two-thirds of the way through
the project, we started working on integration, i.e., synthesizing and
pulling together general conclusions across the individual case studies that made up the project. That was very different for each project
in terms of the outcomes and the project overviews that we created.
In one, we created a series of synthesis papers that were published in
a special issue of a journal; in the second, we created a series of four
edited volumes published by University of Toronto Press; and in the
Partnership Project, we focused on creating a series of five reports that

cut across the key insights and findings from the project, presenting them in a more readable and accessible format.

What did you learn?

The most important thing for the research leader's mental sanity on these large grants is to have the right person responsible for program administration (or sometimes the right two people for large grants, one on the content side and one for the administrative work). These people must have the right skill sets and understand the financial system of your institution. Establishing MOUs with funded researchers also turned out to be a hugely valuable piece of advice. It is a practice I carried forward in subsequent projects, and advice that I've given to other faculty who have been awarded large, multiresearcher grants, both at the University of Toronto and externally.

For all three projects, I learned that the leader of interdisciplinary projects is often the only one who can bridge across all the different research approaches. You must play a role in interpreting from one discipline to another, and in research translation, not just for external stakeholders, but also across the research team members. Research leaders must think through whether the research design will be directed from the top down or implemented bottom-up. The more directed and top-down the research design and research plan is, the easier it is to manage and integrate the work, but the harder it is to get everyone to sign onto it. And even for the first two projects where everyone followed a set research design, we ended up getting different things from different people based on their disciplinary perspectives.

The biggest learnings came from the partnership grant. All three of the projects involved partners such as governments and not-for-profits, but the last partnership grant was different because it had an innovation and economics focus with business partners. These business partners didn't care as much about the normal academic outputs and wanted to know how the findings would help them run their businesses or help them lobby governments for public policy changes. It also created a very interesting dynamic within the project team between the private-sector and public-sector partners.

Around Year 3 of the 5-year partnership project, the business partners started giving feedback that they wanted changes in the way research findings were presented at our annual meetings so that the findings would have more relevance for them. Some of the researchers were presenting at our annual meetings the same way that they would at academic conferences, e.g., starting with a literature review and research hypothesis, comparing across case studies, and generally gearing presentations toward an academic publication like a journal article or a chapter in a book. That was distinctly uninteresting to the business partners, and they started questioning the relevance of the findings for their purposes. I had to do a lot of mediating with the business partners, reorganizing the way we presented our findings at the annual meetings and getting everyone working on the same page.

The things that the business partners wanted placed new demands on the academic team that were, in one instance, extremely time consuming. We created a new process that gave partners the opportunity to provide more input into both the form and the content of the presentations at our annual meeting. In the end, the partners were happier with the result at the final annual meeting, but it was a demanding process to meet their expectations.

There are two big lessons that I learned from the partnership grant. The first is that I should have had other senior members of the team take on some responsibility for interacting with the partners from the very outset of the project. It would have taken some of the load off of the project leader to have shared that with other senior members of the management team.

The second learning from the partnership grant was that we should have involved the partners more extensively in the project design, and made modifications to the design at an earlier stage. In the meeting to develop the full application for the partnership grant, we brought everybody together and had lots of good discussion but didn't follow up by bringing the partners directly into the research design. I subsequently realized that I had missed a step that would have reduced some of the issues farther on.

Do you have any additional leadership advice based on your own experiences or advice that you've received from someone else?

Relationships with partners are very important but take a lot of work to maintain. In the early 1990s, I developed relationships with provincial policymakers when I took a leave from my academic work and worked for the Ontario government. Later, with the SSHRC grants, I developed relationships with people in the federal government. In both cases, maintaining those relationships was very demanding because people in government don't stay in positions for long, sometimes not even for the length of your research project. And the same is true for partners working in the private sector. If they leave, you must develop new relationships with the new people in the roles. Over the length of all three major projects, a considerable proportion of my time and energy was spent maintaining and updating my network relationships. It paid dividends in terms of the way they contributed to the various projects, but don't ever underestimate the degree of effort it takes to manage and maintain partner relationships.

6.18 STEFAAN VERHULST: RESEARCH ENTREPRENEURSHIP TO MOBILIZE A NEW INTERNATIONAL NETWORK

Research Leader: Stefaan Verhulst, cofounder and chief research and development officer, The Governance Laboratory, New York University

What does research leadership mean to you?

My work fits within the rubric of action research where there is already an embedded understanding that we are working to inform decisions. From that point of view, I think there are four elements of research leadership:

- **Strategic:** Specifying and communicating the value proposition of the research and getting the resources to achieve and establish the value. Often this involves showing alignment between the research and the goals of the organization or funder, and understanding who needs to know what, at what time, and for what purpose.
- **Tactical:** Planning and determining the methodologies for the research and establishing standards in terms of research quality. This

also includes building and developing a team or research network
to produce the research by identifying capabilities and who can be
tasked, supported, and incentivized.

- **Inspiring and mentoring:** This includes motivating the people
who are doing the research and also mentoring decision makers to
help them understand why they need research and how to use it.
- **Bridging:** Research leaders need to serve as bridges, across disciplines and between research and practice. They need to show
the value that research can add and demystify research, no matter
what discipline it is.

What leadership situation will you share with readers?

I'm going to talk about the work that I led as chief of research helping
to create the MacArthur Research Network on Opening Governance,
which was funded by the MacArthur Foundation. This was the network that provided the foundation for the creation of The Governance
Lab, where I work now. The idea was to create a network of researchers working on advancing our understanding of open governance in
all its manifestations. This meant pioneering several new lines of research that can inform the opening up of government assets such as
data. It also meant becoming more open to the voices and input from
people who typically aren't involved in research or policymaking.

What did you think and do in that situation?

First, we needed to get an understanding of concepts associated with
opening governance and the ways we could activate different actors in
the field to contribute to a more holistic approach. At the time, opening governance research was siloed between people that work on de-
liberative democracy on the one hand and e-government and gov tech
on the other. The first stage was a broad literature review to gain an
understanding of the topics that are associated with the opening governance space, followed by a mapping of the different actors involved.
From this, we created some categories and clusters and identified who
was active and could provide unique perspectives and research to a
network. We subsequently had a large convening function where we
reached out to those actors to see who was committed to the goals we

shared and would be interested in being part of a broader network that crosses boundaries.

We hosted interactive conversations to try to find the interdependencies between different approaches to opening governance. We invited many players to participate, including policymakers and members from different research communities. In one of the exercises, which we called "If I only knew..." we put people in a room and asked them to fill in the blank. In other words, we asked them what was holding them back from achieving more legitimate and effective governance. It was a methodology to collectively identify questions that could be high impact both in terms of their impact on decision making and in terms of scientific impact, because the questions were novel. Efforts like that led us to develop a short list of questions that we subsequently built teams to address based on who was most excited and capable.

What did you learn?

We figured out that the secret sauce was understanding that the incentives for research are more than just knowledge creation. It is also an incentive for a researcher to be part of a group that includes leading thinkers and to be seen as being part of that epistemic community.

We also learned that, for the kind of action research that we do, "research entrepreneurship" may be a better term than "research leadership." In order to achieve the impact that we want, researchers have to be entrepreneurial and ask questions like "What's the value proposition of this research?" "What are the resources I need?" "What are the resources I have?" and "How do I make rapid progress with the resources, the team, and the network we have in place?" As a research entrepreneur, you cannot control things fully. You steer them and inspire people to join the effort, and deliver their best product.

Also, you must pay attention to the timing of research. Too often we see that the research agenda is misaligned with the decision agenda. It requires some entrepreneurial ownership to figure out how to quickly make progress adhering to the quality standards needed and also how to get resources for short- and long-term engagement. Getting the resources requires a lot more than being a good researcher; it is all about relationship building, and trust building, trying to be where the action is and, without imposing one's views, really adding value. From my point of view, that's a more entrepreneurial way of thinking about research than what we typically have.

Do you have any additional leadership advice based on your own experiences or advice that you've received from someone else?

From a strategic point of view, one of the hardest parts of being a research leader is deciding what you are *not* going to analyze and research. But you have to do that if you are going to prioritize and get the timing of your research right. We've learned that timing is of the essence when it comes to identifying insights that can contribute to a larger goal.

The other advice I have is to always focus on how you can add value. You need to pause and consider how the impact of what you are doing can be widened to make it more valuable to those who might benefit from it. And that doesn't always translate into "big bang" activities and findings. Simple communications approaches, like sharing findings one phase at a time as opposed to only at the end of a project, or creating a short, shareable document that summarizes the findings from a 40-page manuscript, can inspire others to be involved and join the effort.

In the research environment, there can be a lot of busyness, but you want to get past that by being intentional about contributing to a larger objective. It's about asking how you can use research to add value to whatever decision and whatever decision maker you are working with. My understanding of research is a utilitarian one; I feel that research has to add value to society at large and that that can be done in a variety of ways.

6.19 RICH ZEMEL: WORKING WITH INDUSTRY TO CREATE A NEW MACHINE LEARNING RESEARCH INSTITUTE

Research Leader: Richard Zemel, research director, Vector Institute for Artificial Intelligence, and professor in computer science, University of Toronto

What does research leadership mean to you?

There is research leadership in terms of being a leading researcher in a field, but I'm mostly thinking of the practice of leading other researchers. To me, that kind of research leadership means appreciating and, in some sense, mentoring other researchers. It's about being able to understand what other researchers' aims are, what kind of roadblocks there might be, and how they can manage and overcome some obstacles. Research leadership includes helping others in the short term, e.g., helping someone to get stalled research going, and helping them with their longer-term plans too.

What leadership situation will you share with readers?

I'm going to talk about securing funding for, and starting up, the Vector Institute for Artificial Intelligence, a machine learning research institute in Toronto, Canada.

What did you think and do in that situation?

For many years, I had been a faculty member in the machine learning group in the University of Toronto (U of T) Department of Computer Science. Starting around the year 2000, machine learning started growing locally and internationally in terms of importance, hype, and everything else. Many universities, including ours, were losing top machine learning faculty to industry or to big-name universities in the US. At U of T, we had the potential to be a top academic group because we had been one of the leaders of the deep learning tidal wave, largely due to Geoff Hinton's leadership. We had excellent PhD applicants from all over the world who wanted to come to U of T, but not enough faculty to supervise them. We were trying to figure out how to retain really good faculty members and how to grow at a time when machine learning researchers were in high demand.

In addition to being a computer science professor, I was a chief scientist at the Creative Destruction Lab at the Rotman School of Business at U of T. In that role, I advised start-up companies on how to incorporate or improve their artificial intelligence efforts, and I got to meet Tomi Poutanen and Jordan Jacobs. In the summer of 2016, the three of us started talking about building a strong bridge between academic researchers and industry to catalyze the machine learning community in Toronto, and we brought Geoff Hinton in to help brainstorm. To start, we tried to go through the usual routes to secure funding. I applied for grant funding and worked to see what was possible within the university. But it became clear that those weren't going to work for what we wanted to do.

As we were trying to think of other ways to secure funding, Tomi and Jordan spoke to Ed Clark, a very well-known business leader in Canada. It was the turning point because Ed was excited about our proposal and offered to pull out his Rolodex of industry and government contacts. Ed facilitated conversations that led to provincial government funding, many leading companies committing significant funds in the form of sponsorships, and the launch of the Vector Institute in March 2017. Following that, and in partnership with leading machine learning groups in Montreal and Alberta, we worked together to make a strong pitch to the federal government and formed what we called the Pan-Canadian AI Strategy.

To start, my role as the research director was to work across different groups at U of T and do anything that was required to help get the institute off the ground. Early on, I formed a core group of faculty who had similar views and could work well together on the pitch. As we were building the facility, I was pressed into other roles outside my expertise, which was interesting but stressful. When things settled, I concentrated on my primary research director role: overseeing Vector's research foci and hiring.

What did you learn?

One of the things that we learned was that the usual sources of research funding in Canada didn't work for what we wanted to do. There were academic turf wars, e.g., people questioning "Why them? Why not us?" and departments insisting that they retain control. Also, we found that standard grants and fellowships were more suited to gradual growth and couldn't provide the funds that we needed to grow as quickly and with as grand a vision as we wanted. Working with industry, we envisioned creating a high-profile brand and nucleus of top researchers that would initiate a virtuous cycle of talent attraction and investor interest. That, in turn, would lead to a denser machine learning–artificial intelligence (AI) ecosystem, more knowledge economy jobs, and a rising national competitive advantage. So, it was industry funding coupled with government funding that made sense for Vector.

In hindsight, one thing that I wish we'd done differently is to have called ourselves a "machine learning" research institute instead of an "AI" research institute. We went with the term "AI" based on what people in industry called what we were doing, but it created problems on the academic side because AI has a lot of connotations and approaches that don't involve the kind of machine learning research that Vector's core faculty do. I think there is always a trade-off between keeping things kind of narrow and focused (and maybe missing out on opportunities) versus having open and broad scope that is difficult to define. Going with the broad term of AI created tension because once we got the ball rolling, many people started referring to the research that they'd been doing for years as AI and wanted to be part of Vector. At one point, a senior professor I had never met and only knew through their publications called and yelled at me over the phone for the research scope decisions we had made.

The launch of the Vector Institute was not entirely smooth. Among other challenges, the influx of funding and beautiful new space and facilities created tension with other academics. Early on, I was the jack-of-all-trades, even making decisions about the design of the office space, which took up almost an entire floor of a great building in central downtown Toronto. One decision that I'm glad to have made at Vector was to focus on creating great space for the students. The students are the ones who do a lot of the work and are most affected by the working environment. Also, they are the ones who are going to be the next generation of faculty, and if we focus on giving them what they need and making them the most comfortable, they'll be running the show in a few years.

I knew that being the research director for Vector would be a lot of work, but I'm glad that I took on the role. When we created Vector, there were almost no tech companies with research labs in Toronto, so professors or graduates who wanted to work in industry left Toronto and Canada. Now, we have successfully recruited and retained top-notch faculty and Toronto is the largest net gainer of talent in North

America. It has been an amazing turnaround, and machine learning research excellence was at the heart of it all.

Do you have any additional leadership advice based on your own experiences or advice that you've received from someone else?

My main additional piece of advice is about not spreading yourself too thin. If you're the kind of person who gets very interested in lots of things, it is easy to get overwhelmed with students, and groups that you are part of, and emails, and everything else. So, you can't be too ambitious in terms of what you take on. Geoff Hinton, my PhD advisor, had a sign on his door that said, "Just say NO." I think knowing that you can say no is important for people in research leadership positions, because sometimes you get requests solely based on your name or affiliation for work that you don't really need or want to be involved in. So, being able to pick and choose is really important.

Looking back now, at the end of my term as research director, the most rewarding aspect was the research leadership – working with young faculty, as well as postdocs and undergraduates and particularly graduate students. Research is an amorphous endeavor, with a wide variety of paths to, and definitions of, success, so helping these people find their way and maintain confidence in their abilities has been a primary accomplishment. And it is also very enjoyable to share in the intellectual pursuit of interesting challenges!

APPENDICES

Examples of Light-Touch Project Management Documents for Fictional and Generic Research Projects

Scope of a Fictional Graduate Student Thesis Project Expressed in Terms of Deliverables

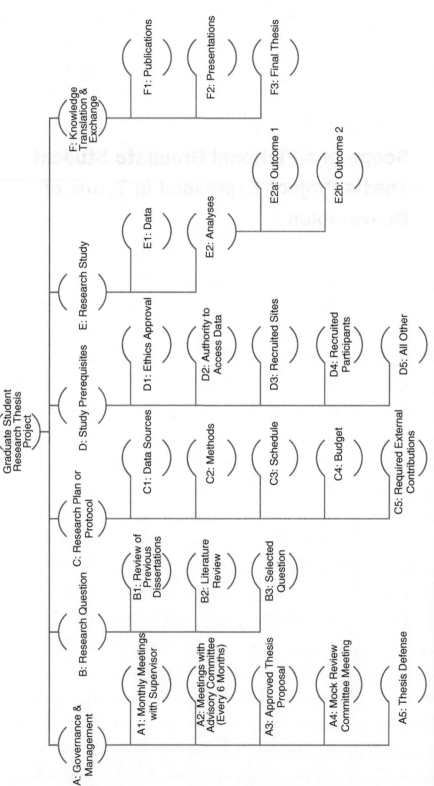

Figure A.1. Work Breakdown Structure for a Fictional Graduate Student Thesis Project

Scope of a Fictional Visual Arts Exhibition Project Expressed in Terms of Deliverables

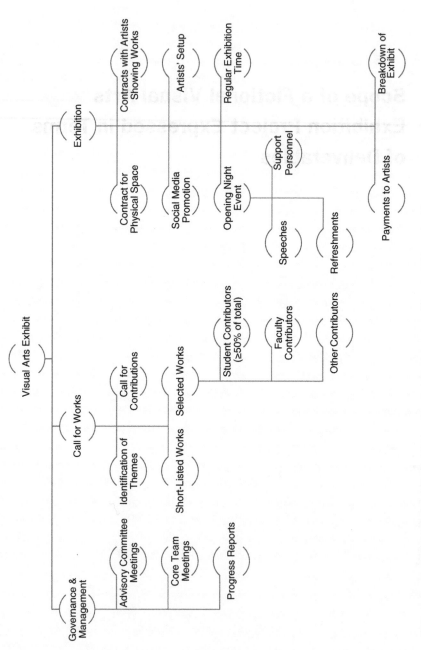

Figure B.1. Work Breakdown Structure for a Fictional Visual Arts Exhibition Project

Scope of a Fictional Systematic Review Project Expressed in Terms of Deliverables

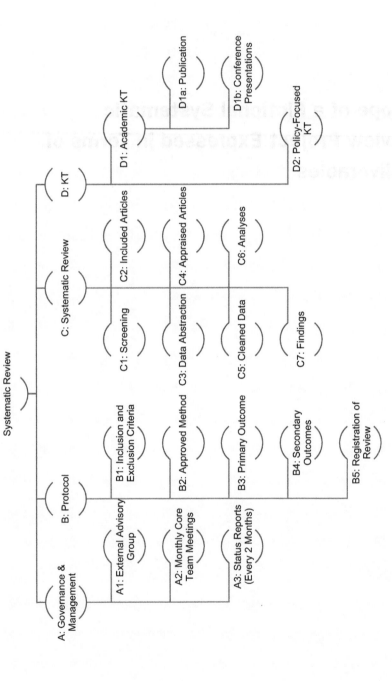

Figure C.1. Work Breakdown Structure for a Fictional Systematic Review Project
Note: KT = knowledge translation.

Three Pages for Planning and Managing a Fictional Seniors' Health Clinics Evaluation Project

BACKGROUND INFORMATION ABOUT THE SENIORS' HEALTH CLINICS EVALUATION PROJECT

A regional health authority (RHA) has established 15 seniors' health clinics for individuals aged older than 65 years to receive comprehensive assessments, immunizations, preventive care, and other health care services. One year after the funding started, anecdotal information suggests that there has been variation in the success of the program's implementation. Some clinics are reporting large numbers of older adults served; other clinics have established only a fraction of their programming and have few clients. Both the RHA and the Ministry of Health are interested in a formative evaluation study to the status of each clinic, the extent to which they are following the planned model of service delivery, the activities and outputs of each clinic, and the impact of these services on other health system metrics. In addition to quantitative analyses, the evaluation should use qualitative methods to shed light on how and why different clinics are experiencing and implementing the program in different ways. The budget is $90,000, and the RHA has requested the results in 9 months.

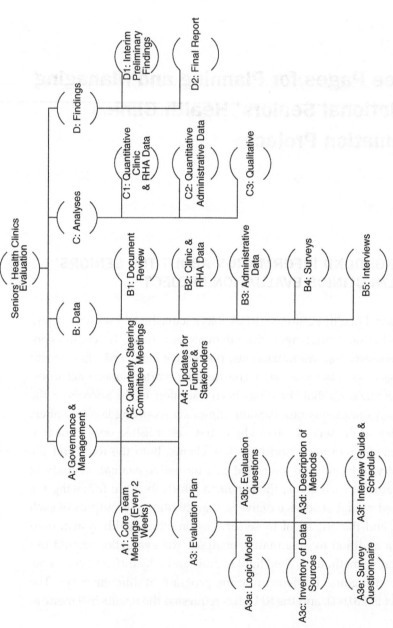

Figure D.1. Work Breakdown Structure for a Fictional Seniors' Health Clinics Evaluation Project

Note: RHA = regional health authority.

[a] The evaluation plan includes A3a: Logic Model, A3b: Evaluation Questions, A3c: Inventory of Data Sources, A3d: Description of Methods, A3e: Survey Questionnaire, A3f: Interview Guide & Schedule

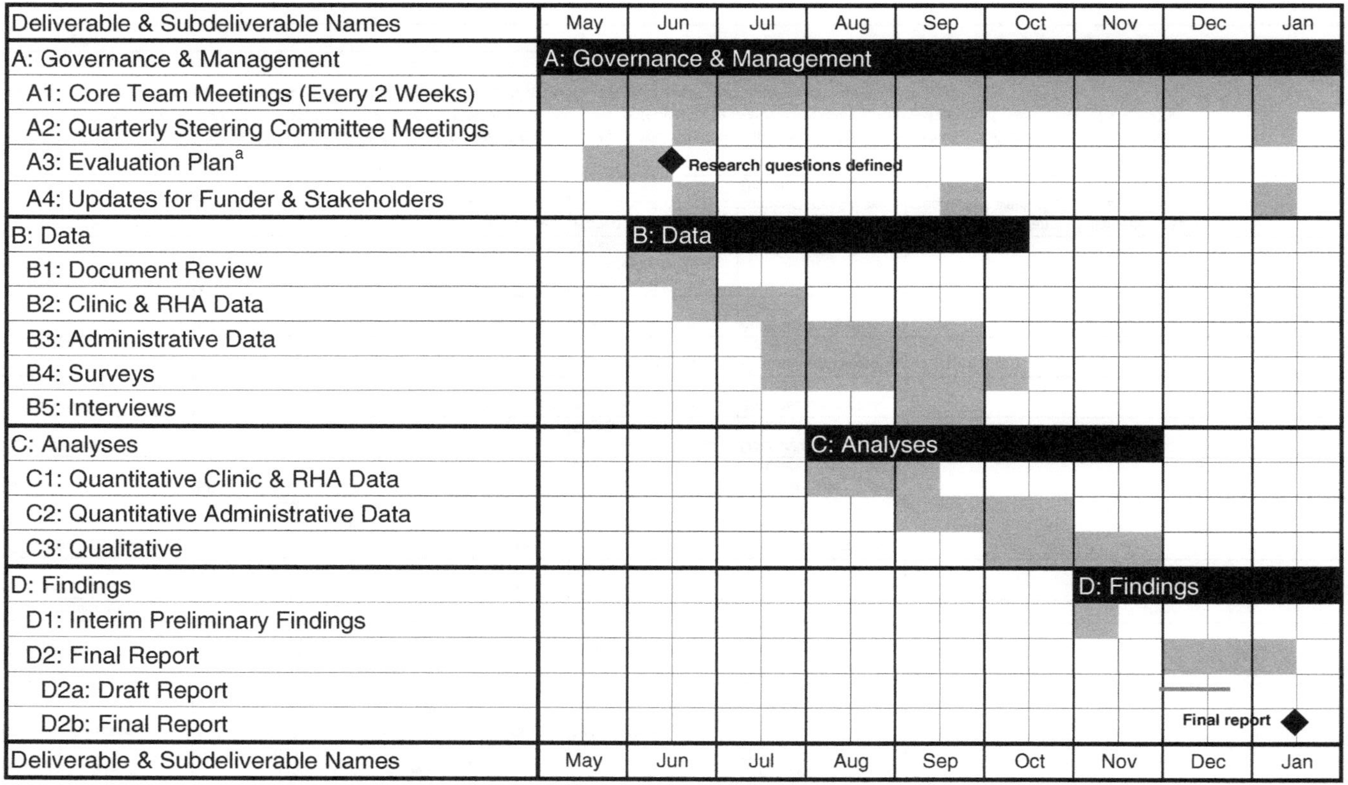

Deliverable & Subdeliverable Names	May	Jun	Jul	Aug	Sep	Oct	Nov	Dec	Jan
A: Governance & Management									
A1: Core Team Meetings (Every 2 Weeks)									
A2: Quarterly Steering Committee Meetings									
A3: Evaluation Plan[a]									
A4: Updates for Funder & Stakeholders									
B: Data									
B1: Document Review									
B2: Clinic & RHA Data									
B3: Administrative Data									
B4: Surveys									
B5: Interviews									
C: Analyses									
C1: Quantitative Clinic & RHA Data									
C2: Quantitative Administrative Data									
C3: Qualitative									
D: Findings									
D1: Interim Preliminary Findings									
D2: Final Report									
D2a: Draft Report									
D2b: Final Report								Final reprt	
Deliverable & Subdeliverable Names	May	Jun	Jul	Aug	Sep	Oct	Nov	Dec	Jan

Research questions defined

Figure D.2. Deliverable-Based Gantt Chart for a Fictional Seniors' Health Clinics Evaluation Project

[a] The evaluation plan includes A3a: Logic Model, A3b: Evaluation Questions, A3c: Inventory of Data Sources, A3d: Description of Methods, A3e: Survey Questionnaire, and A3f: Interview Guide & Schedule

	A	B	C	D	E	F	G	H	I	J
1										
2		Deliverable or Subdeliverable Name	Lead Initials	Last Accomplishment or Completed Task or Milestone	Status[a]	Upcoming Tasks or Milestones and Target Completion Dates[b]				
						1	2	3	4	5
3		A2: Quarterly Steering Committee Meetings	EDP	All Steering Committee members confirmed May 2022	Green	Steering Committee meeting Sep 2022	Final Steering Committee meeting Jan 2023			
4		A3: Evaluation plan	AGD	Evaluation plan finalized and disseminated to team Jul 2022	Completed	Not applicable				
5		A4: Updates for funder & stakeholders	AGD	Status report prepared Jun 2022	Green	Steering Committee meeting Sep 2022	Interim preliminary findings shared Nov 2022	Draft report shared Dec 2022	Final status update Jan 2023	Final report issued Jan 2023
6		B1: Document review	MSP	Completed Jun 2022	Completed	Not applicable				
7		B2: Clinic & RHA data	KH	Data collection started	Green	Data collection completed Jul 2022				
8		B3: Administrative data	SCM	Process to secure approvals to access data initiated Jun 2022	Green	Request for data approved Jul 2022	Data access provided Sep 2022			
9		B4: Surveys	SEB		Green	Data collection starts Jul 2022	Data collection completed Oct 2022			
10		B5: Interviews	SEB		Green	Data collection starts Sep 2022	Data collection completed Sep 2022			
11		C1: Quantitative clinic & RHA data	AGD		Not started	Analyses start Aug 2022	Analyses completed Sep 2022			
12		C2: Quantitative administrative data	SCM		Not started	Analyses start Sep 2022	Analyses completed Oct 2022			
13		C3: Qualitative	SEB		Not started	Analyses start Sep 2022	Analyses completed Nov 2022			
14		D1: Interim preliminary findings	AGD		Not started	Target Oct 2022 to share preliminary results				
15		D2: Final report	AGD		Not started	Work on draft report starts Dec 2022	Draft report shared for comment and review Dec 2022	Close review of draft report – first week of Jan 2023	Final report issued Jan 2023	
16										
17										

[a] Green = progressing well and within schedule, and budget constraints and issues (if any) are minor and likely to be resolved without affecting other deliverables; yellow = low-impact risks have been realized or medium- or high-impact risks have potential to be realized in the near future that could necessitate changes for deliverable or planning; red = progress halted, significant decisions or activities are required to bring stream of work back on track.

[b] Changes relative to last version highlighted in bold italic font.

25 Jun 22

Figure D.3. Microsoft Excel Tracking Sheet for a Fictional Seniors' Health Clinics Evaluation Project (June 2022 Update)

Five-Page Plan for a Fictional Pollution Research Project

BACKGROUND INFORMATION ABOUT FICTIONAL POLLUTION RESEARCH PROJECT

Pollution monitoring around major emitters, such as electrical power generation plants or smelters, is important in assessing the environmental impact of their operations. A three-dimensional profile of the spread of pollution from such sites during various weather conditions is needed to enable the development of mitigation and remediation strategies. A research team plans to measure pollutants in the air within 2 kilometers of an emission site using a drone and comparing and correlating the air pollution results with pollution measured in water and soil at sites distant from the emitter. Completion of the project will require the purchase and programming of the drone and air sampling equipment, drone-based air sampling, physical collection of water and soil samples, analyses of all samples, and comparison and correlation of near-emitter drone-based measurements with distant air and water pollution results. This project is funded by the federal government with $150,000 annually for two years ($300,000 total).

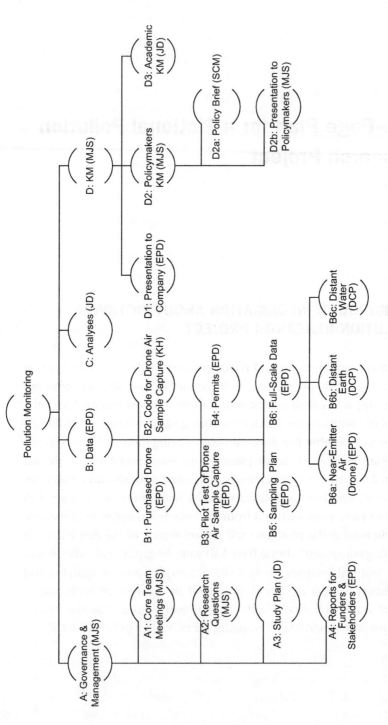

Figure E.1. Work Breakdown Structure with Leads' Initials for a Fictional Pollution Research Project

Note: KM = knowledge mobilization.

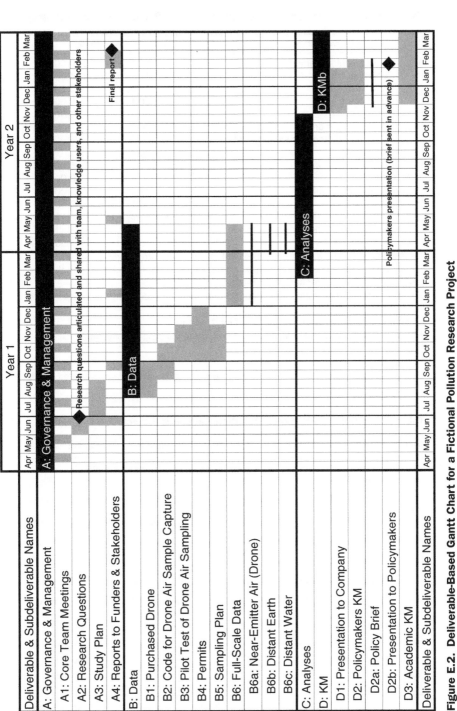

Figure E.2. Deliverable-Based Gantt Chart for a Fictional Pollution Research Project
Note: KM = knowledge mobilization.

Table E.1. Deliverable-Based Budget for a Fictional Pollution Research Project

Workstream or Deliverable Name	Year 1	Year 2
A: Governance & Management[a]	104,500	120,000
Personnel costs[b]	96,500	107,000
Materials costs	5,000	5,000
Travel costs	3,000	8,000
B: Data	45,500	5,000
B1: Purchased drone[c]	30,000	–
B2: Code for drone air sample capture[d]	10,000	–
B4: Permits	500	–
B6: Full-scale data[e]	5,000	5,000
C: Analyses[f]	–	10,000
D: Knowledge mobilization[g]	–	15,000
Total	150,000	150,000

Note: Dashes indicate no budget allocation.

[a] Includes all core costs for the project, including staff time, student compensation, materials, teleconference costs, travel costs associated with sampling, and publication costs; consultant and specialist services costs are excluded from this line and presented below for specific deliverables.

[b] Includes standard host institution benefits and annual compensation increases where applicable.

[c] Estimate $5,000 for 3 drones, $25,000 for 2 air samplers.

[d] Budget for specialist and consultant services related to programming drone.

[e] Budget for rented server space.

[f] Statistician fee.

[g] Budget for open access publication, conference registration, and conference-related travel.

Table E.2. RACI for a Fictional Pollution Research Project

Deliverable	Resources	Approver	Consulted	Informed
A: Governance & management	EPD	MJS[a]	Stakeholders	Funders
A1: Core team meetings	EPD	MJS[a]		
A2: Research questions	EPD	MJS[a] and research executive committee[b]	Stakeholders	Funders
A3: Study plan	EPD, JD[a]	MJS	Stakeholders	Funders
A4: Reports for funders & stakeholders	EPD,[a] JD	MJS	Funders and stakeholders	Entire research team
B: Data	EPD, JD	EPD[a]		Stakeholders
B1: Purchased drone	EPD, SCM	EPD[a]	Vendors	Stakeholders
B2: Code for drone air sample capture	KJH, SCM	KJH[a]		Stakeholders

(Continued)

Table E.2. RACI for a Fictional Pollution Research Project (*Continued*)

Deliverable	Resources	Approver	Consulted	Informed
B3: Pilot test of drone air sampling	SCM	EPD[a]		Stakeholders
B4: Permits	SCM	EPD[a]	Regulators	Stakeholders
B5: Sampling plan	SCM, JD	EPD[a]	Regulators	Stakeholders
B6: Full-scale data	SCM, JD	EPD[a]		Stakeholders
B6a: Near-emitter air (drone)	DCP, JD	EPD	Regulators	Stakeholders
B6b: Distant earth	JD, DCP	DCP[a]		Stakeholders
B6c: Distant water	JD, DCP	DCP[a]		Stakeholders
C: Analyses	EPD, SCM, JD[a]	MJS		Funders and stakeholders
D: Knowledge mobilization	EPD, SCM, JD	MJS[‡] and research executive committee[b]	Stakeholders	Stakeholders and funders
D1: Presentation to company	EPD[a]	MJS	Stakeholders	Stakeholders and funders
D2: Policymakers knowledge mobilization	EPD	MJS[a]		Stakeholders and funders
D2a: Policy brief	EPD, SCM[a]	MJS		Stakeholders and funders
D2b: Presentation to policymakers	EPD, SCM	MJS[a]		Stakeholders and funders
D3: Academic knowledge mobilization	JD,[a] EPD, SCM	MJS		Funders and stakeholders

[a] Deliverable or workstream lead.
[b] The research executive committee consists of MJS (principal investigator), EPD (postdoctoral fellow), and JD (research associate).

RISK MANAGEMENT PLAN FOR A FICTIONAL POLLUTION RESEARCH PROJECT

Table E.3. Negative Risk Management Plan for a Fictional Pollution Research Project

Negative Risk	Likelihood	Impact if Realized	Response(s)
1. Company is not responsive to requests for feedback.	Medium high	Very high	• Tailor communications format and frequency to company's preferences. • Develop relationships with people at multiple levels within the company.

(*Continued*)

Table E.3. Negative Risk Management Plan for a Fictional Pollution Research Project (*Continued*)

Negative Risk	Likelihood	Impact if Realized	Response(s)
2. Insufficient data	Medium	High	• Engage statisticians in study design to ensure enough power. • Oversample relative to anticipated required amount.
3. Staff member leaves	Medium	Medium	• Reserve the last 2 weeks of any person who is leaving the project with advance notice for them to transfer their knowledge and documents to other team members. • Offer a flexible work environment that makes it less likely people will leave for another job.
4. Delayed start of funding results in insufficient time to complete project	Medium	Medium	• Start work on permits for drone approvals before funding starts to increase the rate at which work can be completed once funding is received.
5. Funder withdraws	Low	High	• Tailor communications format and frequency to funder's preferences. • Identify other potential funders to reach out to if there are signals that funder may withdraw

POSITIVE RISK AND RESPONSES

Many team members attend the Canadian National Environmental Protection Conference in person, and there may be an opportunity to fund the travel of additional team members so that an in-person team meeting can be held immediately before or after the conference.

Response: When the dates for the Canadian National Environmental Protection Conference are released, poll team members to determine (a) who has funding and is planning to attend and (b) who would attend if project funding was available and then, on the basis of timing and available funds, make a consensus team decision about whether to organize an in-person team meeting concurrent with the conference (potentially in place of another planned in-person meeting).

ADDITIONAL INFORMATION

This risk management plan was developed by MJS, EPD, JD, and KJM between September and December 2022. The group also identified additional negative risks that were not seen as requiring risk responses at this time. In estimated order of importance (considering both likelihood and impact), the additional negative risks identified were as follows:

- Non-responsive partner
- Insufficient data
- Staff member leaves
- Delayed start of funding results in insufficient time to complete project
- Funder withdraws
- Insufficient quantity of data
- Insufficient quality of data
- Global supply chain issues impact ability to get desired drone in time and within budget.

This risk management plan will be updated before analyses start and if and when new risks emerge that require changes to it.

Example Full Project Plan for a Fictional Natural Sciences Research Project That Is Part of a Multidisciplinary Program

BACKGROUND AND CONTEXT

The 2015 discovery by the University of Toronto's Adrienne G. Di Soto of rareium beneath the shores of Lake Ontario has the potential to transform access to the valuable mineral. Among other impacts, the discovery prompted Rare Minerals International Ltd. ("Rare Minerals") to establish a new Center of the Earth (COTE) exploration and extraction operation.

Because the rareium is deep below the earth's surface, new techniques developed in partnership with universities will be required to optimize extraction. Extraction of rareium offers opportunities for experimental development and basic and applied research. It also has the potential for positive social impacts (e.g., increased jobs, increased ground-breaking knowledge) and negative impacts (e.g., environmental).

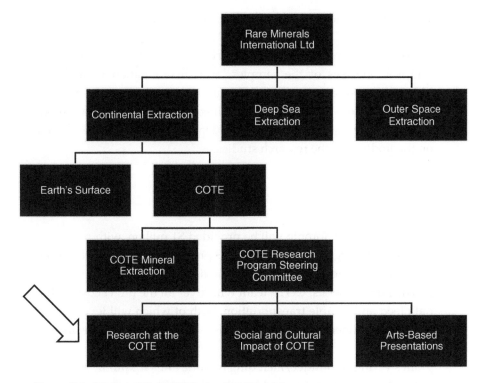

Figure F.1. Fictional RaCOTE Project in Context
Note: COTE = Center of the Earth; RaCOTE = Research at the Center of the Earth.

Building on Rare Minerals' $10 million prior partnerships with the academic sector, the University of Toronto and Rare Minerals have agreed on a comprehensive new 5-year, $2 million program of research beginning in 2038 that includes the following:

- **Research at the COTE (RaCOTE):** Research studies of the physical and chemical properties of samples from deep below the surface of the earth
- **Social and cultural impact of COTE:** Studies of the social and cultural impact of COTE mineral exploration and extraction
- **Arts-based presentations:** An arts-based approach to presenting research findings and other information about COTE.

This plan provides the details of the 3-year, $1.0 million natural sciences RaCOTE project. The RaCOTE project includes joint industry–academica research priorities, extraction of physical samples, analyses of the samples, and dissemination of findings. Multiple meetings are planned, including a summit to ensure that research findings are shared with industry stakeholders. In addition, the RaCOTE project will produce evidence-based policy briefs based on the findings of the research studies.

ASSUMPTIONS

The University of Toronto will be provided $1 million, with payments flowing at the beginning of each year as presented in the budget section. The principal investigator, J.D. Smith, will lead the entire 3-year project.

The Rare Minerals' COTE team will cover all the direct costs of the data feed and sample transportation, both of which will leverage existing Raw Minerals infrastructure. Rare Minerals' COTE team will also cover all costs to establish and support the COTE Research Program steering committee, including honorariums for public members of the steering committee and travel and other meeting costs.

CONSTRAINTS

Rare Minerals must provide prior approval, in writing, for any reallocation of funds that would exceed 10 percent of an individual budget line.

SCOPE

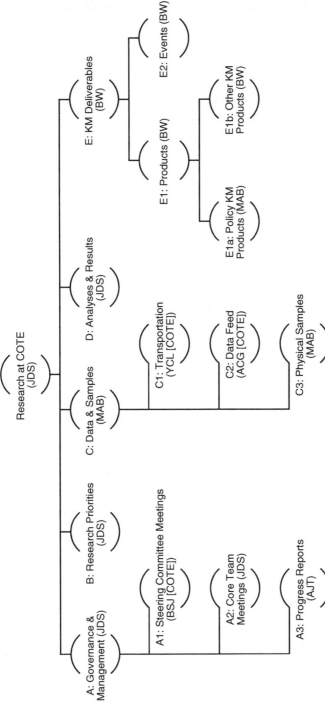

Figure F.2. Work Breakdown Structure for the Fictional RaCOTE Project
Note: COTE = Center of the Earth; KM = knowledge mobilization; RaCOTE = Research at the Center of the Earth.

ROLES, RESPONSIBILITIES, AND GOVERNANCE

The RaCOTE core team members are

- J.D. Smith (principal investigator)
- B. Wang (coinvestigator; lead, knowledge mobilization)
- M.A. Brown (postdoctoral fellow)
- A.J. Tremblay (project manager [part time])
- D.S. Patel (graduate student)
- E.P. Martin (graduate student)
- M. Garcia (research assistant)
- A.P. MacDonald (statistician).

The broader RaCOTE research project team includes core team members and the following people:

- A.G. Gagnon (COTE team data infrastructure lead)
- Y.C. Lee (COTE team transportation lead)
- B.S. Johnson (Rare Minerals vice president of community engagement; knowledge user and COTE steering committee chair)
- T.P. Wilson (Ministry of Environment knowledge user).

It is anticipated that additional knowledge users will be involved in the project (e.g., as members of the steering committee). Generally, these knowledge users will not be invited to be members of the RaCOTE research project team; however, project materials will be shared with them on request and through the project website, and tailored products may be developed for them (see E1b in Figure F.2).

Governance and oversight for the project is provided by the COTE steering committee (terms of reference are available upon request).

SCHEDULE

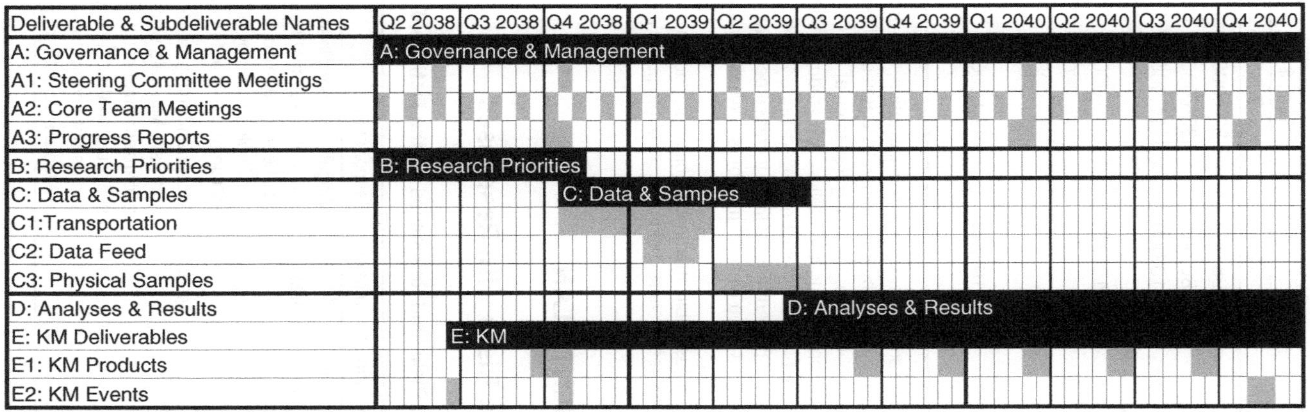

Deliverable & Subdeliverable Names
Q2 2038
Q3 2038
Q4 2038
Q1 2039
Q2 2039
Q3 2039
Q4 2039
Q1 2040
Q2 2040
Q3 2040
Q4 2040
A: Governance & Management
A1: Steering Committee Meetings
A2: Core Team Meetings
A3: Progress Reports
B: Research Priorities
C: Data & Samples
C1:Transportation
C2: Data Feed
C3: Physical Samples
D: Analyses & Results
E: KM Deliverables
E1: KM Products
E2: KM Events
A: Governance & Management
B: Research Priorities
C: Data & Samples
D: Analyses & Results
E: KM

Figure F.3. Deliverable-Based Gantt Chart for the Fictional RaCOTE Project

Note: KM = knowledge mobilization; RaCOTE = Research at the Center of the Earth.

BUDGET

Table F.1. Deliverable-Based Budget for the Fictional RaCOTE Project

Workstream or Deliverable Name	Year, $		
	1	2	3
A2: Core team	195,000	320,000	325,000
Personnel costs[a]	180,000	305,000	310,000
Materials costs[b]	15,000	15,000	15,000
C3: Physical samples materials costs	15,000	75,000	5,000
E: KM Deliverables	–	15,000	50,000
E1: KM products[c]	–	15,000	20,000
E2: KM events[d]	–	–	30,000
Annual totals	210,000	410,000	380,000
Total budget			1,000,000

Notes: Costs for A1 steering committee, sample transportation, and data feed are not included because they are covered by Rare Minerals. Dashes indicate no budget allocated. KM = knowledge mobilization; RaCOTE = Research at the Center of the Earth.
[a] All years include funding for one postdoctoral fellow, two graduate students, one research assistant, and one half-time project manager; Years 2 and 3 also include a part-time statistician and a 2 percent cost-of-living increase per year.
[b] Computers and other supplies used by team members (excludes materials for sample collection and analysis [C3]).
[c] Includes costs for open access publication and webinar production.
[d] Large-scale event with many researchers and members of the public planned for Year 3.

RISK MANAGEMENT PLAN

Selected Negative Risks with Responses

Table F.2. Top Negative Risks and Responses for the Fictional RaCOTE Project

Negative Risk	Likelihood	Impact	Response(s)
Samples not suitable for analysis	Medium high	Very high	Mitigate: Do not close sampling phase until viability of first batch of samples has been confirmed, increase number of samples taken by 50% relative to anticipated amount needed
Rare Minerals work takes priority over research team's use of transportation and data feed	Medium	Medium	Accept and mitigate impact: Accept that Rare Minerals work will be prioritized; build extra time into the schedule so that sufficient samples can be obtained within the time available even if there are delays

(Continued)

Table F.2. Top Negative Risks and Responses for the Fictional RaCOTE Project (*Continued*)

Negative Risk	Likelihood	Impact	Response(s)
Core team member leaves	Medium	Medium	Mitigate impact: For planned departures, use their last 2 weeks for knowledge transfer vs. new project work; adopt the practice that all team members upload a copy of final documents to shared drive
Public concerns about resource extraction	Medium low	Very high	Transfer: response led by COTE program director, who is lead for public assemblies and public involvement in COTE governance

Note: COTE = Center of the Earth

Selected Positive Risks with Responses

Excess capacity on regular Rare Minerals transportation runs allows for the transport of RaCOTE samples more quickly.

Response: Establish holding cases at each end of the transportation channel and educate drivers to transfer samples between the two holding cases when there is capacity.

Public members of the steering committee and members of the communities affected by COTE may be interested in learning more about the project.

Response: Ask steering committee whether there is interest in a tour of the laboratory; if yes, then organize a tour. Monitor who signs up for the email distribution list, and if many members of the public sign up, consider offering a tour to them, too.

Additional Information

The risk management plan was developed by J.D. Smith, B. Wang, M.A. Brown, B.S. Johnson, A.G. Gagnon, Y.C. Lee, A.J. Tremblay, and M. Garcia in fall 2037. Other risks that were brainstormed at that time but not included as top risks to be managed have been captured in a negative risk registry available from J.D. Smith on request. This risk management plan will be updated at least once per year and if and when new risks emerge that require changes to it.

COMMUNICATIONS PLAN

Table F.3. Communications Plan for the Fictional RaCOTE Project

Format and Mechanism	Audience	Frequency
Tracking sheet posted online	Core team, knowledge users (others on request)	Monthly
Core team meetings and related materials	Members of core team (agendas and action or decision items shared with others as needed)	Once per month, with deliverable and workstream teams meeting more frequently as required
Research project team meetings and related materials	Members of the core team plus knowledge users	Kick-off meeting, then quarterly
Steering committee meetings and related materials	Members of steering committee (agendas and action or decision items shared with others as needed)	Three times per year, aligned with the need for advice on deliverables
Status reports	Steering committee, Rare Minerals, knowledge users	Timed to correspond with steering committee meetings
Simple website (repository of downloadable documents and webinar videos)	Core team, knowledge users, community members with an interest; include registration for people who want to receive information about findings by email	Updated no less than every 6 weeks
Knowledge management products: open access publications, webinars, practice and policy briefs	Knowledge users, research team members who join midway through the project, members of the general public who have an interest in the topic	Each publication arising from a RaCOTE product will be accompanied by a webinar and policy practice brief
Annual reports for Rare Minerals in funders' specified format	Rare Minerals and posted on website	Annually

Note: RaCOTE = Research at Center of the Earth.

STAKEHOLDER ENGAGEMENT PLAN

In addition to the communications mechanisms described earlier, J.D. Smith will be available to update and meet with the two main knowledge user partners, B.S. Johnson (Rare Minerals vice president of community engagement, knowledge user, and COTE steering committee chair) and T.P. Wilson (Ministry of Environment knowledge user), using whatever format or mechanism is preferred by the knowledge users (e.g., monthly 15-minute Zoom meeting, quarterly informal meetings, email updates).

As noted under positive risks, if and when there is interest on the part of members of the public, additional mechanisms for stakeholder involvement (beyond their involvement in the steering committee) will be established, such as a tour and tailored communications products.

WORK BREAKDOWN STRUCTURE DICTIONARY

A: Governance & Management: The committees and processes in place to ensure that there is strategic oversight of RaCOTE and that changes made in response to risks and opportunities that arise during the project are informed by expertise within and outside of the research project team.

A1: Steering committee meetings: Scheduled to occur near key milestones and decision points during the project. The steering committee will be established by Rare Minerals to oversee the entire COTE Program. According to the terms of reference (available upon request), the steering committee will include at least three members of the public.

A2: Core team meetings: The core team (see roles and responsibilities for membership) will meet at least monthly, complemented by additional meetings of subteams focused on specific workstreams and deliverables.

A3: Progress reports: Reports written in format specified by funder with plain-language summaries so they are also useful to members of the public and other stakeholders.

B: Research priorities: The defined research questions that the study will address.

C: Data & samples: The combination of physical samples and data from remote sensors that will be analyzed during the project.

C1: Transportation: Refers to the infrastructure that will be used to move physical samples from the mining operation below the earth's surface to J.D. Smith's laboratory for analysis. No new transportation infrastructure is anticipated for RaCOTE; the project will leverage existing transportation channels established by Rare Minerals and the COTE Program.

C2: Data feed: Refers to the infrastructure that will be used to relay information from existing sensors to J.D. Smith's laboratory for analysis. No new data feed infrastructure is anticipated for RaCOTE; the project will leverage existing cables and sensors established by Rare Minerals and the COTE Program.

C3: Physical samples: Refers to the physical samples (e.g., of earth, air, and water) that will be transported from the center of the earth to J.D. Smith's laboratory for analysis. Because the samples will in some cases require specialized storage, the RaCOTE team is responsible for purchasing or constructing containers for physical samples.

D: Analyses & results: Will leverage existing spectrometers and other equipment in J.D. Smith's laboratory. Costs for analyses and results consist only of research team members' time.

E: Knowledge mobilization deliverables: Activities and deliverables to disseminate information about the RaCOTE project, and its findings, outside of the research project team.

E1: Knowledge mobilization products: Peer-reviewed publications (all of which will be published in open access journals) along with webinars and policy and practice briefs. See communications plan for frequency and ways of communicating information within and beyond the research project team.

E2: Knowledge mobilization events: A summit to be held in Toronto or Montreal that will include many stakeholders from Rare Minerals, the research sector, and members of the public.

Bibliography

Advance HE. (n.d.). *Leadership and management*. Retrieved September 3, 2022, from https://www.advance-he.ac.uk/guidance/leadership-and -management

Agile Alliance. (n.d.). *What is the Agile Manifesto?* Retrieved September 3, 2022, from https://www.agilealliance.org/agile101/the-agile-manifesto/

American Society for Quality. (n.d.-a). *What is multivoting?* Retrieved September 17, 2022, from https://asq.org/quality-resources/multivoting

American Society for Quality. (n.d.-b). *What is Six Sigma?* Retrieved September 26, 2023, from https://asq.org/quality-resources/six-sigma

Anthony, S.G., & Antony, J. (2017). Academic leadership – Special or simple. *International Journal of Productivity and Performance Management, 66*(5), 630–7. https://doi.org/10.1108/IJPPM-08-2016-0162

Axelos. (n.d.). *Certifications*. Retrieved September 18, 2022, from https:// www.axelos.com/certifications

Axelos. (2017). *Managing successful projects with PRINCE2®* (6th ed.). Stationery Office.

Beck, K., Beedle, M., van Bennekum, A., Cockburn, A., Cunningham, W., Fowler, M., Grenning, J., Highsmith, J., Hunt, A., Jeffries, R., Kern, J., Marik, B., Martin, R.C., Mellor, S., Schwaber, K., Sutherland, J., & Thomas, D. (2001). *Manifesto for Agile software development*. Retrieved September 3, 2022, from https://agilemanifesto.org/

Canada, National Centres of Excellence. (2018). *Program guide: Networks of Centres of Excellence (NCE)*. Retrieved September 16, 2022, from https:// www.nce-rce.gc.ca/ReportsPublications-RapportsPublications/NCE-RCE /ProgramGuide-GuideProgramme_eng.asp#a2-3

Canada Foundation for Innovation. (n.d.) *Good practices from institutions*. Retrieved September 16, 2022, from https://www.innovation.ca/apply -manage-awards/resources-apply-manage-award/good-practices

Canadian Health Services and Policy Research Alliance. (2015, December 7). *Report from the Working Group on Training*. https://face2face.events /wp-content/uploads/2022/02/6-TMWG-Report-Dec-7-2015.pdf

Canadian Health Services Research Foundation. (n.d.). *Communication notes: Reader-friendly writing 1:3:25*. Retrieved September 16, 2022, from https:// www.cfhi-fcass.ca/innovations-tools-resources/item-detail/2021/04/15 /reader-friendly-writing-1-3-25

Canadian Institutes of Health Research. (n.d.). *Strategy for patient-oriented research*. Retrieved September 13, 2022, from https://cihr-irsc.gc.ca /e/41204.html

Canadian Institutes of Health Research. (2016). *Knowledge user engagement*. Last modified June 8, 2016, from https://cihr-irsc.gc.ca/e/49505.html

Canadian Institutes of Health Research. (2017). *Canadian Health Services and Policy Research Alliance: Training modernization in health services and policy research*. Last modified April 5, 2017, from https://cihr-irsc.gc.ca /e/49883.html

Cassanelli, A.N., Fernandez-Sanchez, G., & Guiridlian, M.C. (2017). Principal researcher and project manager: Who should drive R&D projects? *R & D Management, 47*(2), 277–87. https://doi.org/10.1111/radm.12213

Council for Six Sigma Certification. (n.d.). *Lean Six Sigma green belt certification*. Retrieved Month DD, YYYY, from https://www .sixsigmacouncil.org/lean-six-sigma-green-belt-certification-standard/

Donato, H. (2022, September 22). *Work breakdown structure (WBS), the basic building block for a project plan*. Project-management.com. https:// project-management.com/work-breakdown-structure-wbs/

Ernø-Kjølhede, E. (1999). *Project management theory and the management of research projects* (MPP Working Paper No. 3/2000). Copenhagen Business School, Department of Management, Politics and Philosophy. https:// hdl.handle.net/10398/6308

European Commission. (2022). *Horizon Europe programme guide* (Version 2.0). Retrieved September 3, 2022, from https://ec.europa.eu/info /funding-tenders/opportunities/docs/2021-2027/horizon/guidance /programme-guide_horizon_en.pdf

Goldratt, E.M. (1997). *Critical chain*. North River Press.

Huljenic, D., Desic, S., & Matijasevic, M. (2005). Project management in research projects. In *Proceedings of the 8th International Conference on Telecommunications, 2005. ConTEL 2005* (Vol. 2, pp. 663–9). https://doi .org/10.1109/CONTEL.2005.185981

Innovation, Science and Economic Development Canada. (2022). *Strategic Science Fund: Program guide*. Retrieved September 16, 2022, from https:// ised-isde.canada.ca/site/strategic-science-fund/en/strategic-science -fund-program-guide

Kuchta, D., Gładysz, B., Skowron, D., & Betta, J. (2017). R&D projects in the science sector. *R & D Management, 47*(1), 88–110. https://doi.org/10.1111/radm.12158

Lemieux-Charles, L. (2005, December). *Summary report: National workshop on research leadership and management.* University of Toronto, Department of Health Policy, Management & Evaluation.

Lipmanowicz, H., & McCandless, K. (n.d.). *Min specs.* Liberating Structures. Retrieved September 17, 2022, from https://www.liberatingstructures.com/14-min-specs/

Lippe, S., & vom Brocke, J. (2016). Situational project management for collaborative research projects. *Project Management Journal, 47*(1), 76–96. https://doi.org/10.1002/pmj.21561

Memorial University of Newfoundland, Research Grant and Contract Services. (2018, January). *A project management guide for researchers.* https://research-tools.mun.ca/rpm/wp-content/uploads/sites/13/2018/01/Research-Project-Management-Guide-January-2018.pdf

Miller, K. (2019, July 29). *10 project management tips for non-project managers.* Northeastern University Graduate Programs. https://www.northeastern.edu/graduate/blog/project-management-tips/

Moore, S., & Shangraw Jr., R.F. (2011). Managing risk and uncertainty in large-scale university research projects. *Research Management Review, 18*(2), 59–78. http://files.eric.ed.gov/fulltext/EJ980462.pdf

Mustaro, P.N., & Rossi, R. (2013). Project management principles applied in academic research projects. *Issues in Informing Science and Information Technology, 10,* 325–40. https://doi.org/10.28945/1814

Norris, D., Dirnagl, U., Zigmond, M.J., Thompson-Peer, K., & Chow, T.T. (2018). Health tips for research groups. *Nature, 557*(7705), 302–4. https://doi.org/10.1038/d41586-018-05146-5

Organisation for Economic Co-operation and Development. (n.d.-a). *Gross domestic expenditure on R&D by sector of performance and type of R&D* [Data extracted for higher education sector R&D, PPP dollars – current prices]. Retrieved June 30, 2023, from https://stats.oecd.org/WBOS/index.aspx

Organisation for Economic Co-operation and Development. (n.d.-b). *IHERD reports.* Retrieved September 3, 2022, from https://www.oecd.org/sti/iherd-final-reports.htm

Organisation for Economic Co-operation and Development. (2012). Public research policy. In *OECD science, technology and industry outlook 2012* (pp. 177–80). OECD Publishing.

Organisation for Economic Co-operation and Development. (2015). Annex 2: Glossary of terms. In *Frascati manual 2015: Guidelines for collecting and reporting data on research and experimental development* (pp. 365–82). OECD Publishing. https://doi.org/10.1787/9789264239012-en

Organisation for Economic Co-operation and Development. (2016). What public research will be performed and why. In *OECD Science, Technology and Innovation Outlook 2016* (pp. 134–7). OECD Publishing.

Paprica, P.A. (2021). *Risks for academic research projects: An empirical study of perceived negative risks and possible responses.* arXiv. https://doi.org/10.48550/arXiv.2103.08048

Patient-Centered Outcomes Research Institute. (n.d.). *About PCORI.* Retrieved September 13, 2022, from https://www.pcori.org/about/about-pcori

Philbin, S.P. (2017). Investigating the application of project management principles to research projects – An exploratory study. In E.H. Ng, B. Nepal, & E. Schott (Eds.), *Proceedings of the 38th American Society for Engineering Management (ASEM) International Annual Conference.* Retrieved September 3, 2022, from https://openresearch.lsbu.ac.uk/download/cefd219d929c6ffb423cc379b557f0d91734b96810fe58ae1e520369a8c3e8e1/105272/ASEM%202017_116.docx

Powers, L.C., & Kerr, G. (2009). Project management and success in academic research. *RealWorld Systems Research Series, 2.* https://doi.org/10.2139/ssrn.1408032

Project Management Institute. (n.d.). *Certification framework.* Retrieved September 18, 2022, from https://www.pmi.org/certifications/become-a-project-manager/certification-framework

Project Management Institute. (2021). *The standard for project management and a guide to the project management body of knowledge (PMBOK® guide)* (7th ed.). Project Management Institute.

Riol, H., & Thuillier, D. (2015). Project management for academic research projects: Balancing structure and flexibility. *International Journal of Project Organisation and Management, 7*(3), 251–69. https://doi.org/10.1504/IJPOM.2015.070792

Sambunjak, D., Straus, S.E., & Marušić, A. (2006). Mentoring in academic medicine: A systematic review. *JAMA, 296*(9), 1103–15. https://doi.org/10.1001/jama.296.9.1103

Straus, S.E., & Sackett, D.L. (Eds.). (2013). *Mentorship in academic medicine.* John Wiley & Sons.

Vom Brocke, J., & Lippe, S. (2015). Managing collaborative research projects: A synthesis of project management literature and directives for future research. *International Journal of Project Management, 33*(5), 1022–39. https://doi.org/10.1016/j.ijproman.2015.02.001

Index

Notes: The letter *b* following a page number denotes a box; the letter *c*, a leadership advice crosswalk box; the letter *f*, a figure; and the letter *t*, a table.

diversity, 68, 84, 103–4, 107*b*, 175, 183, 218–20, 223. *See also* Brown, Elspeth; EDI (equity, diversity, and inclusion); gender; marginalized communities; stakeholders

early career researchers: leading deliverables, 37; understanding expectations related to tenure, 205–6, 207–8; using the handbook, 22*b*
EDI (equity, diversity, and inclusion), 175. *See also* diversity
Edwards, Aled, 67*c*, 184–6
environmental enrichment, 209
equity, 68, 68*c*, 188–9, 211–12, 213
executive committees: governance and management hierarchy, 100*f*; guiding leadership, 198–9; for large projects, 92, 92–3*b*; principal investigators and, 102–3; relationships with core and project team, 90, 91*f*
executive directors. *See* program administrators; project managers
experimental development, 2*b*, 66, 166

Farber, Steve, 186–9; budget follows the work, 60*c*; involving stakeholders, 67*c*; project management skills within the team, 88*c*; on research leadership, 186–7; start large projects with a meeting, 119*c*
flexibility: of leaders, 20*b*, 183, 185; non-time constrained deliverables, 46; to retain staff, 78*b*; schedule compression and, 48; through budgeting tactics, 57, 64, 65; your research plan should not be rigid, 72*c*

Flood, Colleen, 189–93; know when to say no, 55*c*; research leaders secure funding, 115*c*
funders: budget requirements and considerations, 56–8, 64, 65; priorities reflected in budget, 58–9; risk they will withdraw from project, 78*b*; schedule compression and, 55; seeing work breakdown structures (WBS), 31. *See also* funding; grant applications; stakeholders
funding: for BIPOC researchers, 175; for equity-focused research, 211–12; from industry, 237–8; managing multiyear, 229; need to diversity streams of, 206–7; for postdocs and students, 205; responding to negative decisions, 226; role of, 19*b*; shifts in culture of, 227. *See also* grant applications

Gantt charts: for budget management, 229; in communications status reports, 131–4, 133*f*; created in a spreadsheet program, 24*b*, 134; fast tracked year, 48–9, 50*f*; the one person team, 90*b*; pollution research project (fictional), 45*f*, 46–7, 255*f*; project plan for natural sciences research project in a multidisciplinary program (fictional), 264*f*; relaxed year, 48–9, 51*f*; schedule compression, 48–53, 50*f*, 54*f*, 251*f*; triple constraints and, 69. *See also* schedules, deliverable-based
gender, 175, 208, 218–19. *See also* diversity
Goldratt, Eliyahu M., 53–5
governance, open, 233–4

roles and responsibilities *(continued)*
85*f*; leaders, 178; the meeting
chair, 147–9, 148–9*b*; the one
person team, 89, 90*b*; principle
investigator and project manager
intertwined, 86–9, 120*t*; principle
investigator and sponsor,
101–2; professional attributes and
competencies, 97, 98*b*; program
administrator, 22*b*, 87, 126, 182,
230; project management skills
within the team, 88*c*; project
managers, 22*b*, 86–9, 120*t*, 126,
140–2; the RACI as tool to
define multiple roles, 93–6, 94*t*,
140; relationships among core,
executive and project team,
90, 91*f*; subteams, 91*c*; value
of understanding, 83. *See also*
individual roles

Sackett, David, 220, 221
saying no, 20*b*, 55*c*, 193, 207, 221, 239
schedules, deliverable-based:
avoiding multitasking, 53–6,
54*f*, 55*f*; constraints, 44–6, 47;
developing Gantt charts, 45*f*,
46–7; importance of timing, 46*c*;
schedule compression, 47–53,
48*f*, 49–53, 50*f*, 51*f*, 52*b*, 54*f*, 55,
139; triple constraint, 69–71, 70*f*;
using work breakdown structures
(WBS) to develop, 43–4
Schull, Michael, 68*c*, 91*c*, 157*c*, 200–4
scope, project: affect of increases
on staffing, 179; based-on
deliverables produces tangibles,
30–1; common deliverables for
research projects, 31–4; "define,
then deliver" mindset, 25–6,
25*b*, 27*f*; establishing a common
understanding of, 34–43, 36*f*;
generic Work Breakdown
Schedule (WBS), 29*f*, 30–1, 33, 34,

39*f*, 40*b*, 41; plans must change
if scope does, 71*c*; relationship
to vision, 28*c*; triple constraint,
69–71, 70*f*; Work Breakdown
Schedule (WBS) as tool to
articulate, 27–30
seniors' health clinics evaluation
project (fictional), 249, 250*f*, 251*f*,
252*f*
Sherwood-Lollar, Barbara, 110, 204–8
Shoichet, Molly, 144*c*, 208–11
Siddiqi, Arjumand, 67*c*, 68*c*, 211–14
Six Sigma, 13
skills and abilities needed by
research leaders: accepting advice,
217; accountability, 87*c*, 200–1,
204; being open to doing things
differently, 198, 215; building
teams, 88*c*, 182, 191–2, 194–6,
201–3, 223, 232–3; capacity
building, 96*c*, 218; communication,
128*c*, 192, 193; continual learning,
20*b*, 97*c*, 181, 209–10, 214, 217,
224; decision-making, 98*c*, 199;
entrepreneurial mindset, 205, 207,
208; flexibility, 20*b*, 72*c*, 183, 185;
listening, 18–20*b*, 88–9, 174–5, 176,
180, 183, 223; mentorship, 96*c*, 218,
221, 236; nurturing, 211; saying no,
55*c*, 193, 207, 221, 239; showing
respect, 216, 217, 221; skills
and abilities needed, 202, 204;
supporting others in research,
218, 221, 222, 227; understanding
the needs of stakeholders, 134*c*.
See also project management,
research leadership
considerations
Soré, Zaïna, 214–17; start large
projects with a meeting, 119*c*
sponsors, 101–2, 104–6, 109*b*
stakeholders: budget reflects their
priorities, 58–9; communication
needs, 134, 134*c*; defined, 135;

About the Author

P. Alison Paprica is a professor (adjunct) and senior fellow at the Institute for Health Policy, Management and Evaluation at the University of Toronto and Associate Graduate Faculty, Laboratory Medicine and Pathobiology, in the Faculty of Medicine at the University of Toronto. She is also a senior fellow at Massey College and principal of the boutique consultancy Research Project Management. Alison has previously held executive-level positions with independent research institutes, including Health Data Research Network Canada, ICES (formerly the Institute for Clinical Evaluative Sciences), and the Vector Institute for Artificial Intelligence. Before holding these roles, she was director of the Planning, Research and Analysis Branch at the Ontario Ministry of Health, where she was responsible for up to $60 million in annual applied health research investment and knowledge translation activities to bring research evidence into policy and practice. Prior to working in the public sector, Alison held scientist and management positions at three different international pharmaceutical companies.

Alison holds an Honours Combined BSc in biochemistry and chemistry (McMaster University) and a PhD in organic chemistry (Western University), and she was a fellow in the Healthcare Excellence Canada (formerly Canadian Foundation for Healthcare Improvement) Executive Training in Research Application program from 2011 to 2013. Her main research interests are data governance and research data infrastructure, public involvement in data-intensive health research, evidence-informed policy, and the leadership and management of research as a topic in its own right. She has been coinvestigator, principal applicant, or coapplicant on 13 Canadian federally funded research grants totaling more than $80 million and has published 27 peer-reviewed journal articles, of which she is first or last author on 12. She has served as a peer reviewer for leading scientific journals, including *PLOS, Nature, Science, British Medical Journal,* and *Journal of the Canadian Medical Association,* and she is a member of the Canadian Institutes of Health Research College of Reviewers and the International Advisory Board for Health Data Research UK.

Alison is an early adopter of project management and among the first 3 percent of the more than one million people around the world who hold Project Management Professional certification from the Project Management Institute. As a strong supporter of research and an expert practitioner of project management, she has led work to adapt the most relevant subset of globally accepted project management tools and processes so that they work for research projects and other initiatives with high uncertainty. Since 2013, she has developed and delivered courses, workshops, and capacity-building sessions focused on the management and leadership of academic research to more than 1,000 people at the University of Toronto, McMaster University, Cornell University, the Canadian Evaluation Society, the International Institute of Tropical Agriculture in Nigeria, the Canadian Institutes of Health Research Health System Impact Fellows, the Social Sciences and Humanities Research Council Partnerships Grants Start-Up Meeting, National Science and Engineering Council–funded Collaborative Research and Training Experience programs, and others.

Printed and bound by CPI Group (UK) Ltd, Croydon, CR0 4YY

09/06/2025

14685787-0001